Global Studies Research

For all from whom I have learned:

Students

Teachers

Friends

Family

Global Studies Research

Pamela A. Zeiser

University of North Florida

FOR INFORMATION:

CQ Press

An imprint of SAGE Publications, Inc.

2455 Teller Road

Thousand Oaks, California 91320

E-mail: order@sagepub.com

SAGE Publications Ltd.

1 Oliver's Yard

55 City Road

London EC1Y 1SP

United Kingdom

SAGE Publications India Pvt. Ltd.

B 1/I 1 Mohan Cooperative Industrial Area

Mathura Road, New Delhi 110 044

India

SAGE Publications Asia-Pacific Pte. Ltd.

18 Cross Street #10-10/11/12

China Square Central

Singapore 048423

Acquisitions Editor: Anna Villarruel

Editorial Assistant: Lauren Younker

Production Editor: Astha Jaiswal

Copy Editor: Deanna Noga

Typesetter: C&M Digitals (P) Ltd.

Proofreader: Theresa Kay

Indexer: May Hasso

Cover Designer: Dally Verghese

Marketing Manager: Jennifer Jones

Printed in the United States of America

ISBN: 9781506396286

This book is printed on acid-free paper.

19 20 21 22 23 10 9 8 7 6 5 4 3 2 1

Contents

Preface

As International Studies Program Director at the University of North Florida, I became committed to teaching interdisciplinarity. Having been an interdisciplinary International Affairs major as an undergraduate myself, I had always loved when what I saw as the "puzzle pieces" from my different disciplinary courses—geography, history, languages, politics—snapped together in my mind. I learned over time how useful the ability to integrate information from different sources was to my academic, professional, and personal lives. I wanted to offer that to my students. *Global Studies Research* is the result of my efforts to do so.

Overview

Our world has always been and remains complex, because the deceptively simple phrase "how the world works" encompasses the many countries in the world, their many interactions with each other and with other global actors such as international organizations, globalization, and a host of global issues and problems. Students in Global Studies, International Studies, or International Affairs programs need not only descriptions of the world, these actors, and their activities, but also a set of tools to understand, evaluate, apply, and, most important, integrate the information available to them in an interdisciplinary major. Yet most undergraduate Global Studies programs require their students to take a *disciplinary* research methods course; few programs emphasize the synthesis and integration that is the goal of interdisciplinarity (Brown, Pegg, & Shively, 2006). Students' ability to understand and assess the complex problems in our world—and their careers—is improved by understanding and integrating information and scholarly analyses from different disciplinary perspectives, but exactly how to ensure that is problematic both pedagogically and, in university settings where Global Studies "borrows" courses from the discipline, structurally. Building on the general interdisciplinary studies literature, I offer an integrative research process specific to Global Studies.

From a teaching standpoint, modern interdisciplinary studies is most usefully "defined as a process of answering a question, solving a problem, or addressing a topic that is too broad or complex to be dealt with adequately by a single discipline or profession" (Klein & Newell, 1997, p. 393). Global issues such as the HIV epidemic and terrorism are exactly the type of complex problems and topics that interdisciplinary Global Studies focuses on—and why interdisciplinary studies is usefully case-based.

The literature on interdisciplinary theory includes numerous research models to explain why and how we integrate material from different disciplines to study complex topics. What all models of the process have in common are steps for gathering,

[handwritten margin note: what are these tools? how are they developed]

[handwritten margin note: if different approaches don't agree on the causes of or solutions to a problem, how can they be effectively combined]

comparing, and combining information and scholarly insights from multiple disciplinary sources so as to more fully understand the subject under study. *Global Studies Research* explains and demonstrates an interdisciplinary, integrative approach based on common critical thinking and comparison skills, utilizing the metaphor of a jigsaw puzzle. Students will learn how to first prepare for a research project, then gather, compare, and combine information and insights (puzzle pieces) from common Global Studies disciplines of anthropology, economics, geography, history, and political science through application to case studies centering on the global HIV epidemic and terrorism as global issues (each of which is a completed jigsaw puzzle picture). The textbook introduces interdisciplinarity, provides basic building blocks of relevant disciplinary knowledge, explains a process for integrating knowledge from multiple disciplines, and models this interdisciplinary Global Studies Research Process in its presentation of the case studies. This familiarizes students with not only the disciplinary tools to study the world, but more so how to gather, compare, and combine disciplinary information and insights at the same time it presents substantive Global Studies subject matter in the case studies.

Benefits for Faculty and Students

Interdisciplinary teaching is not always easy; I seek to provide a textbook that will enable faculty to teach an overtly integrative process for research as well as to teach more easily outside their discipline when they themselves usually are trained within a single discipline and many course reading materials (textbooks, journal articles, research books) also emerge from a single discipline. *Global Studies Research* will help faculty resolve these problems without going outside the (inter)discipline of Global Studies to general interdisciplinary studies texts. This textbook provides them with a single, interdisciplinary source of information about integrative research for their students—one that introduces five disciplines, their contributions to Global Studies, and how these disciplines together provide information and insights to answer research questions related to Global Studies. It also explains how to determine additional relevant disciplines. The case studies enable faculty to illustrate to students the process for and utility of the integrative Global Studies research process and provide faculty with the flexibility to tailor the course to their own interests, backgrounds, and specific teaching goals by focusing more in depth on one of the case studies in the textbook or introducing their own case studies. *Global Studies Research* provides faculty members with ready-made content, examples, and assignments for teaching outside their own disciplines.

It provides students with an introduction to the disciplines of anthropology, economics, geography, history, and political science. In doing so, it exposes students to the perspectives of multiple disciplines. Through the Global Studies research process, it provides students the opportunity to develop and practice integrative skills to understand and manage complex problems. Direct inclusion of critical thinking, comparative analysis, and research skills in *Global Studies Research* supplements the synthetic skills built through an integrative approach.

This book emphasizes how the combination of information and insights from five disciplines provides a fuller understanding of each case than just one discipline would. The textbook enables faculty to offer and students to gain from active, interdisciplinary Global Studies learning techniques by building them into the content and process of the textbook. It also offers students the opportunity (which faculty can use as assignments) to practice those skills themselves through the inclusion of active learning "Take a Step!" boxes.

Student Learning Objectives

Whether students end up in international affairs careers or one of the many U.S.-based careers impacted by globalization, learning an integrative thought process is vital to success. Thus, the goals or learning objectives of this textbook are that students

- identify and describe the basic subjects of study, concepts, research methods, and theories that create the perspectives of common disciplines for Global Studies (anthropology, economics, geography, history, and political science);

- recognize and explain the ways in which these disciplines provide information and insights necessary to research and understand today's complex world, including globalization, global actors, global issues, and the relationships among them;

- identify, describe, and, through active learning components, apply a comparative, integrative process for researching and reporting on Global Studies topics, modeling the process through two global issues case studies: the global HIV epidemic and terrorism;

- through active learning components, identify and apply comparative and integrative skills along with Global Studies content; and

- through active learning components, demonstrate and build research, critical thinking, and writing skills.

Plan of Book

To follow through on these learning objectives for students, Chapter 1 introduces Global Studies research by explaining that our world and how it works are complex subjects of study because of processes, interactions, and topics like globalization, global actors, global issues, and differing points of view. It introduces the jigsaw puzzle metaphor and offers readers an understanding of interdisciplinarity and its definitions. Global Studies is then described and defined as an interdisciplinary endeavor. The importance of disciplinary perspective is explored before the research process is briefly introduced.

Chapter 2 focuses on five contributing disciplines: anthropology, economics, geography, history, and political science. It provides students with basic knowledge about these disciplines and their respective perspectives, based on subjects of study, key concepts, research methods, and theoretical approaches. Using the jigsaw puzzle analogy, Chapter 3 then presents the Global Studies research process, detailing the "prepare, gather, compare, and combine" steps needed to study topics related to our complex world.

Chapter 4 presents an integrated essay on the HIV epidemic as a global issue, providing an overview of how international organizations respond to it, and an example of the results of the Global Studies research process. Chapter 5 "examines pieces of the puzzle" to explain exactly how the prepare, gather, compare, and combine steps from Chapter 3 were applied to the study of the global HIV epidemic to produce the integrated essay in Chapter 4. Chapters 6 and 7 do the same thing for the terrorism case study. While Chapter 5 demonstrates the basic integrative process, Chapter 7 introduces common challenges to interdisciplinary research and suggests process-related solutions. Chapter 8 concludes the book by summarizing the steps and challenges of Global Studies research as well as reiterating the value of the integrative skills offered, especially for career preparation.

Active Learning

Activities within these chapters prompt students to prepare, gather, compare, and/ or combine disciplinary information through active learning. Active learning utilizes "instructional activities involving students in doing things and thinking about what they are doing" (Bonwell & Eison, 1991, p. 2). Active learning focuses on engaging students in more than just passive learning (Bonwell & Eison, 1991). As a tool to manage the complexity of learning about the world, Global Studies requires us to evaluate and compare disciplinary information and scholarly analyses, then combine them into a complete, whole picture. The goals of active learning are completely in line with the goals of Global Studies, and this book utilizes "Take a Step!" text boxes as suggested assignments to take students through the steps of the Global Studies research process and give them practice in utilizing it as an approach to studying the world.

Acknowledgments

This book grew out my efforts teaching the Capstone Seminar for International Studies majors at the University of North Florida. Together, my students and I worked to ensure they left the program with interdisciplinary integration skills—for research projects, graduate school, careers, and more. I relied heavily on the general interdisciplinary studies literature, and so am grateful to the scholars in that field, especially those cited throughout this book. I am particularly grateful to Allen F. Repko's *Interdisciplinary Research: Process and Theory*, which prompted me to adapt interdisciplinary studies methods specifically for Global and International Studies. Additionally, challenges in teaching the material in Repko's book sparked my use of comparative analysis to develop the idea of supplementary and complementary integration. I am equally grateful to the many University of North Florida (UNF) students who enrolled in the Capstone Seminar across the 4 years I spent developing this approach. Their enthusiasm, flexibility, and feedback were invaluable.

I could never have finished *Global Studies Research* without the support of many wonderful family, colleagues, and friends. I am extremely grateful to my family: to the memory of my grandparents Bernadette and Francis and Letty and Thomas. To the memory of my aunts Dorothy, Sister Doris Marie (SND), Patricia Van Ruiten, and my uncle Thomas. To my immediate family for their encouragement, interest, and patience: Noel E. Zeiser and Bich Uy Thi Dang; Kathleen A. Zeiser; Andrew Zeiser; and Judith, John, Sarah, and Rebekah Krum. I know that my late brother Shane Zeiser would have been equally supportive. To my close friend and cousin Karen Minson, who was an unfailing source of encouragement; I am sad she can't see the published book and thank her posthumously. To my aunts and uncles: Paul Rosenthal and the late Beverly Rosenthal, Mary Zeiser, John Zeiser, Ruth and Gene Miller, Paul Zeiser, Jean Walker and Joyce Hellums, Peggy Bailey and the late Herb Bailey, Johnny Van Ruiten, Mary Edge and the late Joe Edge, and to my cousins in Florida and Georgia: Anne Rosenthal, Debbie Scott, Ronald Edge, and David and Martha Edge.

I am lucky to have colleagues who are also great friends: Berrin Beasley offered me a sounding board and feedback on drafts, held me accountable, and is a constant source of friendship and encouragement. Mary Borg granted me her expertise in economics and comments on drafts as well as her friendship and support. Alison Bruey has been the valued other end of our "writing line" for a decade; she is an example of the scholar and writer I wish to be. David Schwam-Baird challenged me on theory, commented on drafts, and allowed me to vent when frustrated; I am grateful to David and Shira for years of friendship. Suzanne Simon helped me stay positive and keep the big picture in mind and shared her expertise in anthropology. Nancy Soderberg offered me encouragement, feedback on drafts, and more than one necessary reality check. Colleagues Denise Bossy, Dale Clifford, Rosa DeJorio, Doris Fuchs, and Sucheta Pyakuryal shared their expertise with me, in reviewing the disciplinary summaries or other parts of the manuscript. Any errors that remain are mine and mine alone.

I am grateful to Matt Corrigan, Natasha Christie, Mike Binder, and other colleagues in the Department of Political Science and Public Administration for their interest and support. I thank Michael Boyles in UNF's Center for Instructional Research and Technology for his assistance with the figures for this book.

I was fortunate to have great research assistants, so I thank Steven Holmes, Rebekah Krum, Sarah Krum, Murshed Ramos, and Kellie E. Borg. I appreciate the following former students and now friends who read drafts and gave me valuable feedback from their perspectives: Robert Conrad, Ashley Harrington, Leah Huber, and Ryan McDonagh.

I am grateful to a number of friends who supported me through the writing of this book: Shoshana Altrichter, LeAnn Anderson-Vincecruz, Melissa Barnard, Kate Beardall, Carla Fells, Linda Finley, Don Hood, Marty and Dick Jones, Leslie Kaplan, Kristina Lopez, Frances Marquez, Melissa Mashburn, Vikram Mukhija, Bina Nicpon, Cecelia and the late Bob Pearce, Wendy Rahman, Eric Reichman, the late Joan Russell, Kelly Vallecillos, and Cary Yamamoto. I thank Jane Sievers for attempting to keep me sane—and the failures in that regard are also on me.

I also thank the reviewers, whose feedback helped me improve my original manuscript: Alison Holmes, Humboldt State University; Yi Edward Yang, James Madison University; and Austin Trantham, Jacksonville University.

This book would not exist without the hardworking and helpful people at SAGE Publications: Scott Greenan, Lauren Younker, Jennifer Jones, Astha Jaiswal, Anna Villarruel, Theresa Kay and Deanna Noga. I am grateful to Chris Gill for connecting me with SAGE in the first place. And I thank Michael Kerns, Carrie Brandon, and Duncan Marchbank for assistance earlier in the process.

About the Author

Pamela A. Zeiser is an Associate Professor and spent 7 years as the International Studies Program Director at the University of North Florida (UNF) in Jacksonville. She has taught interdisciplinary International Studies courses such as Global Issues in Contemporary Politics and Capstone Seminar: International Studies. In the discipline of political science, she offers a broad range of International Relations and Comparative Politics courses including International Law and Organization, Politics and Society in Britain and Ireland, and Politics of *Harry Potter*. Her publications are on the topics of global health, U.S. foreign policy, pedagogy, civic education, and social media. Dr. Zeiser has taken students on study abroad programs in Europe and serves as an Academic Lecturer for World Affairs Council of Philadelphia study travel programs. She earned her PhD in Political Science and Master of Arts in International Studies at the Claremont Graduate University. Her Bachelor of Arts from the University of Nevada, Reno, was in interdisciplinary International Affairs.

1 Interdisciplinary Global Studies

1914–1915

- World War I begins

- United States intervenes in Mexican Civil War

- Ottoman Empire undertakes genocidal massacres against its Greek population

- British ocean liner *Lusitania* sunk by German submarine, killing 1,198 passengers

- First successful (non-direct) blood transfusion

- Earthquake in Avezzano, Italy, kills 29,800

- German-American Erich Muenter explodes bomb in U.S. Senate Reception Room to protest U.S. sales of weapons to UK and France during World War I; none killed

- First transatlantic radiotelephone message from Virginia to Paris

- 25,000 American women march in New York City for the right to vote

- Typhoid Mary, a carrier of the disease, recaptured and quarantined to prevent further spread of disease in New York City

2014–2015

- Death toll in Syrian Civil War reaches 130,000 with 4 million displaced

- Russia intervenes in the Ukraine and annexes Crimea

- Journalists investigate Myanmar's genocidal actions against the Rohingya minority

- Malaysian Airlines Flight MH17 shot down over Ukraine, allegedly by Russian-supported separatists, with 283 killed

- A human intestine is generated in a laboratory using stem cells

- A magnitude 7.8 earthquake strikes Nepal, killing 8,000

- More than 140 killed by Al-Shabaab gunmen at Garissa University College, Kenya

- Spacecraft *Philae* lands on comet 317 million miles away

- Women in Saudi Arabia register to vote for the first time

- Ebola outbreak in West Africa kills at least 11,000

Our world changes, and it stays the same; it has been and still is complex. Between 2014 and 2015, we saw the rise of the Islamic State, continued civil wars in the Middle East, and terror attacks throughout the world. As these and other global news headlines indicate, over 100 years our world has changed much—and little. War continues, though in 2014 and 2015 we saw many small conflicts rather than the World War of 1914–1915. Natural disasters continue, though we know today that some, such as climate change, are exacerbated by human activity. Epidemics also continue, complicated by rapid air travel. Technological advances amaze, shifting from the first transatlantic phone call to space exploration and mobile phones, but also include identity theft and hacking. Medical advancements and human rights successes change lives for the better. Terrorism, so much in the headlines throughout the world today, seems relatively new but terrorist acts occurred in the United States and other countries in 1914 and 1915 and well before, though of course the damage can be more extensive today.

Despite the 100-year gap, the above major news headlines from the respective years provide examples of continuity and change in our world, but to understand fully such global events and issues—in and of themselves as well as across time—we must appreciate the "big picture" and learn how to study both the big picture and all the smaller details that help create the whole. We must know at least a little bit about a lot of things to understand our complex world, including the past, culture, economics, geographical locations, and politics. The Global Studies research process enables us to learn about and combine all these topics as we study the world and how it works.

A Complex World

Our world is a fascinating and challenging subject of study because it is complex. There are so many global actors, political systems, organizations, cultures, economies, geographical boundaries, and conflicts—and the interactions of all these together—to understand. We can include all this in the phrase "how the world works." Yet for all its complexity, our world is well worth studying, for the fun and challenge of learning about it, to help prepare for careers in the globalized economy, to better understand the foreign policy choices governments make, and to simply be aware of the world around us and our place in it. The complexity of our world is visible especially in processes like globalization and in global issues, global actors, and differing points of view.

Globalization

Globalization is an important subject of study to understand the complex world. In fact, today, this subject frames many others in our study of the world—and is arguably one reason why Global Studies is necessary and important. Despite its frequent usage since the 1990s, the term *globalization* can be pretty fuzzy because it's applied to many different activities and is ill-defined. When talking about **globalization**, an economist usually means something different than a philosopher would. We can try to encompass these differences by utilizing a broad definition: **"the intensification of economic, political, social, and cultural relations across borders"** (Holm & Sorenson, 1995, p. 1). We can add to this definition the idea that globalization is a *process* of establishing and intensifying these relations and interconnections. By emphasizing process, we can include not just the products or results of globalization but also the causes and activities of globalization. This definition helps us grasp that globalization is a multifaceted process that can affect not only economic connections throughout the world but also interconnections of many types.

Because there is no agreed on definition of globalization, there are many debates and disagreements over the word itself and what it describes. In addition to varying definitions, there is also the question of whether globalization is something new beginning in the mid- to late twentieth century, when the term itself came in to use, or something that has existed throughout history. If it is not new, is it different in form or character from previous time periods? Is globalization today, as political scientist Joseph S. Nye (2002) asserts, "thicker and quicker" due to technology and instant communication (p. 85)? When talking specifically of economic globalization, there is disagreement over whether it has to mean expansion of the current global market economy or whether it could be a process of promoting a different economic system emphasizing equality and provision of a social safety net. When talking specifically of cultural globalization, there is disagreement over whether it must be the unavoidable spread of Western culture (sometimes described in shorthand as the Americanization or CocaCola-ization of the world, because of the spread of American culture and products worldwide) or whether it includes more balanced interconnections between many cultures. Given the multiple understandings of and questions and arguments about globalization, the subject of globalization is part and parcel of our complex world.

Why has american culture spread so much?

Global Issues

Certain complex issues or problems in the world are considered "global" because they cannot be successfully addressed by a single country on its own; they can only be tackled together by the countries affected by the issue. A **global issue** is one that **gains attention or "has aroused concern throughout much of the world"** (Soroos, 1990,

p. 310) and is generally one of four types: (1) transnational, (2) tragedy of the commons, (3) parallel, or (4) externally relevant (Soroos, 1990; Zeiser, 1998). First, global issues can be "transnational—that is they cross political boundaries (country borders)" because they "originate in one state but have ramifications for others" (Soroos, 1990, pp. 310–311; Snarr, 2008, p. 2). Examples of such transnational problems include acid rain, where pollutants released in one country can be deposited in neighboring countries, and refugee flows, when large numbers of people flee to a neighboring country for reasons such as war or genocide. The second category, tragedy of the commons, concerns use (and often misuse, hence the tragedy) of resources all countries and peoples share in common, such as the oceans or atmosphere (Soroos, 1990, pp. 310–311). The final two types of issues exist within individual countries but still receive international attention. Parallel global problems get international attention because they are common to many states. The global HIV epidemic and other health issues can be examples. Externally relevant issues become global when "what occurs within a given state is of concern to the outside world" (Soroos, 1990, pp. 310–311; Zeiser, 1998). Such global issues include major violations of human rights such as the Tiananmen Square incident in China in 1989, when the Chinese government used deadly military force to disrupt protests for government reform. The four types of global issues can overlap: If we talk about the HIV epidemic within individual countries, it is a parallel global issue. But if we talk specifically about the spread of HIV from one country to others, it becomes a transnational global issue. Depending on the situation, terrorism can be externally relevant, parallel, and transnational. Global issues are generally problems, and because of interdependence they cannot be solved or managed without coordinated global action. Globalization can contribute both to the existence of and the response to global issues. If we are studying the complex world, we end up studying global issues and how the world responds to them. Ultimately, understanding complex problems allows actors to take action to help manage or solve global issues.

Global Actors

Although many think first of countries, there are a variety of actors at the global level that are part of globalization and respond to complex global issues, including countries, international governmental organizations, international and local nongovernmental organizations, international businesses, individuals, transnational social movements, and media. *Countries*, or what some contributing disciplines call *nation-states*, are key actors in the world. Often the actions countries take (or do not take) contribute to complex global issues and attempts to solve them. We can group countries: The wealthier, industrialized or service-oriented democracies such as the United States, Europe, and Japan are developed countries while those such as Burkina Faso, Georgia, or Timor-Leste that struggle to join the global economy or move beyond resource-based economies, are unable to provide basic services like infrastructure and education, and/or are sometimes politically unstable are developing countries. They are also called resource-poor countries. Organizations such as the

World Bank also commonly categorize countries as high-income, middle-income, and low-income. This categorization has led to the acronyms HIC for high-income countries and LMIC for low and/or middle income countries. Another classification is the "global North" for richer countries and "global South" for poorer countries, based on the fact that most developed countries fall into northern latitudes and most developing countries into southern latitudes on the globe (though this categorization isn't entirely accurate). United Nations reports have even simplified it further, using simply the terms *rich* and *poor* countries. The categories aren't perfect—and are sometimes considered offensive to "poor" countries—and different people sometimes place a country in different categories. The point is that our complex world works differently for powerful, wealthier countries than it does for struggling, poorer countries. The categories help us comprehend and refer to those differences.

How do we allocate resources better? →

When many countries choose to cooperate, they often do so through organizations where national governments make up the membership—*international governmental organizations* (*IGOs*) like the United Nations and World Health Organization. As global actors, IGOs provide forums for discussion, coordinate responses to global issues, and develop guidelines for how countries might behave as they respond. IGOs can be multipurpose, just as the United Nations covers a broad range of issues such as security, economic development, human rights, and other priorities. Or an IGO can have a specific purpose, such as the International Atomic Energy Association's focus on nuclear technology, especially on stopping the spread of nuclear weapons while promoting safe use of peaceful nuclear technologies. IGOs can be universal or, like the United Nations, made up of most countries in the world. They can also be regional: The European Union coordinates policies only among countries of geographic Europe.

Nongovernmental organizations (*NGOs*) are, as their name suggests, organizations whose members are *not* governments or countries. The members of local or national NGOs are usually individuals, while international NGOs can include individuals and/or groups of individuals who make up national chapters of the international organization. NGOs are more likely to have a specific purpose, such as Amnesty International's efforts regarding human rights or the World Wildlife Fund's emphasis on conservation of nature and endangered species. Religious organizations are also NGOs, such as the World Council of Churches and the Jewish Joint Distribution Committee. NGOs can be open to anyone, or they may be limited to specific types of members (such as scientists, members of a particular religion, or businesspersons). International NGOs are more active at the global level but, as we will see in the case of the global HIV epidemic, local NGOs can influence global activities.

As global actors, NGOs often serve to draw attention to global issues and to pressure governments and IGOs to act, propose responses and work cooperatively with governments and IGOs to enact them, and fill the gap when other actors fail or lack the resources to act. For example, Médecins Sans Frontières (Doctors Without Borders) offers treatment to malnourished children in poverty-stricken countries whose

BOX 1.1
LEARN MORE
The United Nations

The United Nations (UN) was founded in 1945, based on an international treaty known as the United Nations Charter. The Charter describes the institutions, membership, powers, and purposes of the United Nations. Following World War II, its purpose was to serve as a forum for discussion—a center of diplomacy—and thus prevent another world war. It has three broad areas of focus, into which most global issues fall: international peace and security, economic and social development, and human rights and international law. It has universal membership; basically, any recognized country can join if it wants to, and most do. There are currently 193 member countries. When someone says "the United Nations did" something, they are actually saying "most countries in the world agreed to do" something. The UN cannot act independently of its members, though it does have some discretion in implementing the various policies and programs agreed on by its members. To do so, the UN has developed a very large bureaucracy. The UN is funded by dues from the member countries.

The main active bodies of the UN are the General Assembly, Security Council, Economic and Social Council, International Court of Justice, and Secretariat. All member countries attend General Assembly meetings to discuss a wide range of global issues and to develop recommendations and guidelines. The Security Council focuses on international peace and security. It is made up of 15 member states, five of them permanent, that act together to encourage peaceful resolution of international disputes, enact sanctions against countries in violation of Security Council resolutions, and recommend use of force when necessary to resolve an international dispute. The International Court of Justice (ICJ) is the judicial branch of the UN. Member countries can take disputes to the ICJ for settlement, and the ICJ can offer advisory opinions on questions of international law.

The UN Secretariat handles the day-to-day administration of the organization. The Secretary General leads the Secretariat and has the diplomatic task of representing the UN to all its member countries. For 2018–2019, the UN had a budget just over US$5 billion and approximately 44,000 staff working throughout the world. The UN is not a single organization but a system or "family" of organizations. Programs like the United Nations Development Programme (UNDP) operate within the UN structure and budget, and report to the General Assembly on its activities to promote economic, political, and social development in countries through attention to poverty, the environment, human rights, building democracy, and preventing crises. Specialized agencies are independent and have their own budgets and staff, but work within the UN. The World Health Organization (WHO) and World Bank are examples of specialized agencies. WHO was founded as part of the UN; the World Bank was not, but later entered into a partnership agreement with the UN.

For more information on the United Nations: www.un.org

governments cannot offer health services themselves. We also find public-private partnerships, where nongovernment and government entities act jointly in response to a global issue; the Global Fund to Fight AIDS, Tuberculosis, and Malaria (discussed in Chapter 4) is an independent, nonprofit, public-private foundation.

We generally consider NGOs to be organizations that contribute positively to the world. Technically, however, terrorist organizations or transnational crime groups are nongovernmental organizations. To differentiate those nongovernmental actors whose intent is to harm from those whose intent is to help, we call the former *suspect organizations*. This term can be controversial; think about the common phrase "one man's terrorist is another man's freedom fighter," which emphasizes that what we might call a suspect organization could be seen as entirely legitimate by others. However, there is general agreement by many global actors that certain organizations are suspect. The Colombian Cali Cartel serves as an example. It dominated the global illegal trade of cocaine in the 1990s, until it was dismantled through coordinated efforts of governments and law enforcement agencies in Colombia, elsewhere in Latin America, the United States, and Europe.

International businesses are another type of global actor, particularly when it comes to the global market economy. Specific terms vary, including MNCs for multinational corporations, MNEs for multinational enterprises, and TNCs for transnational corporations. Whichever term one prefers, we are talking about business enterprises that have factories, stores, facilities, or other assets in at least one country in addition to their home country. McDonald's, Walmart, and Coca-Cola are American-owned international businesses that produce, distribute, and/or sell products in other countries. BP (formerly British Petroleum) is a United Kingdom-based business with global operations. International businesses find supporters when they create jobs and economic growth, but are criticized when they are perceived as having too much political influence in developing countries, violating human rights laws through poor labor or safety conditions, or contributing to environmental disaster. International businesses may also enter into public-private partnerships, as NGOs do.

While *individuals* serve as leaders of countries and make up NGOs and international businesses, we can also study individuals on their own as global actors. Individuals (and groups of individuals) become victims of human rights abuses or natural disaster and contract disease. Individuals also respond to global issues. Prominent political, religious, business, or social leaders within a single country can gain authority and influence internationally even if they are not representatives of government, particularly when their personal behavior and beliefs have an impact on the world beyond that of their governments' policies. The late Nelson Mandela serves as a worldwide symbol of freedom of oppression and discrimination for fighting against apartheid and helping found a truly representative democracy in South Africa—much of his effort came decades before he served as president of that country from 1994 to 1999. Celebrities can use their fame to promote global causes, such as U2 singer Bono's work to draw attention to poverty and the HIV epidemic in Africa and actor George Clooney's efforts to raise awareness of those issues along with genocide in Sudan and preventable diseases such as malaria.

Individuals can work together through formally organized structures, such as NGOs, but can also work together temporarily or informally through *transnational social movements* (*TSMs*). Social movements are groups of people who seek political, economic, or social change (*or* to prevent change), and they become transnational when groups are active in more countries than the government being targeted or when the target of influence is the global community as represented by IGOs or international law. The 1990s movement to ban the use of landmines in conflict serves as an example: One individual contacted and encouraged coordinated effort by activists around the world, some of whom then did the same until the movement ultimately involved over 1,300 organizations in 95 different countries. This movement resulted in the Ottawa Treaty of 1997, which bans the military use of anti-personnel landmines by any country ratifying the treaty. TSMs like the International Campaign to Ban Landmines (see www.icbl.org) can include representatives of NGOs and can develop into NGOs over time if, for example, a formal or permanent structure is necessary to achieve their goals.

The *media*—broadly defined to include print, broadcast, and Internet communication of news and information—can be both a tool for other global actors and an actor in and of itself. While the media does not make policy or solve global problems, it contributes to both efforts by announcing what other actors do and through what gets covered as news. Global actors can utilize the media as a tool to disseminate information and policy positions as well as to persuade other actors to agree with their policy positions or take some sort of action. When George Clooney gave a 2011 interview on CNN about contracting malaria in Sudan and used that opportunity to raise awareness of the disease's impact on African countries among viewers, the media was a tool of an individual global actor. When newspapers and television news broadcasts reported on the government of Bahrain's use of force against pro-democracy protests in 2011, the media could be considered an actor itself, raising awareness among viewers of the protests and the violent government response. Directly or indirectly, this may have prompted countries, IGOs, NGOs, international businesses, and individuals to take action, propose policies, or further raise awareness of human rights abuses in that country and elsewhere.

We know there can be significant disadvantages as well as advantages to social media, particularly when the accuracy or intent of posts is questionable. Nonetheless, platforms like Twitter and Facebook are cost-effective tools that enable individuals, TSMs, and NGOs, especially, to organize and influence others regarding global issues. Twitter, in conjunction with the Experience Project, sponsors TwitCause, a Twitter account (@TwitCause) individuals can follow to learn about a variety of nonprofit causes. Individuals can retweet to show support for a cause as well as donate to organizations related to that cause. TwitCauses can be global as well as local, and global TwitCauses have included reducing child hunger and protecting endangered species.

[handwritten margin note: does the media cause more harm than good? Has it contributed to faster globalization?]

Differing Points of View

If globalization, global issues, and global actors are common subjects of Global Studies, so are the many different points of view about and within these very subjects. There are as many points of view about the interactions between and interconnections among countries as there are countries and peoples in the world. Knowing just our own national point of view limits our ability to understand and study our complex world. We need to be exposed to and open to the variety of points of view throughout the world—and the debates and disagreements that result. With knowledge of these points of view, debates, and disagreements, we can decide for ourselves what we believe about the complex world and why it works the way it does.

The International Monetary Fund (IMF) serves as an example. The IMF is an international governmental organization created following World War II and designed to create a more stable global economy as well as reducing poverty and improving the economies of member countries. When the IMF makes loans to developing countries, it sets conditions that it believes will enable the country to bring its economy in line with the global market economy. These conditions have included reducing government spending and removing price controls or subsidies. From the IMF's point of view (and those of many developed countries), the global market economy benefits most countries in the world and developing countries will also benefit from adhering to that economic system. The point of view of the citizens of the country receiving IMF loans and being held to the conditions, however, could be very different. Reducing government spending could mean that the government cuts funding for pensions, education, or other social services its citizens rely on. And removing price subsidies could radically increase the cost of food, fuel, and other necessities for those citizens—increases that are especially hard for the poor within that country to afford. While criticisms of IMF structural adjustment programs led to some reforms in the early 2000s, conditions for funding still remain.

In Indonesia in 1998, government policy changes made in response to IMF conditions—and the pace at which they were made—caused such economic hardship for the people that widespread rioting occurred and contributed to the fall of Indonesia's President Suharto. The United States had positive views of the IMF, because the IMF shares the United States' view of the global market economy. But many in Indonesia had a very negative perception of the IMF. Evaluating the value and actions of the IMF throughout the world would be difficult without understanding these differing opinions and points of view. Ultimately, knowing the points of view of others informs our own.

The Jigsaw Puzzle Metaphor

We can effectively study globalization, global issues, global actors, and differing points of view utilizing an interdisciplinary approach. Interdisciplinary Global Studies as a field of study and the Global Studies research process allow us to understand and

How do we listen and empower those in need to allow them to help themselves?

How do we develop a humble attitude when considering world issues?

utilize the social sciences and other relevant disciplines to help us engage, intellectually and practically, with our complex world. Ultimately, the goal of understanding and explaining how our world works is to better understand and manage the complex and never-ending interactions between countries, international organizations, and other global actors as well as understand processes such as globalization and to solve or manage new or ongoing global issues. It is not enough to learn facts, figures, past events, or current patterns and trends; we must also *learn how to learn about* our ever-changing world, the actors operating within it, and the problems or issues that develop.

A helpful (if imperfect) metaphor for studying our complex world through interdisciplinary Global Studies is a jigsaw puzzle—a very large, detailed picture with many, many pieces to the puzzle. It is a jigsaw puzzle that we build with only a general idea of what the picture will turn out to be—there can be many equally valid pictures—and one that is never finished. What you can see of the picture—of the world—is enough to figure out what you are looking at and to see some useful, intriguing detail. But there are gaps within the picture, the edges are not complete, not all the pieces fit neatly together, and there are always plenty more pieces of the puzzle on the table with which to add to our current picture or craft a new picture entirely. Jigsaw puzzles, especially those with thousands of pieces, are very complicated pictures. And the world is just such a complicated jigsaw puzzle.

What is different and challenging about the world as a jigsaw puzzle is that many pictures are possible and informative. And any particular picture is never complete, even when we may think it is. If we choose to study a single country such as France, we learn all we can about that single country and put many puzzle pieces into a nice picture, and then discover it is still incomplete around the edges. This is because we cannot study just France in isolation—we have to study it in relation to other countries. We have completed one section of the puzzle, but find more pieces and begin to fit them around the edges of that section to create a larger, fuller picture.

The 2003 War on Iraq is a good example. While some countries supported the U.S. invasion of Iraq to depose Saddam Hussein, two countries particularly opposed to the U.S. intervention were France and Germany. Public opinion in these countries showed that 75% of the French and 69% of Germans were against the U.S. invasion of Iraq (The Pew Global Attitudes Project, 2003), and their governmental leaders spoke out against it. Americans who supported the war felt baffled and betrayed by the reactions of our traditional allies, which resulted in a drop in respect for both countries and protests at French and German consulates around the country. Americans, disillusioned with their allies, took a set of puzzle pieces and created a picture they thought was complete. The puzzle pieces they used came from studying the interactions among the United States, France, and Germany regarding the 2003 War on Iraq from the point of view of being allies and their political relationships since World War II—and the picture that emerged displayed their feelings of betrayal by and unhappiness with France and Germany.

But that particular jigsaw puzzle was, in fact, incomplete. Other news articles, right alongside those on consulate protests, discussed the North Atlantic Treaty Organization

(NATO) taking command of the International Security Assistance Force (ISAF) in Afghanistan in 2003, where the United States and allies had been fighting against the Afghani Taliban and Al Qaeda since 2001. Those who thought they had the complete picture—of French and German opposition to the U.S. invasion of Iraq—unintentionally or intentionally failed to see additional puzzle pieces that were available, pieces that added significantly to the puzzle's picture. Partly because NATO took command of the ISAF and increased the number of troops in Afghanistan—troops from NATO nations including France and Germany—the United States could redirect its efforts and troops toward Iraq.

Without recognizing these additional pieces to the puzzle, we would never notice that, despite their public denunciation of the War on Iraq, France and Germany helped make it possible by supporting NATO engagement in Afghanistan. Such contradictions and complexities are often present in international relations; governments have to simultaneously keep their own voters happy in the short-run while maintaining long-term alliances and agreements with other countries. Governments often don't mind if their own people (or the people in other countries) fail to notice the contradictions, because it can make the governments' attempts to balance domestic and international demands easier. Those Americans involved in protests against France and Germany never noticed that France and Germany contributed, even if indirectly, to U.S. efforts in the War on Iraq, because they failed to see or ignored certain pieces to the puzzle and put together an incomplete picture.

As fascinating as the complexity is (or as many puzzle pieces as there are), our global puzzle could be *too* challenging and overwhelming without tools for managing that complexity and facilitating our study of the world, its inhabitants, their interactions, and their interconnections. Global Studies provides us with these tools. If the world is our puzzle, interdisciplinary research is how we find the pieces and figure out how to put them all into place to make our picture as complete as possible, even if we recognize it will never be fully complete.

Being Interdisciplinary

What if two approaches are at odds ?

In the face of our complex world and all there is to learn, understand, and explain within it, Global Studies helps us manage that complexity because it is one within the larger class of interdisciplinary studies. An interdisciplinary approach allows us to utilize information and scholarly analyses from many disciplines when one discipline alone will not provide us with the necessary puzzle pieces to create a full picture. Once we review what a discipline is and why it is useful to integrate them, we can examine why and how interdisciplinary Global Studies provides us with tools for understanding how the world works—for finding and placing puzzle pieces into a global picture.

In a university setting, disciplines are established, specialized fields of study. Dating back to the Greek philosopher Aristotle, scholars have tended to break complex topics into smaller sub-topics to make them easier to study. They then focus on certain subtopics as subjects of study. To go back to our puzzle metaphor, they take complete pictures and break out individual puzzle pieces to better examine each individual puzzle piece. Scholars traditionally apply this "divide-and-conquer strategy" to their studies (Newell, 2007, p. 260). For example, when faced with a problem such as environmental disaster, a biologist might look at the scientific causes; an economist might study the economic consequences for businesses, governments, and individuals; and a political scientist might examine possible government policies to reverse or prevent environmental damage. Eventually, the structure of most universities came to follow these specialized fields of study, or academic disciplines; therefore, universities have a Department of Biology and a major in Biology, a Department of Economics and a major in Economics, and so forth.

Each discipline has its own subjects of study, key concepts, theories, and accepted research methods. Individuals typically specialize in a discipline and, sometimes, a certain subject of study within that discipline. Specialization became institutionalized through university structures and the resulting education they provided to their students.

There is value to specialization; much knowledge and many scientific developments resulted from studies of ever-more-specific subjects. But the divisions between disciplines are artificial, created to help simplify subjects of study and enable scholars to better learn and study each subject through narrow research topics. Broader research topics—especially those related to complex global processes, issues, actors, events, interactions, and points of view—often cannot, however, be effectively studied by a single discipline alone. Specialization can make us too narrow to find answers to all our questions about how the world works. The creation of subdisciplines within social science disciplines demonstrates this. Subdisciplines, also called subfields, are specific areas of research within an academic discipline. As the subjects of study within disciplines got increasingly specific, scholars acknowledged the artificiality of the divisions between disciplines and how those divisions limited their ability to fully study their subjects. As a result, they began to expand their subjects of study and create new subdisciplines that again crossed disciplinary lines. Examples of such subdisciplines include political economy within the discipline of political science and economic geography within the discipline of geography.

There are problems in the world, such as environmental disasters, that we can only solve with the joint efforts of biologists, economists, and political scientists, among others. Political scientists can propose certain governmental policies to fix the damage and prevent another disaster, but would those policies be successful if they do not understand the biological causes of the environmental disaster, or if they do not understand what the damage costs those involved, including the very government that must make policies? While specialization helps us better understand certain aspects of a problem, we often cannot solve a complex problem unless all the specialists share and combine their knowledge. And that is where interdisciplinary studies or interdisciplinarity comes into play.

The idea of *interdisciplinarity* continued to exist alongside disciplines because there have always been topics that can be better explained and problems that can be better solved or managed by utilizing knowledge from more than one discipline. *Inter* simply means among or between; so interdisciplinary is among or between disciplines. The divisions between disciplines have always been artificial, if well-built and long-standing. They can hamper the study of and finding solutions for complex problems. As a result, interdisciplinarity became an educational goal during the 1900s in the United States. Going back to the early 1800s, U.S. university and college structures relied on disciplinary departments. By the early 1900s, the number of departments and subjects available in universities had expanded in response to student demand and there was a growing concern that students were becoming *too* specialized. During the 1910s and 1920s, attention focused on the creation of a common curriculum—or general education—that combined disciplines and was thus interdisciplinary even though it was not called such. Immediately prior to and then also following World War II, attention to studies of regions throughout the world, complex foreign and defense policies, and technology led to an increase in interdisciplinary teaching and research. By the 1960s and 1970s, interdisciplinarity was seen as a revolutionary approach to "boring" universities that were not keeping up with the times (Lattuca, 2001). Universities and professors became concerned about the artificial, if necessary, divisions between disciplines and their impact on what students were learning. Concerned that students were less able to study and solve complex problems, they began concerted efforts to cross and recombine the disciplines, or at least the knowledge generated by them, through creation of interdisciplinary courses, majors, research projects, and general education programs. There was, in other words, a growing push to develop *and teach* completed puzzle pictures by emphasizing why and how to put all the disciplinary puzzle pieces together again.

Although a variety of definitions for *interdisciplinary* exist, many of them generally emphasize **an interdisciplinary approach** as **a process for managing complex topics and problems, those which are too complex to be effectively explained by individual disciplines**. Any interdisciplinary approach "draws on disciplinary perspectives and integrates their insights through construction of a more comprehensive perspective" that is ultimately "complementary to and corrective of the [individual] disciplines" (Klein & Newell, 1997, p. 394). Building on earlier definitions, Repko, Szostak, and Buchberger (2014) define the term as "a cognitive process by which individuals or groups draw on disciplinary perspectives and integrate their insights and modes of thinking to advance their understanding of a complex problem with the goal of applying the understanding to a real-world problem" (p. 28).

Interdisciplinarians—people who utilize such a process to integrate information and scholarly analyses from two or more disciplines in their teaching and research—often use very specific terms to distinguish exactly how the disciplines are brought together. Two such terms are multidisciplinary and interdisciplinary. *Multidisciplinary* refers to gathering together information from several disciplines in a way that is cumulative but does not alter or necessarily combine the information. We can still identify

how specifically do we do this?

which information comes from which disciplines. A common example is a panel presentation on a topic such as terrorism. Panelists could include historians, political scientists, and sociologists. Each panelist talks individually about his or her discipline's perspective on terrorism, but no linkages are explicitly made—except perhaps in the minds of the audience. *Interdisciplinary* refers to an integration of information and scholarly analyses so that the end result is fundamentally different (and, as the saying goes, greater) than the sum of all its parts. The information and scholarly analyses of the contributing disciplines are so well combined that they no longer stand out on their own.

An effective metaphor for the differences between multidisciplinary and interdisciplinary is based on fruit, fruit salads, and smoothies (Augsburg, 2006; Nissani, 1995; Repko, 2012; Repko, Szostak, & Buchberger, 2014). Each individual discipline is a particular fruit: History is strawberries, geography is blueberries, and political science is raspberries. Multidisciplinary is a fruit salad: The individual disciplines or fruits are combined by adding each in with the others, but we can still tell which contributions are from which disciplines just as we can still see and taste the differences between the strawberries, the blueberries, and the raspberries. Interdisciplinary is a smoothie: The various disciplines or fruits are so well blended that they have become an entirely new product. We neither see nor taste the original fruits individually, but instead experience a new taste and texture as a result of blending. Both multidisciplinary and interdisciplinary efforts help us explore the complexity of how the world works; the focus here is on the integration inherent to interdisciplinary efforts.

While the idea of an interdisciplinary approach may be new, the simple fact is that, without realizing it, we all undertake a similar process of gathering, comparing, and combining information all the time. If I am running late for work and need to figure out the fastest route to get there, I might check traffic reports, consider what time of day it is and whether I have to deal with rush hour traffic, think about where there are construction zones, and factor in the weather. I gather and integrate all that information, along with the potential routes I might take, and make a decision. Doing this may not seem like I have solved a complex problem, because we all do it so often. But I have done exactly that. In fact, research shows that

> the human brain is designed to process information integratively.... A person's ability to make a series of complex decisions without consciously reflecting on all the parts of those decisions is an example of a person's natural capacity to process information integratively. (Repko, 2008, p. 276)

Every day, people make decisions in their lives and careers that involve the gathering, comparison, and combination or integration of information from multiple sources. One purpose of discussing Global Studies as an interdisciplinary process is to reflect on the fact that we already know how to undertake a similar thought process—and regularly do so. We can learn to apply a similar, if more directly analytical, process to research the world using interdisciplinary methods.

Global Studies

If our complex world—and all it encompasses—is what we are studying, interdisciplinary Global Studies provides us with effective tools to understand and manage that complexity because it combines knowledge gained from the social sciences and other relevant disciplines into comprehensive descriptions and explanations of our world. To know about how the world has worked in the past is vital, but history alone does not fully explain how it works today. To know about trade and financial interactions in the world is also vital, but knowledge of economics alone also does not fully explain how the world works. We need to add in politics, culture, and geography as well. Combining, for example, anthropology, economics, geography, history, and political science tells us more about how the world works because together they describe more facets of how the world works than any one of these disciplines does individually.

Global Studies is one of the many interdisciplinary efforts to survey relevant disciplines and recombine the knowledge generated by them to understand and manage complexity—in our case, of how the world works. As an interdisciplinary approach, Global Studies emphasizes why we recombine the information and scholarly analyses of separate disciplines and provides us with an approach for doing so. Chernotsky and Hobbs (2013) define *Global* (or *International* in their case) *Studies* as "a field of inquiry that examines the broad array of human relationships that involve cross-border interactions" (p. 3). If we build on this definition to focus on process, we can adapt the definition for general interdisciplinary studies (above) to design a definition specifically for **Global Studies: a process that utilizes the social sciences and other relevant disciplines to describe, analyze, and explain how the world works and prompt solutions for managing the complex global problems in our world.** Global Studies is a process of gathering, comparing, and combining[1] the information and scholarly analyses generated by contributing disciplines to learn about our complex world and solve or manage its complex problems. This definition can be tailored by listing disciplines specific to a particular interdisciplinary research project or a university's academic major in Global Studies. For example, based on the disciplines it includes in its Global Studies major, one university might define Global Studies as a process that utilizes information from the disciplines of anthropology, economics, geography, history, and political science to describe, analyze, and explain how the world works and prompt solutions for managing the complex global problems we face today. Other universities might include fewer or more disciplines, such as art history, communication and/or journalism, languages, literature, philosophy, religion, and sociology. Other interdisciplinary fields, including area studies such as Middle Eastern Studies or European Studies, can also contribute information and insights to Global Studies. A tailored definition can help students better understand their major, the courses included within it, and

---

[1]The "prepare, gather, compare, and combine" research process presented throughout is adapted primarily from the interdisciplinary studies process defined by Repko (2008, 2012) and Repko and Szostak (2017), and also includes ideas found in Klein (1990), Newell (2007), and Szostak (2002).

the competencies they can expect to develop before graduation. In Global Studies research, specifically, it is the complex problem under study that ultimately determines the relevant disciplines. How to determine which disciplines are relevant is covered in Chapter 3, on the Global Studies research process.

It is not only the contributing disciplines that differ from university to university; the name of the interdisciplinary major (or program) can vary as well. Global Studies, International Studies, and International Affairs are common names for interdisciplinary majors today, and World Studies is an older name still utilized by some universities. Scholars disagree about whether or not these names for the majors are interchangeable. For many, "Global" Studies is more inclusive and analytical because they see "international" as restricted to only nation-states or countries. That is, after all, what *international* means: among or between nations; the definition excludes other global actors such as NGOs. Other scholars, however, believe the term *international* has evolved and now has a connotation that includes many global actors and the interactions between them. While I use the term *Global Studies* for this book, I hope that all interdisciplinary programs studying our world—no matter the name—will find the process useful.

The social sciences are at the core of Global Studies and the field may include additional disciplines. For the purposes of this book, we focus on the disciplines of anthropology, economics, geography, history, and political science as disciplines contributing to Global Studies. This is because Global Studies majors at universities and colleges across the United States (and the similar interdisciplinary majors called International Studies or International Affairs) commonly include these disciplines in their programs.[2] Again, as noted above, some universities may include other disciplines and students should ensure they understand the disciplines included in their program of study and/or needed to complete Global Studies research.

Each of these disciplines can be considered a social science, and the social sciences are disciplines that study human behavior and interactions (broadly termed *social interactions*) in our world. More specifically, the social sciences focus on the interactions of human beings within a society. In Global Studies, we extrapolate this definition beyond human beings to countries, organizations, and other global actors—made up of human beings—and their interactions within the global system. We can use the social sciences—specifically anthropology, economics, geography, history, and political science—to understand these interactions. "The social sciences seek to explain the human world and figure out how to predict and improve it" (Repko, 2012, p. 5).

The social sciences are closely related and mutually reinforcing. We know the dividing lines between them are artificial, even if they allow for specialization. Anthropology, economics, geography, history, and political science are related to one another as social sciences and there can be overlap among them. For example, while geography specializes in studying space, place, and locations, each of the other disciplines

---

[2]Based on a 2015 review of the online mission statements and curricula of roughly 80 International Studies, Global Studies, International Affairs, and other such interdisciplinary, international programs at U.S. colleges and universities.

BOX 1.2
LEARN MORE
The Social Sciences

Colleges and universities group disciplines and majors into several large categories including the natural sciences, humanities, and social sciences. The natural sciences study the natural, physical world and include such disciplines as biology, chemistry, and physics. The humanities are the disciplines such as arts, languages, literature, and philosophy that study human creativity and what it means to be human.

The social sciences are different from the previous two in that they study the social relations and societies of human beings. Disciplines in the social sciences include anthropology, communication, economics, geography, political science, and sociology. There is debate whether a discipline such as history would be a social science or one of the humanities—because history not only studies the records produced by human beings, much as the fields of art and literature do, but also studies past social relations and societies. This tells us that the categories, while useful, are not without their overlap or critics.

contributing to Global Studies can also produce information about geographical location and its impact on the past, politics, economics, and culture. For example, prior to the advent of air travel, whether or not a country had access to a seaport was important to politics, trade and economics, and how isolated their culture was—and so scholars in the disciplines of politics, economics, and anthropology had to take geographical location into account in their studies. Each of these social science disciplines studies human beings and their behavior, but focuses on a slightly different aspect of human behavior. Each offers unique contributions and, therefore, is of value to Global Studies. Other social sciences and even disciplines in the natural sciences or humanities may be useful to Global Studies; while these five are common, your university or professor—or more important, your research project—may require other or additional disciplines to understand and explain how the world works.

Anthropology provides us with in-depth knowledge of how people live their daily lives, including family life, religion, identity, gender, and traditions—which create patterns of behavior shared by groups of people that we call *cultures*. More specific to Global Studies, anthropology contributes an understanding of the variety and impact of cultures throughout the world on how the world works and the impact of how the world works on cultures.

Economics studies the distribution of resources (or lack thereof), including the structures and functioning of the systems that produce and distribute economic resources. This can include decision making under situations of scarcity and the institutions that make those decisions. The discipline of economics considers resources and their distribution as motivators of human behavior (Repko, 2008), and so economies and how they operate are integral to Global Studies subjects of study, particularly in situations of scarcity.

Geography provides us with an understanding of space, place, and locations—and how we as humans interact with them. Where we live can impact many types of human activity, including agriculture, development, identity, languages, migration, and population. This is true at several scales or levels from the local to the global, so geography contributes information about the varied impacts of space, place, and location on Global Studies.

History examines past human behavior, particularly processes of social, political, and cultural change over time, looking for patterns and trends that help us explain how we got to where we are today—and possibly to inform where we might be going in the future. History provides the background and context for all Global Studies research—we can better understand how the world works today by understanding how it worked in the past.

Political science studies politics, or more specifically power, political ideologies, political decision making, and institutions such as governments and their relationships with their citizens. Within political science, the subfield of international relations

FIGURE 1.1   Global Studies

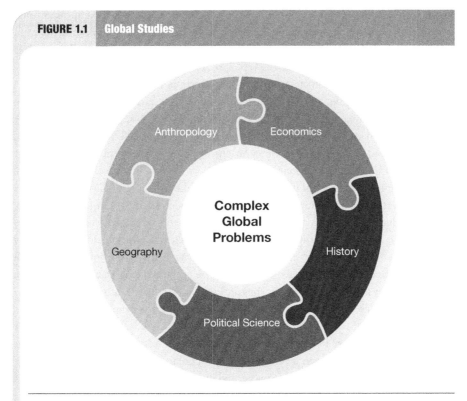

Source: iStock/theseamuss

more specifically studies governments' relationships with each other and other global actors such as international organizations. Interactions between global actors, power, and political decision making—especially as they relate to conflict or cooperation—are fundamental to all Global Studies subjects of study.

Because these disciplines make contributions to our understanding of how the world works, the facts, figures, and analyses they produce become the pieces of our global puzzle. Understanding the causes of war, for example, requires understanding how factors such as the past, politics, economic resources, culture, and geographical locations interacted to lead to conflict. To successfully use these disciplines to understand how the world works, we need to be familiar with each one individually and with how together they provide us with an understanding of our world. Anthropology, economics, geography, history, and political science may all study human behavior, but each discipline also offers its own unique contribution through its use of subjects of study, concepts, research methods, and theories that together make up a discipline's perspective (Repko, 2012).

Disciplinary Perspective

Perspective is a point of view or a way of "seeing" the world—it is the "lens" through which we view globalization, global issues, and global actors and their international interactions we want to understand. "Perspective does not mean opinion; it refers to point of view—literally, point from which something, an object outside the mind, is viewed" (Appleby, Hunt, & Jacob, 1994, p. 256). As we learn and understand the subjects of study a discipline focuses on, the key concepts it utilizes, the methods with which it gathers its data, and the theories that create its frameworks for analysis, we also learn the context within which researchers from that discipline choose to situate their experiences, analyses, opinions, and beliefs (Newell, 2007; Repko & Szostak, 2017). We begin to "see" the world as an anthropologist, economist, or geographer would. Understanding disciplinary perspectives is key to interdisciplinary studies: The lens through which a discipline views the world is its most distinctive feature, as the incorporation or integration of disciplinary perspectives into a larger, more holistic perspective is the chief distinguishing characteristic of interdisciplinary studies (Newell, 1998, p. 215). It is important to remember that while we consider disciplinary perspective a "lens" shared by those within a discipline, this does not mean that all scholars within a discipline agree on all the features that make up that lens. As can be seen in Chapter 2, theoretical approaches and research methods, in particular, are features around which debates within a discipline can center. For example, in recent years scholars within each contributing social science discipline have taken a "critical turn" or employed critical theory to question the assumptions and accepted knowledge in their respective disciplines. Yet even when disciplinary scholars disagree, it often is to change or defend a feature of that discipline's accepted perspective—and so even disagreement and debate informs us about disciplinary perspective.

One common criticism of interdisciplinary studies is to question whether students can learn enough about several disciplines to effectively utilize their information and insights (Benson, 1982; Newell, 1983; Newell, 2007). After all, doesn't it take graduate school to "master" a discipline? Interdisciplinarians acknowledge "it takes many years to learn a discipline" but counter that "it takes only a few readings to begin to develop a feel for how that discipline characteristically looks at the world, its angle of vision, its perspective" (Newell, 1998, p. 217). Global Studies researchers—in classrooms and in practice—could find themselves part of collaborative interdisciplinary teams but also working as "solo interdisciplinarians" (Newell, 2007, p. 247). Especially for the latter,

> at this point in the process, the required breadth of knowledge in each discipline is quite modest: command of the few relevant concepts, theories, or methods from each discipline that are applicable to the problem under consideration, and a basic feel for how each discipline approaches such a problem. . . . If the problem can be illuminated adequately using a handful of introductory-level concepts and theories from each discipline, and modest information is readily and simply acquired, then a solo interdisciplinary researcher or even a first-year undergraduate student can handle it. Luckily, one can get some useful initial understanding of most complex problems using a small number of relatively basic concepts and theories from each discipline. (Newell, 2007, p. 253)

Global Studies research requires that we understand disciplinary perspectives and, to have that understanding, we need to be familiar with each contributing discipline's subjects of study, key concepts, research methods, and theoretical approaches.

Subjects of Study

Subjects of study are just that: **the subjects researched within each discipline**. As mentioned above, the included Global Studies disciplines, as social sciences, study humans and human behavior. In the "divide and conquer" tradition of disciplines, however, each studies different manifestations of human activity. The disciplinary summaries in Chapter 2 briefly describe each discipline's focus, emphasizing their role in understanding the world around us.

Key Concepts

A **concept** is **an abstract idea generalized from particular instances or examples of things** (Neufeldt & Guralnik, 1991, p. 288). Such abstract ideas become key to a discipline when there are many of the particular instances or examples it is generalized from—when the idea is so common within the discipline that it becomes necessary for anyone studying within that discipline to understand it. One example is the concept of power in political science. Power can be defined as "the capacity to do things and in social situations to affect others to get the outcomes we want" (Nye, 2011, p. 6). Because there are so many instances of one leader or country trying to influence other leaders or countries, every student who seeks to study politics must grasp the concept of power.

That does not always mean concepts have widely accepted definitions, even within a single discipline. Nye's is but one definition of power. Although they may all contain similar elements, there are at least half a dozen definitions in the discipline's literature. When there are multiple definitions within a discipline, researchers must be clear in their own writing about which definition they utilize for a "fuzzy" concept. When several definitions exist, choosing one to clearly present in the research project offers readers clarity as well as researchers the firm grounding needed to determine which disciplines are relevant.

There can be overlap between concepts and other elements of disciplinary perspective—such as subjects of study and research methods. Culture is a subject of study for anthropology, but is also a concept. The very lack of clear definition tells us it is an abstract idea—a concept. One difference, however, is that concepts generally apply to and help us understand more than one subject of study—and, thus, to understand disciplinary perspective.

Research Methods

Research methods are simply **the techniques and strategies used to do research—to gather data** to learn how the world (or anything else) works. Global Studies disciplines can both have unique and shared research methods. Historical methods emphasize the gathering of primary sources such as census results, letters and diaries, and oral histories. Historians also rely on secondary sources, or what scholars have previously written about a subject of study, and those secondary sources might come from another discipline. Anthropology is often differentiated from the other social sciences by its reliance on lengthy periods of fieldwork to observe peoples and how they live their daily lives, although the disciplines of geography, history, and political science also rely on fieldwork. Economists are likely to emphasize statistical analysis of data, although the other contributing disciplines do as well.

Most scholarly books and journal articles explain their use of research methods, and there are two main categories of research methods in the social sciences: quantitative and qualitative. *Quantitative research* is about studying the "amount of something" based on "counts and measures of things" (Berg & Lune, 2012, p. 3), such as an economist studying the amount of money spent on the HIV epidemic by a country, organization, or the world as a whole. Quantitative methods often utilize experiments and "number-crunching" or "the tools and techniques of statistics, from simple graphs and tables to sophisticated multivariate techniques" (Remler & Van Ryzin, 2015, p. 61). The purpose of quantitative research is to measure, count, categorize, and classify information. The advantages include the ability to gather and process large amounts of data that allow results to be generalized into larger patterns and trends, to do so precisely and relatively efficiently, and to maintain the objectivity of the researcher. The main disadvantages are that quantitative data lacks detail and context.

Qualitative research is about studying the "nature of things" using "the what, how, when, where, and why of a thing" including "meanings, concepts, definitions, characteristics, metaphors, symbols, and descriptions" rather than numbers to understand the why and how of an issue or event (Berg & Lune, 2012, p. 3). Qualitative research has the advantage of being rich in detail and it relies on the subjective personal experiences and background of an expert researcher for interpretation, but it can be time-consuming to gain that expertise and gather the detail. Qualitative methods include observation, interviews, focus groups, and textual analysis.

While quantitative methods can tell us how much money a country is spending on the HIV epidemic, qualitative methods can tell us the human impact of that money: If a country is unable to afford to provide medical care for individuals with HIV or AIDS, how does that impact the individuals' lives? The lives of their families? Quantitative research can tell us about the financial cost whereas qualitative research can tell us about the human cost. "It is not the topic of the research that makes it qualitative or quantitative—the distinction lies in the nature of the data and methods of analysis" (Remler & Van Ryzin, 2015, p. 61).

Case study is also a qualitative method, one that involves the description and explanation of an event, issue, organization, or person as one example of a larger category of events, with the goal of using the one example as a way to partially describe and explain the larger category. The global HIV epidemic is an example of the larger category of global health issues, and thus to describe and explain the global response to the HIV epidemic provides information about how the world responds to other global health issues. Case studies are particularly useful when we need to study something "within its real-life context, especially when the boundaries between phenomenon and context are not clearly evident" (Yin, 1994, p. 13). This is often the true within Global Studies, and so Global Studies research is demonstrated here utilizing case studies of the HIV epidemic and terrorism as global issues.

In some of the social sciences, there have been ongoing debates among scholars over whether quantitative or qualitative methods are "better." Ultimately, both have their place: "A discipline tends to link with certain problems that in turn link with certain theories that in turn link with certain methods" (Repko, 2012, p. 211). While, traditionally, economists tend to rely more on quantitative methods and anthropologists on qualitative, each discipline can use both. In doing Global Studies research, we will be accessing publications that include or blend both quantitative and qualitative methods.

Research methods are an advanced topic for study within a discipline. For our purposes, we need basic knowledge of how each Global Studies discipline gathers and analyzes its information to understand the sources we read. To solve the problem of getting to work on time, mentioned earlier, I need to know where construction zones are slowing traffic. I do *not* need to understand the reasons for the construction project or the specific engineering tasks that must be carried out to finish the construction project; I need only know how the construction zone affects traffic flow at the particular time on the particular day that I will be driving to work. Similarly, in Global Studies we do not necessarily need to do original research ourselves at this point, but we do need to understand how disciplinary information and insights we rely on were gathered to use them effectively. A deeper understanding of research methods and the ability to do original research may come with additional college or university courses. Original research could then become part of your Global Studies research process, as could research in teams made up of representatives of relevant disciplines.

Theoretical Approaches

Theoretical approaches and research methods work together because theory enables a researcher to analyze the data gathered, draw conclusions, and develop scholarly insights. The use of the word theory differs between everyday life and the academic study of the social sciences. A common use of theory in everyday life is as a hypothesis—a possible explanation based on little evidence that can guide further investigation. In the social sciences, however, a **theory** is a tool we use to make sense of data we have gathered (possibly to test a hypothesis). We use theory to **analyze the relationships and patterns among facts in evidence** to draw conclusions from our information. There are many different definitions of theory across the social sciences. According to Joseph Nye (2007), a well-known political scientist, "theories are the road maps that allow us to make sense of unfamiliar terrain" (p. 8). One way is to view theories as **mental maps or frameworks we apply to information** to better understand it. Theory helps us simplify reality; without theory, we may become so lost in facts that we can only describe what we learned and are unable to analyze for relationships and patterns. However, social scientists must remember that theory can simplify reality but not replace it. As we find patterns among our facts in evidence, theories help us put our facts in a larger context as part of our analysis. Ultimately, theory serves to allow us to describe and explain our subjects of study and, in social science disciplines, to attempt to predict future patterns based on those descriptions and explanations. Theory allows us to produce insights, or scholarly analyses, from information (Newell, 2007; Repko, 2008). Across the social sciences, the terms approach, framework, and model may be used synonymously with theory.

Global Studies disciplines encompass many theories and theoretical approaches—there is no single theory that explains human behavior in general or an individual discipline's subjects of study. Depending upon the discipline, multiple approaches may coexist or compete for attention because over time theories have been proposed, tested, and criticized—and then revised or discarded. When theories coexist, we can think of them as tools in a toolbox: For our task at hand, we pull out whichever tool best allows us to accomplish that task. While both a hammer and a wrench will help us pound a nail into a wall, clearly the hammer is the better choice. The same is true of theories: We have many to choose from, but one theory may be better suited to one research topic than another. The discipline of anthropology is one that celebrates eclecticism in theories: Many coexist, such as Marxism, postmodernism, and environmental approaches, and scholars utilize whichever theory best allows them to study the subject about which they want to learn.

In the political science subfield of international relations, however, theories compete. Many scholars seek to find a single theory that best explains international relations; they object to having many tools in the toolbox and seek instead a single multipurpose tool—like a Swiss army knife that includes a knife, scissors, corkscrew, pliers, screwdrivers, file, and other implements all in one design. Debates therefore continue over international relations theories such as realism, liberalism, and constructivism as each vies to be the multipurpose tool that best explains how, for political scientists, the world works.

Because they are all social sciences studying human behavior, there are theoretical approaches common to all the contributing disciplines included here. Some scholars call these "grand theories" and hope that, because they can apply to all these disciplines, common theories may develop into that multipurpose tool. Within each discipline, they may be more or less valued. Examples of theories that are common across Global Studies disciplines include Marxism, postmodernism, and feminism.

Theory, like research methods, is an advanced topic for study within any discipline. What is important for our purposes is that theory produces the insights that result from a discipline's perspective and its unique contributions to Global Studies.

Descriptions of five contributing disciplines are in Chapter 2, emphasizing the disciplines' subjects of study, key concepts, theories, and research methods to provide an overview of its disciplinary perspective. One goal of these disciplinary descriptions is to provide you with the basics of each discipline—to allow you to effectively engage with each discipline and its perspective. Disciplinary courses in your major should also contribute to your knowledge of contributing disciplines and their perspectives.

It important to know, however, that just as the world they study constantly changes, so do the Global Studies disciplines: Advances in research and technology, the borrowing from discipline to discipline, and debates or disagreements among scholars within the disciplines can alter them over time. For example, the advances of information and communication technologies and explosion in their usage has created the need in political science for studies of e-governance, or government agencies' use of the Internet and other technologies in providing citizens with services. In anthropology, fieldwork traditionally meant travelling to and living in another country to study communities and their cultures. With the advent of the Internet, however, some anthropologists may never leave home, instead immersing themselves in online communities to study their cultures. While Chapter 2 covers the basics of each discipline here and now, those basics can change over time and future Global Studies research may require you to update as well as expand your knowledge of the contributing disciplines.

find sources from experts in every discipline related to a topic?

Global Studies Research

To learn about our complex world and how it works, we can gather information about the past, politics, economic resources, culture, and geographical locations to achieve the "big picture." To get all this, we must gather information from more than one discipline. We need to build on the knowledge of each discipline by being interdisciplinary. Interdisciplinarians tend to define the process as a series of steps, although there are many models and differing numbers of steps (Augsburg, 2006; Klein, 1990; Newell, 2007; Repko, 2006, 2012; Repko & Szostak, 2017; Szostak, 2002). What all models of the process have in common are steps for preparing, gathering, comparing, and combining information and scholarly analyses from multiple disciplinary sources so as to more fully understand the subject under study. *Global Studies Research* explains and demonstrates an interdisciplinary, integrative approach based on common critical thinking and comparison skills, utilizing the metaphor of a jigsaw puzzle. Students will learn how to gather, compare, and combine information and scholarly analyses (puzzle pieces) from the contributing disciplines of anthropology, economics, geography, history, and political science.

To undertake interdisciplinary Global Studies research, we follow a process that enables us to bring together published, secondary source research resulting from each contributing discipline's perspective and combine it into a comprehensive depiction of our subject of study. To go back to earlier metaphors, the interdisciplinary Global Studies Research process enables us to make smoothies—a final research product that combines the knowledge gained from the contributing disciplines into a fundamentally different end result. While the smoothie metaphor best describes the end goal of interdisciplinary Global Studies research, it is the jigsaw puzzle metaphor that best demonstrates the process of producing that end goal of integrative research.

We first prepare to research, by choosing our research subject and question—selecting the type of picture that our jigsaw puzzle will portray. Just as jigsaw puzzle pictures might be landscapes, city scenes, animals, or maps, our Global Studies research subject might be globalization, global issues, global actors and the interactions between them, or differing global perspectives. We then gather our research or knowledge produced by the relevant disciplines; this stretches our metaphor a bit, because instead of a single jigsaw puzzle packaged in a box full of pieces, we have to go out and find the puzzle pieces for ourselves. They are instead stored in a series of boxes, or within disciplinary and other types of research. Finally, we figure out which pieces fit together and snap them into place in the jigsaw puzzle picture—we compare and combine research results from the contributing disciplines into a comprehensive new research product. Chapter 3 goes into this research process in detail, but first Chapter 2 introduces the five contributing disciplines included here: anthropology, economics, geography, history, and political science.

2 Contributing Disciplines

nterdisciplinarians value the separate disciplines: "[T]he disciplines are founda-
tional to interdisciplinary studies because they have produced the perspectives and
insights that contribute to our ability as humans to understand our world" (Repko,
Szostak, & Buchberger, 2014, p. 29). However, "the (various) disciplines . . . were not
designed to address such complex situations, though the partial insights they provide
are absolutely essential to understanding individual aspects of a complex situation"
(Newell, 2010, pp. 9, 11). For Global Studies, the social sciences and other relevant
disciplines provide us with the necessary information and scholarly analyses and
perspectives to study, understand, and potentially solve or manage complex global
processes and issues. They are the "necessary precondition for and foundation of the
interdisciplinary enterprise" (Repko et al., 2014, p. 28). To build on that foundation,
we must have a basic understanding of relevant disciplines and their perspectives.
As noted in Chapter 1, different universities and colleges may include different
disciplines in their Global Studies, International Studies, or International Affairs
majors. Five disciplines that commonly contribute to Global Studies majors are
included here: Anthropology, Economics, Geography, History, and Political Science.
Suggestions for how to learn about additional disciplines and their perspectives are
provided later in this chapter.

Anthropology

Translated literally from the Greek, anthropology is the study of humanity. That
is, of course, a very broad subject and one that also includes the subjects of other
disciplines contributing to Global Studies. Anthropology is intentionally interdisciplinary to begin with; some anthropologists argue that anthropology "encompasses
all other disciplines related to humans" (Magli, 2001, p. 2). Yet it is still possible
to differentiate anthropology from other social sciences disciplines: Anthropology
encourages the study of how human life began and evolved and how human beings
lead their daily lives. In the United States, the discipline is broken down into four
subdisciplines, which include archeology, linguistics, physical anthropology, and
cultural anthropology.

Global Studies commonly includes cultural anthropology.[1] This is because, while all subdisciplines of anthropology contribute to our knowledge of the world, understanding the similarities and differences between—and within—the cultures of the various countries and peoples of the world especially helps us manage complexity in our world. As the American Anthropological Association (2018) points out, "a central concern of anthropologists is the application of knowledge to the solution of human problems."

Modern cultural anthropology dates to roughly the turn of the 20th century, but has roots that go much further back. We know ancient scholars such as Plato were interested in the worldviews of different peoples, and worldview is a fundamental aspect of culture. As European countries sought colonies in the 17th, 18th, and 19th centuries, members of their militaries, missionaries, colonial administrators, and travelers began telling and publishing stories of the different peoples they encountered and how they lived their day-to-day lives in their local communities. Such stories were usually based on each person's experience with other peoples' religions, traditions, families, and food and shelter, not academic analyses. However, throughout this period this secondhand data was used by European thinkers to lay the foundation for the scientific study of other cultures. Today's trained anthropologist studies many of the same subjects, but from a very different perspective.

Subjects of Study

Cultural anthropology focuses on understanding how people in different countries, different communities, and different groups live their lives, how they view the world, and how they view their place within the world. There is, however, no single agreed-on definition of culture. When possible, many anthropologists seek to use more specific terms in place of the ill-defined term *culture*. Anthropology started as the study of other cultures understood to be discreet units as they were discovered during colonial eras; anthropology has proceeded to become more diversified and complex through the decades due to modernization, globalization, and so forth. As a discipline tied to real-world problems, anthropology itself has also become increasingly complex and, consequently, many cultural anthropologists are less dedicated to the study of "culture" per se and more dedicated to complex problems for which culture provides significant context.

Anthropologists study the formation of identities, social relationships, and group affiliations, often broken down into smaller topics such as kinship, family, and marriage. Religions, rituals, and traditions also make up our daily lives and so anthropologists

---

[1] *Cultural anthropology* is the term used in the United States; the American Association of Anthropologists uses the term "cultural anthropology" for the subdiscipline while at the same time utilizing "sociocultural anthropologists" for those within the field. European, particularly British, anthropologists utilize the term *social anthropology*.

study them. Individual and community conceptions of health are important to how people live their lives. Common daily activities such as preparing and eating food, labor (employment), and leisure activities are all subjects of study. As are the economic exchanges that may be needed for people to grow or obtain food and other objects, necessary or desired. Society can be a subject of study and a term that can also be ill-defined, but generally refers to the groups formed as individuals choose to live and interact with one another, including the structures, functions, and rules of those groups. Monaghan and Just (2000) make the distinction that "we may *have* a culture, but we *belong* to a society" (p. 53; emphasis in original). Within societies, humans often live within or identify with even smaller groupings, so additional subjects of study can include language and communication, socioeconomic class, race/ethnicity, gender and sexual orientation, age, and personhood. Interactions between and across societies and countries also impact culture, so transnational activities and globalization are subjects of study, as are geographical location and the natural environment. Laws and customs governing all this—including politics—also constitute what anthropology studies.

Key Concepts

Culture encompasses all this—and more. As noted above, disciplinary subjects of study and concepts can overlap. Culture remains a complex concept in anthropology in part because it remains under study and debate. While there is no single, agreed on definition, most definitions include an emphasis on identifiable, if evolving and varied, behaviors or ways of life common to a particular time, group, and/or place that people learn and share through social interactions. Anthropologists must understand culture as a concept at the same time they refine it through further study.

When Magli (2001) asserts that anthropology "aims at understanding the global significance of a people's life, calling that significance—though with countless different shades of meaning—'culture'" (p. 8), she is explaining not only culture but also raising the equally important concept of comparison. Just as concepts can overlap with the subjects of study, they can also overlap with research methods; comparative analysis is common in the social sciences and is, quite simply, the search for similarities and differences. In the case of anthropology, that would be the similarities and differences between cultures and their ways of life. Anthropologists can use these similarities and differences to generalize about cultures—or to criticize other anthropologists' generalizations.

Comparison is inherent to as well as a tool to study different cultures' systems of classification. Classification is the act of separating people, animals, objects, ideas, events, and such into different categories to define and order them. Categories help humans understand, for example, that a chair is something one sits on, even if there are many different types of chairs—rather than relearning each time one sees a new type of chair that it is an object to sit on. A single person, object, or idea may fit more than one category, because categories can overlap and change in meaning over time as well as place. Race is another example of classification, where humans divide themselves and

to what extent can we do this? (if issues are intertwined)

each other into categories based on physical characteristics. Historically, some believed that different races were divisions or subspecies among humankind; today, we know from DNA technology that there are no such divisions or subspecies—only culturally assigned understandings of physical differences. Anthropologists seek to understand the similarities and differences between the classification systems of various cultures, as such systems can help us understand how a culture and individuals within it see the world and their place within it.

Researchers must be very careful in how they make their comparisons, create categories, or study classifications systems, however. During the 18th and 19th centuries, some anthropologists understood culture to be a measure of how "civilized" a society was based on such things as art, architecture, and technology. European colonizers thus believed themselves superior to the "primitive" peoples in the new lands they discovered and conquered. Believing they could enlighten and civilize "the natives," imperial Europeans changed the ways of life in their colonies without understanding the inherent cultures. This was destructive in many ways and, coupled with the economic exploitation of colonization, has had lasting detrimental effects in many former colonies even now that they are independent nations. Today, we use the term *ethnocentrism* to describe the feeling that one's own group is superior and anthropologists actively work to ensure that cultures and classification systems are seen as different, not better or worse.

To avoid the racism and prejudice built into ethnocentrism, Frank Boas, a German emigrant known today as a founder of American anthropology, developed the concept of cultural relativism, which insists that every culture should be examined on its own merits and that no culture is superior to another. Cultures can be carefully compared, to understand the similarities and differences, but not judged as better as or worse than another. While unscrupulous scholars can misuse cultural relativism— most notably during Apartheid in South Africa (Lavenda & Schultz, 2008)—it should enable anthropologists to set aside their own prejudices as they study other cultures and communities.

Holism and context are related, key concepts for the discipline of anthropology. Holism is, simply put, the idea that the whole is greater than the sum of all its parts: As individuals interact to learn, share, and influence their ways of life, "culture" is created and that culture amounts to more than just the individual interactions. Culture includes behaviors, institutions, and structures that existed prior to the current generation of individuals and will outlast those individuals. Later generations will, in turn, learn, share, and influence culture as well. Understanding the whole—the culture— gave meaning to individual interactions. The concept of holism remains the basis for cultural anthropology's fieldwork-based methodology.

Anthropologists came to debate the concept of holism because some feel that referencing the whole devalues the individual, because if the individual has meaning only in relation to the whole, we have erased individual actions and agency from the equation. For this reason, the use of the concept holism has arguably diminished and been replaced, to an extent, by the similar idea of context. Context considers the interconnections between individuals and between individuals and their wider communities—even the wider world, as encompassed by globalization and transnationalism. The context is the whole, and it can be greater than the sum of its individual parts—if perhaps more temporary and limited than the institutions and structures of holism. Every interaction can have more than one possible context. Some anthropologists replace holism and context with the ideas of scale of integration, to make the point that the emphasis is on the interactions that link the individual parts within the whole. Whichever the preferred term, the emphasis is on the big picture and understanding individual people, groups, events, and so forth within that bigger picture. Anthropologists seek to ensure that the parts are viewed within the appropriate whole.

Anthropology, like the other contributing disciplines, has more concepts, both in terms of number and specialization, than can be introduced here. Students utilizing research from anthropology must ensure they understand the necessary concepts, and may need to engage in further study of the discipline in order to do so. Additionally, when concepts such as society are broadly defined because their meanings are controversial and changing, it is even more important to understand them within each discipline and disciplinary perspective, as meanings can differ for a concept common to more than one discipline.

Research Methods

Anthropologists of all four subdisciplines utilize a wide variety of qualitative and quantitative research methods. The hallmarks of cultural anthropology, however, are fieldwork and ethnography. Also called participant observation, the main data-gathering method of many anthropologists is to spend extended periods of time with the population under study. Traditionally, this has meant anthropologists reside in other countries with their subjects of study, living as they live, observing and interacting with them to learn about their daily lives and how they view the world. Pioneering ethnographer Bronislaw Malinowski undertook a study of the Triobriand people of New Guinea, publishing *Argonauts of the Western Pacific* in 1922. More recently, "fieldwork" can occur within one's own society, such as corporations or other organizations, and has even moved online or across the boundaries between the physical and virtual worlds when anthropologists study digital communities.

Fieldwork requires considerable preparation; anthropologists will study the necessary language(s), history, and existing knowledge and literature of their subject people, groups, or community. Rather than attempting to study entire cultures, as in the past, today's anthropologists undertake problem-based ethnography and develop a research proposal presenting their research methods, theoretical approaches, and, possibly, hypotheses and expected results. They use their proposals to apply for funding and academic, ethical, governmental, and other necessary permissions and permits to undertake their fieldwork.

Once in the field, anthropologists may use a variety of research methods, such as oral histories, surveys, focus groups, archival research, review of art or artifacts, genealogical research, and so forth. For many anthropologists, however, a key method for gathering data is the in-depth interview—talking to the research subjects, usually called informants or participants. This can be in a formal, structured interview or very informally over a meal or drink. An effective anthropologist values the "serendipity" of "being there" to observe, interact, and learn when something significant or enlightening happens with the group, community, or organization under study (Eriksen, 2004, p. 45; Monaghan & Just, 2000, p. 22).

Ethnography is the written product that results from an anthropologist's process of describing and analyzing the data gathered during fieldwork. These can include reports, academic journal articles, or books. The production of ethnography is an ongoing process that occurs both during fieldwork and after, when anthropologists reflect on and further analyze the data gathered. The anthropologists' goal is to understand the information gathered as the informant would—to see life and the world the same way their informants would—so as to add insights and information to the global store of knowledge. The content and styles of ethnography have changed over time, between more positivist approaches that seek the "objective truth" about a culture or group under study and more humanistic approaches that consider the anthropologist's experience.

This is why the concepts of comparison and context are so important to anthropology. Anthropologists will consider the similarities and differences between their own perceptions and those of their informants. They seek to adopt their informants' self-understanding as best they can so as to analyze how those narratives compare to others and how those perceptions fit within the "bigger picture" created by the multiplicity of viewpoints in our world today. Cultural relativity and avoiding bias are also vital as anthropologists analyze their fieldwork data and experience.

A number of academic journals publish anthropological research. The American Anthropological Association has over 20 journals, including *Annals of Anthropological Practice*, *Medical Anthropology Quarterly*, *Culture, Agriculture, Food & Environment*, and *Journal of Latin American and Caribbean Anthropology*, and *Cultural Anthropology*.

Theoretical Approaches

If theoretical approaches are tools in the anthropology toolbox, today there is an extensive set available to guide anthropologists as they analyze data gathered through fieldwork or other research methods. Early, now discredited, anthropological theories of evolutionism and diffusionism assumed that societies and cultures evolved from "primitive" to "modern." Such theories presumed European societies as advanced whereas others were backwards, justifying colonialism and European intervention in the "primitive" societies of Africa, Asia, and South America. Boas' concept of cultural relativism was a response to and critique of evolutionist views of the "civilized" overseeing the "savages."

Moving into the 20th century, anthropologists ceased ranking societies and cultures but continued to study them as a whole. Structural functionalism emphasized how people interacted within a society or culture and how those interactions created institutions such as marriage or norms such as taboos. All this together, to advocates of structural functionalism, made up the social structure of a society and helped maintain that society.

Critics of this approach argued that the emphasis on society as a whole—studying the collective—left out an understanding of individuals, some of whom would or could not adhere to the societal institutions or norms accentuated by structural functionalism. The role of individuals in society became a focus of anthropological studies, even privileged over societies and cultures for some anthropologists. These may be termed psychological anthropology or cognitive anthropology. The resulting dispute over studying *either* individuals or the collective eventually subsided and scholars acknowledge the importance of *both* individuals and social structures to understanding how peoples lived their daily lives.

Marxism influenced all social sciences, including anthropology. Marxist anthropologists and others who built their approaches on Karl Marx's ideas (even if, especially in the United States, they don't call themselves Marxist) focus on how economic, material, and ideological factors impact and can prompt change in culture. This can include studies of production, consumption, and materialism. A related approach considers how technology and access to it affects culture. This was not a return to evolutionism or an assumption that low-technology societies are primitive. Instead, the emphasis is often on economic development and inequality. The impact of material factors also plays into environmental and ecological approaches to understanding how people live their daily lives and how the environment can put pressure on culture. For example, anthropologists can study pollution resulting from production or economically driven overuse of natural resources such as fisheries.

As, over time, scholars tested and debated existing theoretical approaches, a group of newer approaches developed that were critical of historical and existing theories. Clifford Geertz's emphasis on "thick description" arguably led into the development of critical theories such as postmodernism and feminism. Geertzian interpretivism suggested that detailed description and a single anthropologist's interpretation of a culture was enough to add to knowledge. Cultures were "texts to be read" and different anthropologists could develop different interpretations of them. Postmodernism believes that different scholars will see cultures differently, because they assume that knowledge is contested and political in nature. Postmodernists question the ideals of rationality and science, emphasizing that much in our world—including and perhaps especially culture—is socially constructed and thus subject to interpretation. Feminists also question what we know (or think we know), particularly about women and existing power relationships that result from traditional understandings of gender roles and their impact on societies and cultures.

While brief, this overview of theoretical approaches in anthropology makes it clear that the discipline accepts a multiplicity of approaches. Today, most anthropologists have given up on finding a single, grand theory and instead recognize that different approaches can illuminate different subjects of study.

Anthropology as a discipline has "humanity" as its all-encompassing subject of study and yet it makes its own distinct contributions to the social sciences in general and Global Studies specifically. Eriksen (2000) argues "the task of anthropology is to create astonishment, to show that the world is both richer and more complex than it is usually assumed to be" (p. 7). He also concludes:

> anthropology is so broad that it moves . . . in the frontier areas [near other disciplines], at the same time as it . . . retains its own identity. The shared identity that keeps the discipline together . . . can be summed up as an insistence on regarding social and cultural life from within, a field method largely based on interpretation, and a belief (albeit variable) in comparison as a source of theoretical understanding. (p. 80)

Economics

The discipline of economics focuses on a variety of factors related to resources, be they natural, human, or material. Economics has, therefore, been of interest to thinkers and scholars for millennia—going back to ancient Greece, India, and China. An independent discipline today, economics emerged from the discipline of philosophy. Many fundamental questions and concepts of economics came from early Western philosophers such as John Locke and David Hume; Adam Smith, one of the most famous names in economics, was a moral philosopher. He is considered the father of modern economics and as his famous 1776 book *An Inquiry Into the Nature of Causes of the Wealth of Nations* suggests, early economic thinkers were especially interested in political economy, as in "economy of the polity." Economics (initially called economic science) became an independent discipline in the late 18th to early 19th centuries.

Economics studies the distribution of scarce resources and the decision-making processes related to that distribution. The discipline considers three main questions: (1) what will be produced, which is related to allocation; (2) how it will be produced, which is related to resources; and (3) who is going to get it, which is distribution. There are many subdisciplines of economics; microeconomics, macroeconomics, international economics, and development economics are all important to Global Studies. Micro-economics examines single or specific factors of the economy and individual decision making while macroeconomics emphasizes how the individual factors interact and work together to create an economic entity—such as the economy of a nation-state. International economics concentrates on international differences in resource allocation and distribution as well as the international organizations that influence them. Development economics studies and seeks to improve the economies of low-income countries, where resources are often most scarce or poorly distributed due to a host of historical, political, cultural, and geographic factors.

Subjects of Study

The subfields of economics relevant to Global Studies help introduce the discipline's subjects of study. Resources of all kinds are considered, though the main categories are often land or national resources, labor or human resources, and capital or productive resources such as equipment and technology. Economists study the allocation and distribution of resources through the economic market, or system of decisions related to the exchange of goods and services. There are two main theoretical types of economies: (1) the free market economy where decisions and prices are dictated by supply and demand and (2) a centrally planned or command economy where decisions and prices are determined by the government. In reality, most modern economies are a mixture of both types, though usually predominantly one or the other. A free market economy puts emphasis on the private sector, or the part of the economy not owned, controlled, or provided by the government though the government may institute regulations. Subjects of study related to the private sector include employment and profits. The public sector is that part of the economy owned, controlled, or provided by the government, including monetary policy, fiscal policy and taxation, deficit spending, and provision of social services. Poverty and how to reduce it is an important topic within and among countries, particularly low-income countries or low-income regions within high-income countries. Borrowing, saving, and investing as well as socio-cultural factors such as gender inequality, racial inequality, and access to and quality of education are subjects of inquiry for economists, both generally and in relation to poverty (Dasgupta, 2007). International trade and finance encompass the flows of goods, services, labor, capital, and currency across national borders. Economists also study international organizations such as the World Bank, International Monetary Fund, and United Nations Development Programme, which can influence what happens in both private and public sectors of the economy.

Key Concepts

Just as there can be for other contributing social science disciplines, there is overlap between subjects of study and key concepts within economics. The concept of the free market system, based on supply and demand, is central to today's global economy. This system is not universally appreciated, however, because of the tension between efficiency and equity. Related to efficiency is the concept of opportunity cost, or the benefit lost from other alternatives when one choice is made. Theoretically in a market system, prices determine the efficient allocation of resources and goods; those who can make the most effective use of resources and goods, without waste, can obtain them. However, not everyone has the same resources to begin with, so this creates inequity in the system. Inequity and market failures, or "when markets fail to perform efficiently or fail to perform according to other widely held social values," can be reasons for government intervention in the economy. If market failures limit resources or goods related to basic human needs such as food or housing, societal values can impact the market through demands for government redistribution of resources and goods through social welfare policies such as housing subsidies, supplementary income for food, and the like (Orvis & Drogus, 2019, p. 317).

Societal values also interact with the idea of public goods. Private goods are "rivalrous and excludable": if I can protect my food from you (excludable) and I eat it all, you cannot share in it (rivalrous). Public goods are "non-rivalrous and non-excludable." If a government provides its people with national security, then everyone within the country shares in that security (non-excludable) and what security one receives does not prevent any others from also receiving security (non-rivalrous). However, because they are non-excludable and people can obtain them for free (free-rider problem), the private sector does not normally supply public goods. If a public good is important to a society, the government must provide it (Dasgupta, 2007, p. 52).

Another well-known economic thinker was David Ricardo, who proposed the concept of comparative advantage. This is the idea that "through free trade, all countries . . . would develop and could become wealthy by focusing on producing the products they themselves did better than they did other products." Ricardo was also a member of Parliament and his ideas influenced British—and eventually global—economic and trade policy. International trade results from and increases interdependence, or "the mutual connections that tie states and other players to each other. No state is fully independent and able to provide for all its needs and manage all its problems" (Scott, Carter, & Drury, 2019, pp. 25, 236).

Common measures of how wealthy countries are (or are not) include Gross Domestic Product (GDP) and Gross National Product (GNP). GDP "is the total value of all goods and services produced in the nation in a year" and GNP adds to that the net income from foreign investments (Weaver, 2017, p. 78). While common, GDP is also a controversial measure of national wealth, as it arguably does not account for human well-being. Additional measures have been introduced; the GINI coefficient highlights inequality by measuring the distribution of wealth across a nation's population. The Human Development Index, created by Indian economist Amartya Sen and Pakistani economist Mahbub ul Haq, and its variant the inequality-adjusted Human Development Index, incorporates per capita economic measures but also life expectancy and education levels.

The concept of development, which buttresses the subdiscipline of development economics, describes economic and social growth in countries, particularly the process that "allow(s) people to escape poverty and lead longer and healthier lives" (Goldin, 2018, p. 148). Considerable research—in economics and other disciplines—addresses the challenges and opportunities facing low-income countries and their peoples. Sustainable development is a related concept. The world recognizes that the processes that allowed high-income countries to develop negatively impacted the Earth's environment. This was largely due to the concept of externality: "transactions that do not include the full costs or benefits of production in the price" (Orvis & Drogus, 2019, p. 317)—in this case, a cost in the sense of pollution or other damage to the environment. "Economic development is sustainable if, relative to its population, a society's productive base doesn't shrink." Sustainable development efforts today seek to ensure that "society's productive base" includes our natural environment and resources (Dasgupta, 2007, p. 129).

Research Methods

Economics as a discipline relies heavily on quantitative research methods, employing mathematical and statistical models and methods for theoretical and applied research. Economics employs both normative and positive research, the former being theoretical- or opinion-based research on how the economy should work and the latter being evidence-based and applied research on how the economy does work. In reality economics, like the other social sciences, finds that the line between normative and positive is sometimes blurred. Value-based judgments about poor social outcomes like poverty and inequality often lead to positive economic analysis about how to provide better outcomes through economic policies. The discipline uses a blend of inductive and deductive reasoning to solve economic problems, with inductive reasoning being positivist and deductive reasoning allowing economists to analyze how to make economic outcomes better.

Qualitative methods are not generally associated with economics. However, Starr (2014) asserts that there has been growing interest in qualitative methods and mixed methods (combining quantitative and qualitative methods) in the discipline for the last 10 to 15 years. She reviews more than two dozen qualitative or mixed-methods studies of economic subjects ranging from price stickiness to innovation in industry to development and poverty to household saving, spending, and borrowing. Qualitative methods used alone or in combination with quantitative methods by economics scholars include interviews, focus groups, life histories, and case studies. These methods appear especially useful to economists seeking to understand the economic lives of women, refugees, the low-income, and those with health issues, including mental illness.

The American Economic Association (AEA) is a professional association for the discipline, as is the European Economic Association. AEA journals include *American Economic Review, Journal of Economic Perspectives,* and *The American Economic Journal: Applied Economics.* Other important scholarly journals for the field are *Journal of the European Economic Association, Economy Theory,* and the *Journal of Development Economics.*

Theoretical Approaches

Economic theories center on the main modern economic systems: capitalism, communism, socialism, and mixed economies. Each system is based on theory—the theory of capitalism, for example—and no currently operating economic system fully matches the theorized version. Thus, additional theories develop to explain why and how the economy operates under various conditions and to suggest solutions to economic challenges. In general, economic theory can be positive or normative.

Capitalism combines the free market system with private ownership of property. Though not the first, Karl Marx is one of the best-known critics of capitalism. Writing in the mid-1800s, Marx argued that all societal changes reflect economic changes and that societies develop through a series of stages: from the primitive communism of hunter-gatherer days to the feudal system seen in Europe in the middle ages to capitalism and then on to socialism, where goods and services would be distributed according to need, and finally to communism. Theoretically, communism would happen when human nature had changed to allow for stateless and classless societies. Communist systems such as the Soviet Union were command economies that did not fit Marxist theory. Theories of socialism also grew out of Marxism and are particularly concerned with solving the societal problems of capitalism, such as poverty. Socialism encompasses a wide range of economic forms and has no single definition. What most socialist economies—as well as mixed economies, which combine features of socialism with features of capitalism—have in common is government intervention in the economy to create a substantial welfare state that meets basic human needs and promotes individual autonomy through provision of social services. While many capitalist countries offer at least some social services to low-income citizens, in a socialist country there is a wider range of benefits available universally.

Because today most countries are capitalist (or mixed) and the global system is as well, most economic theories serve as frameworks to understand, explain, and manage challenges to capitalism. Historically, as capitalism developed, free trade was not the global norm. Economic nationalism, also called protectionism or (in the past) mercantilism, involves utilizing trade policy to protect national interests. Economic nationalists believe it is appropriate to limit trade to protect national industries and employment. Tools of economic nationalists include tariffs and quotas. Tariffs are essentially taxes on imported goods, making them more expensive than domestically produced goods. Quotas are limits on the number goods, such as automobiles, that can be imported from abroad.

Two prominent economic theories in the 21st century are Keynesianism and neo-liberalism, both of which address economic downturns. In the 1930s, John Maynard Keynes suggested that "governments can manage the business cycles of capitalism via active fiscal policy and monetary policy, including deficit spending when necessary" (Orvis & Drogus, 2019, p. 322). This macroeconomic theory argued nation-states could run a short-term deficit to stimulate the economy and clear the deficit when the economy improved (Orvis & Drogus, 2019, p. 322). Keynesianism held sway until the 1970s–1980s, when neo-liberal, or free market, polices reemerged to compete with it. Associated with Milton Friedman and Friedrich Hayek, neo-liberalism is against deficit spending. This theory holds that the "government should balance its budget and minimize its role in the economy to allow the market to allocate resources to maximize efficiency and thereby economic growth" (Orvis & Drogus, 2019, p. 324). The Global Recession beginning in 2008 reflected the debate between these two theories; the United States relied primarily on the Keynesian model while some countries in Europe adopted neo-liberalism and austerity.

Also important in the 20th and 21st centuries are development theories, through which economists (and policy makers) have sought to decrease poverty and improve economic growth; there have been a number of approaches to understanding "why are some countries rich and others poor?" As former colonies gained independence, global efforts to promote economic growth in their economies assumed there was one way for all countries to develop—the path that Europe and the United States took. Modernization theory reflected this view, emphasizing the need for developing countries to engage in international trade and acquire a "free market mindset" as well as for developed countries to reduce aid. These priorities failed, as did modernization theory as an approach to development, in part because the "one size fits all" approach did not take into account the impact of colonization on the recently independent countries. Building on this history, dependency theory gained traction by suggesting that developed countries continue to exploit the former colonies and "the only way that countries could escape the trap of . . . underdevelopment was to end their dependence on the advanced economies by stopping import of manufactured goods and export of primary goods" (natural resources). This resulted in import substitution industrialization and government intervention to protect growing sectors of the domestic economy. By the 1970s and 1980s, neo-liberalism also reemerged in development theory, and policies shifted toward privatization, reduction of government spending, removal of price subsidies, and deregulation. Despite some success stories, many countries remained underdeveloped at the close of the 20th century. Moving into the 2000s, development approaches have taken on a more holistic view, looking not only at the economy but also political stability and governance as well as aspects of human well-being such as education and health. Nonetheless, the challenge of development remains (Goldin, 2018).

This holistic approach to development reflects the complexity of that challenge, and the world faces many complex economic challenges. As Weaver (2017) points out, there is a difference between the academic discipline of economics and the economy itself: "[T]he discipline of economics provides one way to view the organization and operation of the economy, but researchers must think critically about the particular viewpoint proposed by the discipline of economics" (pp. xiv–xv). The discipline is, of course, made up of more than one viewpoint but they are all informed by the discipline's perspective, based on subjects of study, key concepts, research methods, and theoretical approaches. Anthropology also does what Dasgupta (2007) credits to economics in that both "tr(y) to uncover the processes that influence how people's lives come to be what they are" (p. 7). The difference is disciplinary perspective—and the economics perspective is necessary to Global Studies.

Geography

Geography as a discipline studies the Earth's surface and humans as they interact with that surface. As Bonnett (2008) suggests, "the world is geography's logo" (p. 2). That imagery suggests the discipline's broad arena of interests and activities. Like anthropology, geographers see their discipline as inherently interdisciplinary and, according to John Nietz (1961), the "'mother of many other subjects'" (as cited in Bonnett, 2008, p. 104). Others see geography as developing from the disciplines of history or anthropology.

The discipline includes two main subfields: physical geography and human geography. As the Association of American Geographers explains, human geography focuses on "the spatial aspects of human existence" while "physical geographers study patterns of climates, landforms, vegetation, soils, and water" (American Association of Geographers, 2018). Some geographers consider the discipline a bridge between the natural sciences and social sciences, as physical geographers are often more comfortable with the natural sciences and human geographers engage with and are influenced by social sciences. Human geography is often more commonly seen in Global Studies, but both subfields can be relevant.

The study of geography has ancient origins, going back at least to Ancient Greece and Rome. "The oldest literatures we have are geographies," such as The Odyssey and the tale of the Golden Fleece (Bonnett, 2008, p. 7). The ancient Chinese study of geography was highly developed, including the use of triangulation and coordinates. As Europe entered the Middle Ages and much knowledge from the Greeks and Romans was lost, Islamic countries continued to expand geographical knowledge and information. In the 10th century, Arab geographer Al Muqaddasi began what would become known as fieldwork. Where earlier geographers had relied on the information of others—explorers and travelers—he "would not present anything as fact to his readers unless he had seen it with his own eyes" (Holt-Jensen, 2018, p. 24).

Geography as an academic discipline was also preceded by popular geographical societies and associations such as the Société de Géographie de Paris and the British Royal Geographical Society in London. These organizations or clubs mixed members from the scientific community with the political, economic, and social elite. Given the inclusion of the elite, many associations also served to support imperialism and political interests. They funded expeditions and research, collecting data and insights from abroad (Holt-Jensen, 2018). Geographical societies were an "essential means of communication between the explorers and the general public, including their sponsors" (Matthews & Herbert, 2008, p. 2).

While geography was a subject offered in British universities as early as the 16th century, the academic discipline generally dates from the 1870s to 1880s, when European and American universities began to have professorships in and departments of geography (Holt-Jensen, 2018; Matthews & Herbert, 2008). There are a number of subdisciplines or specializations within geography, such as cartography, cultural geography, economic geography, geographic information systems, human-environment interaction, natural hazards, political geography, population geography, and regional geography (American Association of Geographers, 2018).

Subjects of Study

There is logical overlap between these specializations and the subjects of study in geography. Common subjects of study include culture, language, and religion, particularly the geographic distribution or geographic patterns of each. Geographers look at the economy as it relates to such topics as agricultural regions and production or the locations of industry and manufacturing. The subjects of study related to human interactions with their geographical environment include population density and distribution, migration, resilience to natural or man-made disasters, and environmental problems such as climate change. Politics or political geography is a common subject of study, ranging from public administration and urban planning at the local level to international relations at the global level, including the boundaries of states, regional cooperation such as the European Union, and war. Natural resources are also a topic of research for geographers, whether as a physical aspect of the Earth or as a factor in economics, environmental issues, or political decision making. Development would also be a subject of geographic study that links with other topics such as economics, environment, and politics.

Key Concepts

Key concepts help geographers understand and approach their subjects of study. Many geography textbooks agree on two concepts key to understanding the discipline: space and place. Definitions of space have changed over time, in conjunction with shifts in theoretical approaches and disciplinary politics. Space generally refers to a location or position on Earth's surface; it can be absolute space measured through objective means such as geographical coordinates or distances or it can be relative space, which relies also on human perceptions of that position. Whether absolute or relative, space can also be defined as "the physical gap or interval between two objects" (Rubenstein, 2011, p. 489). Place is what we casually think of as location. It is "a meaningful portion of space" (Cresswell, 2006, p. 356)—space that has boundaries to make up recognizable territory or characteristics. Like space, place also involves human perceptions because place can be delimited by human understandings of a particular "portion" of space. Our "mental maps" of a neighborhood may differ from the lines on a government map or the tax or police districts that neighborhood falls into.

Other than space and place, there is less agreement on the key concepts of geography. For Global Studies, orientation, environment, distribution and related concepts, and scale are also important. As interdisciplinary researchers, if we need to understand additional key concepts we can consult geography textbooks or experts to learn more.

Mental maps are a form of orientation; as humans we assign meaning to places based on physical or human characteristics, such as the Cold War political views of "West" being Europe and the United States and "East" being areas controlled by the Soviet Union. Eastern Europe is made up of countries such as Poland, East Germany, Czechoslovakia, and Romania but geographically doesn't exist (it is Central Europe). During the Cold War, however, eastern Europe was a political and geographic reality, given the controlled and patrolled boundaries between the East and West.

Environment can take on several related meanings in geography. Most generally, it can be our "surroundings" (Fellman, Getis, & Getis, 2007, p. 516). It is the physical and natural environment, but understanding the link between humans and their physical surroundings has been a long-term goal of geography so the term can also apply to the processes of human and natural interaction. Environmental damage or degradation can result from that relationship, so the term is also used in the popular sense of environmental issues, problems, and crises.

Distribution is "the arrangement of objects across surfaces." Geographers may look at the distribution of natural resources, buildings, languages, or political systems across the earth's surface. Diffusion is the process through which the objects come to be distributed. Languages and ideas can spread through space, as can policies or products. Density is a related concept that describes "the frequency with which something exists within a given" space. Population density is a common subject in geography. Pattern is also a related concept, which considers not just if there is an arrangement of objects in space but whether or not that arrangement is geometric—such as the grid pattern of streets common in U.S. cities (Rubenstein, 2011, pp. 32–33, 484).

In Global Studies and globalization, there is much discussion of the local and the global. Both are scales in the geographic sense, which refers the size or scope of the area under study. It can also refer to a comparison between the size of the area under study and the size of a larger area covered on a map—or the earth as a whole. In political geography, scales can include local, national, regional, and global, such as a local disease outbreak or a global epidemic.

Research Methods

As a discipline, geography utilizes a wide variety of social science research methods, both qualitative and quantitative. Geography is a social science within which there has been debate over the value of qualitative and quantitative methods. As human geography developed, from the early- to the mid-20th century there was an emphasis on both regional geography and the interaction between humans and their environment, including culture. This human-oriented research was generally qualitative. Quantitative methods such as statistical analyses became more popular in the 1950s and 1960s, because geographers sought to avoid descriptions about what was unique about places (especially regions) and better follow scientific methods. Quantitative "spatial science" developed and dominated the discipline for a decade or two. By the 1970s, the interest in culture and interpretation had returned and many became critical of quantitative methods. Today, the discipline sees fewer dramatic shifts between methods and more use of both as appropriate to subdisciplines and subjects of study. Holt-Jensen (2018) calls this a "multi-paradigmatic" approach, reflecting many options ranging from "hard" quantitative methods to "soft" humanistic or qualitative approaches (p. 134).

Geographers consider their discipline to be closely identified with fieldwork. Early in the discipline's history, they conducted fieldwork to undertake cartography—to create maps. Explorers traveled to discover and map new parts of the world—and to stake claims for their respective countries and identify resources available. Within known territories, surveys were conducted to identify natural and artificial features of an area as well as significant locations, distances, and directions. In the 20th century, geographic fieldwork took on more human and cultural as well as physical investigations, with geographers being influenced by anthropologists such as Bronislaw Malinowski and Clifford Geertz. Today, fieldwork goes beyond mapping to include tools such as interviews, surveys, photography, and observation to gather geographic information and data. The comparative method can be utilized in analyzing data, as can classification. Geographers will analyze and evaluate their fieldwork data and likely reflect on the experience (as anthropologists do) before communicating their findings in published research, including in journals such as *Geographic Review* and *Journal of Geography in Higher Education*.

By the 21st century, computer technology added new dimensions to mapping, both physical and human—as well as combining the two. Geographical Information Systems (GIS) use computer programs to combine data, statistical software packages, and computer graphics software to create maps. "Computer-assisted cartography" can combine data into layered maps, such as one where, for the purposes of city planning, the basic terrain is layered first with utility lines and grids, then property lots and lines, and then voting or school districts (Fellman et al., 2007, p. 26).

GIS is complemented by 21st-century technological advancements in Earth observation as well. Observation of Earth's surface from a distance is not new; early geographers used first balloons and kites, then (and still) aircraft before technology made remote sensing possible by drones, spacecraft, and satellites. Together, GIS and remote sensing have drastically increased the flexibility, complexity, and accuracy of mapping, as well as the speed at which maps are produced (Fellman et al., 2007). Academic journals include *International Journal of Geographical Information Science* and *International Journal of Remote Sensing*.

Theoretical Approaches

The discipline of geography is "multi-paradigmatic" in theory as well as in research methods. In fact, geography more so than other social sciences emphasizes the direct relationship between theory and research methods (Del Casino, 2006). Over time, the discipline has seen repeated shifts between more scientific and more humanistic theoretical approaches and research methods, until today variations of both make up the geography toolbox.

In the 1800s, understandings of human geography were firmly based in physical geography. Prominent German geographers Alexander von Humboldt and Carl Ritter encouraged the scientific study of geography, seeking to generalize patterns as they developed the theory of environmental determinism, which argued the physical environment governed human behavior. For example, "mountainous areas produce dispersed forms of settlement and the plains foster nucleation" (Matthews & Herbert, 2008, p. 53). As environmental determinism became discredited, possibilism emerged. This theory recognized that while the physical environment did impact human behavior, it did not solely determine it. Humans could also impact their environment through innovation and technology. As possibilism dominated, there was a concurrent shift toward human geography and qualitative methods. The emphasis, particularly in regional geography, was on what was unique about places. Today, possibilism remains in force and is a basis for cultural ecology or the study of human-environment interactions.

Del Casino (2006) presents four main categories of modern theory: (1) spatial science or quantitative geography, (2) humanism, (3) critical realism, and (4) post-structuralism. Spatial science was a reaction to the qualitative methodologies and interpretation common in regional geography. Especially during the 1950s and 1960s, spatial science as a combination of theory and quantitative methods sought to generalize, replicate, and find patterns. Walter Christaller's central place theory, though developed earlier, became popular and is an example of spatial science. He explained locations of settlements and market towns and consumer behavior in traveling the distances to them (Matthews & Herbert, 2008).

By the 1970s, humanistic and cultural approaches reasserted themselves, with many (not all) in human geography moving away from quantitative data to qualitative analysis focused on "meanings, values, and on diversity of human behavior." The critical realism phase began then, as "new cultural geography" concentrated on perceptions and people's mental maps (in addition to physical ones) as shaped by experiences and preferences. Structuralist theories are also included in the category of critical realism, as they explored "hidden structures of empowerment and control." An example of structuralism would be Marxist geographers' assertions that inequality resulted from "distributions of wealth and poverty . . . (in) the workings of a capitalist society" (Matthews & Herbert, 2008, pp. 56, 59). Socio-cultural features such as language, values, beliefs, and prevailing societal narratives served as a point of continuity between structuralism and the post-structuralism of the 1990s and beyond. Structuralism was more deterministic—hidden structures dictate human behavior—whereas post-structuralism underscores human decision making despite structural forces.

Overall, theoretical paradigm and methods shifts represent changes in geography between seeking to find similarities and generalize or to find differences that explain uniqueness in humans' interactions with the physical world. Both trends are now ongoing parts of a discipline that believes Earth and its environment are central to understanding human behavior and seeks to study their interaction in a holistic way. For geography, history, culture, economies, and politics are important—as they relate to human-environment interactions. As Alistair Bonnett (2008) insists, geography's "ambition is absurdly vast. But we know it would be more absurd to abandon it" (p. 28). Thus, the discipline of geography makes contributions to Global Studies necessary to understanding complex, spatially related aspects of how the world works—like territorial conflict, historical and current global trade, and cultural differences or similarities worldwide.

History

History is the study of the past, including people, places, and global issues from different times and events that have already happened. Historians describe and explain these past people, places, issues, and events. Sources for historical narratives can be written documents, oral traditions, or, with more recent technology, digital recordings. Generally, history is told in chronological order and focuses on particular times. History is more than a simple chronicle of what happened; professional historians attempt to tie the past to a larger context by interpreting or analyzing what happened, sometimes to help explain the present. History is, in the words of British professor E. H. Carr (1961), "an unending dialogue between the present and the past" (p. 35).

Subjects of Study

The main subject of study in history is both simple and vast: the past. Subjects of study have changed over time as different topics became "important" to scholars. Early historians studied their leaders and countries—because, like Thomas Carlyle, they considered great men and great nations important. Given the global dominance of Europe and the United States, Western historians examined countries and communities considered powerful and important, overlooking people and countries they considered powerless and unimportant as subjects of history. Over time, however, the subjects broadened to include average people and how they lived; known as new social history, this movement focused on history from the bottom up rather than the top down and broadened the subjects under study, including an emphasis on the untold or, more accurately, ignored histories of minorities, women, former European colonies, and less-powerful countries. Different subfields of history exist, including environmental history, gender history, Indigenous and American studies, and African and Diasporic studies. They also include regions of the world, such as Latin American history or Asian history, and types of history, like religious history and the history of science and medicine. All these subjects of study, together, make up the discipline of history.

Key Concepts

In history, key concepts emphasize the process of "doing history." As they offer interpretations and search for larger patterns, historians are making arguments in favor of their interpretations and analysis. Thus, a key concept within the discipline is the development of an argument. Historians develop research questions in their search for larger patterns, and then seek historical facts to help them answer that question. "A historical fact is something that happened in history and can be verified as such through the traces history has left behind" (Evans, 2002, p. 4). Using historical facts as evidence, the answer to a research question becomes a historian's argument or interpretation of what happened.

How historians use facts as evidence ties to the concepts of objectivity, credibility, and bias. An objective view of the past accepts the world as it was, whereas a subjective view is one that sees the world as we wish it had been. Debates exist within the discipline about whether any historian can be truly objective, but for many historians the goal is to be as objective as possible—to approach a subject of study with as few preconceived notions as possible. Historical facts must be accepted as they exist in valid sources, not manipulated or deliberately misused to support an argument. We cannot select only the evidence that supports our argument and ignore what does not. If historical facts exist that fail to support an argument, historians must acknowledge them and either alter the argument or explain why the facts that support the argument are more persuasive or preponderant than those that do not. Doing so makes the results believable or credible. Bias is related to objectivity, and serves to acknowledge that, even when they strive to be, no historian can be truly objective. Choices of subjects of study, sources, theories, perspectives, and other decisions undertaken by historians will directly or indirectly affect the resulting arguments. Both historians and readers of history must compensate for bias. Historians must do their best to be objective and acknowledge their personal and professional limitations, while readers must evaluate the resulting historical arguments. Readers can grant credibility to historians who seek objectivity and are aware of their own biases.

the choices made by the researcher matter

As historians undertake their studies, they often search for larger patterns. Doing so is one way to analyze the past. Larger patterns can include relationships of cause and effect. Explaining the causes of past events or situations is one way history provides us with context about how the world works. What happened is still in the past, but understanding causes—and their consequences—can help us understand what is happening in the present and perhaps plan for the future.

When historians look for larger patterns, they can also look for continuity and change. Some historians study the past to see what continues or what happens repeatedly, and to try to determine why there is continuity from one time to another. Conversely, they can look for what is different—for change. Or a historian may look for both continuity and change at the same time.

Research Methods

The simplest explanation of historians' research method is data collection, because it is the historian's goal to gather and analyze as much data as possible related to a research topic. While many historians undertake qualitative history, both qualitative and quantitative methods are used. Economic historians, for example, engage in statistical analyses.

Historians collect two main types of sources as data for their research: primary sources and secondary sources. Primary sources are original historical records. Primary sources include many different types of records from the past: business records (such as bills, invoices, and inventory records); government records (such as tax registers, census records, and council meeting minutes); legal records (such as statutes, wills, and trial documents); school records (such as lists of pupils or exams for teaching certification); personal journals, diaries, and correspondence; newspaper articles or news broadcasts; interviews and oral histories; and church records (such as birth, marriage, or death records). Even paintings, photographs, poetry, and plays can be historical records. Once they are determined to be authentic, these are all examples of original documents, records, or objects that contain historical information, but not always explanations or interpretations of that historical information.

Bias is an important concept when reviewing primary sources, because the sources themselves can reflect biases of the writer, government policies, or societies at the time they were produced. For example, until the 1860s, Native Americans were not included at all in the U.S. Census. The 1980 census was the first time there was an attempt to count the homeless and the first time the form allowed women to indicate their status as military veterans. As valuable as census data and other primary sources can be, they are incomplete and include misclassifications because of political climate or societal norms.

When historians study original records, analyze or interpret them, and write up their conclusions, the resulting books or academic journal articles becomes secondary sources—because they include the explanation, analysis, and/or interpretation of primary sources. Today's secondary sources, however, could be carefully used as the future's primary sources (Arnold, 2000). In 1990, physician and historian Mirko Grmek wrote *History of AIDS: Emergence and Origin of a Modern Pandemic*, the first major international history of the global HIV epidemic. He acknowledged that less than 10 years into the pandemic was early to write a history—and that secondary sources can become primary sources, stating that "I hope not only to shed light on this problem for the contemporary reader, but to provide a testimony for the future historian" (Grmek, 1990, p. ix).

Historical research is published as scholarly books and in a variety of academic journals, including *American Historical Review, The Journal of African History, Journal of Latin American Studies, Contemporary European History,* and *Perspectives on History.*

Theoretical Approaches

For historical research, there are generally two approaches to analyzing the relationships among historical facts gathered from primary and secondary sources: those who examine facts for relationships based on preexisting frameworks and those who do not. Those who argue there is no theory in history are those who argue they approach each research project without preexisting frameworks; instead they seek only to determine the relationships existing within and between the sources gathered. Relationships would vary from project to project. Historians who utilize theory, on the other hand, approach projects with preexisting frameworks. A Marxist historian is most interested in the role of economics in history and thus would examine sources based on a preexisting economic framework, looking within the sources gathered for relationships among economic classes, types of economies, types of production, and so forth. Historians who utilize theory generally remain flexible; if a particular theoretical framework isn't helpful, they may combine it with elements of other theoretical frameworks.

We can often group historians based on the theories or types of theories they utilize—and it is often theory that divides them, especially for those who deny history utilizes theory. Main historical theories include those from the *Annales* School, modernization, postmodernism, and Marxism. In telling the history of history, scholars group historians into different theoretical categories. Some break it down by philosophers and thinkers, such as Karl Marx, whose theory of Marxism (as noted above) emphasized the role of economic forces on history, above all else. The *Annales* School in France, named for their main academic journal, disagreed with Marxism's emphasis on economics and sought to consider a "total history" that would include tools from all the social sciences. The group known as American modernization theorists emphasized history as the process of modernization: how countries, economies, and societies modernize. They recognized that economic forces were an important, but not sole factor, in historical change; to them the key factor was modernization (Appleby et al., 1994). More recently, in the United States, we see historians who utilize postmodernism as a theory, where the emphasis is on the construction of language, culture, identity, and meaning—and who has the power to construct those structures and narratives. Sometimes, the theories chosen by a historian may reflect an ideological approach or the subfield or subject under study. Each of these theoretical groups—and more—can exist at the same time and in competition with one another, though they can also drop out of use, as has been the case with American modernization theory. There can be deep divisions within the theoretical groups; postmodernism as a label encompasses a wide range of approaches, some of which contradict one another.

History's perspective—the way in which we can differentiate it from other disciplines—relies most heavily on its main subject of study and its research methods. History is the only discipline whose main goal is to study the past; that past may include political events or cultural traditions, but those things become subjects of study for the historian primarily because they *happened in the past*—and the past explains the present. The opposite is true for a political scientist or an anthropologist, for whom political events or cultural traditions are the focus and the history surrounding them is context. As the only discipline to focus exclusively on the past, history's methods also differentiate it. Historians rely on and engage with primary sources far more than any other Global Studies discipline.

Political Science

Though most of us have a general sense of what "politics" encompasses, there is no single, accepted definition of politics. One definition that is both to the point and broad enough to encompass the variety of interactions is American political scientist Harold D. Lasswell's (1958) "who gets what, when, and how." Implied in Lasswell's definition is politics as a process—a series of actions and interactions proceeding toward a specific endpoint or goal. Politics, then, can be further defined as "the process through which power and influence are used in the promotion of certain values and interests" (Danziger, 2009, p. 4). That is a decision-making process, one that can result in public policies. According to the American Political Science Association, the field's main professional organization, political science as a discipline is "the study of governments, public policies, and political behavior. Political science is a social science which uses both humanistic perspectives and scientific skills to examine the United States and all countries and regions of the world" (American Political Science Association, 2017). In the United States, political science has a number of subfields: American politics, comparative politics, international relations, political theory, public administration, and public law.[2]

All these subfields contribute to our understanding of how the world works, but comparative politics and international relations are most relevant to Global Studies. Comparative politics studies governments, policy issues, and political behavior in countries and regions other than one's own. International relations (IR) refers, quite literally, to the relations between and among nations. The relations between nation-states can be of many types: political, economic, cultural, social, and so forth—and political scientists study them all. The subfield of IR today, however, studies not only interactions among countries (known in IR as nation-states) but also a variety of other actors, including international organizations, multinational corporations, transnational social movements, ethnic groups, indigenous groups, media, terrorist and criminal organizations, and even globally relevant individuals. Because these interactions are fundamental to globalization, global issues, and differing points of view, the focus here is on the disciplinary perspective of IR as a subfield of political science. To have an understanding of political science as a discipline, however, you may need to research comparative politics or other subfields for Global Studies research, depending on your topic.

Subjects of Study

Definitions of political science inform us of a number of subjects of study: governments, policy issues and policies, political behavior, political processes, political values, and power, among others. Two main subjects of study in international relations are conflict and cooperation. Conflict is a historically ever-present fact of the international system and is a subject that IR scholars and practitioners alike seek to understand, whether it be world war, terrorism, trade disputes, or diplomacy to resolve tensions between global actors. One particularly prominent focus for international relations is the study of the causes of war.

Conflict may be a key feature of international relations, but so is cooperation. The international system includes efforts to avoid conflict and promote peace and security. These efforts are often promoted by international organizations, governmental and nongovernmental, both of which IR scholars study. International political economy focuses on the intersection between politics, markets, and policies, including trade and finance as well as questions of economic growth and stability. In understanding how the world works, we must understand not only conflict but also the extent to which countries work together and rely on one another. Globalization and global issues can reflect both conflict and cooperation, and are also subjects of study for political scientists as well as Global Studies. Domestic politics of nation-states can be relevant to Global Studies, as they can influence how a state behaves internationally. For example, in democracies a country's legislative can determine foreign policy, so domestic tensions between political parties or factions may be a subject of study.

---

[2]In countries other than the United States, American politics would fall within the subfield of comparative politics and countries' own domestic politics might be considered a subfield (for example: British politics, German politics).

Key Concepts

Many political science concepts are important to Global Studies, both from the field generally and from the subfield of International Relations specifically. As noted above, there can be overlap between subjects of study and key concepts; power is a key concept because political scientists frequently study it and thus those in the field must understand it. Power is a term with many definitions. Political scientist Joseph S. Nye Jr. (2011) defines it as "the capacity to do things and in social situations to affect others to get the outcomes we want" (p. 6). Globalization, as defined in Chapter 1, is also both a larger subject of study and key concept.

Other concepts flow from subjects of study. To research conflict and cooperation in our world today, we have to understand that the process of international politics depends on two important IR concepts: anarchy and sovereignty. Some scholars assume politics at the international level is very different from politics at the domestic level because of anarchy or the lack of any higher, governmental authority to enforce rules or dictate the behavior of nation-states. In other words, there is no world government to determine who gets what, how, and when in the international system. Sovereignty refers to the right of a nation-state to control what goes on within its own borders, without outside interference. A nation-state can determine for itself its government, laws, policies, and actions. Under sovereignty, because no higher authority exists to force political interests or values on a nation-state, each nation-state is legally equal to all other nation-states (if not always in practice).

Nation-states compete to achieve their goals, or national interests, including protecting themselves from military attack by other nation-states (national security), opportunities for trade and economic expansion, the well-being of its population, and control over the wide variety of people, goods, and information crossing their borders. In the process of seeking to achieve national interests, nation-states come into conflict with one another, which can be resolved through diplomacy or the use of military force. Nationalism can complicate international as well as domestic conflict. This concept refers to identifying with and having loyalty to a nation, which itself refers to a group of people in a particular territory. Instead of loyalties attaching to a single individual as king, as in the past, loyalties today may attach to the people living in a certain geographic area.

Nation-states also cooperate to achieve their national interests. Cooperation can occur in international governmental organizations (IGOs) or through the vast numbers of treaties and agreements forged by and among nation-states, known collectively as international law. Cooperation can bring the concept of sovereignty into question, because when nation-states work together, especially within the rules of international organizations and international law, they are allowing themselves to be subject to outside interference. Interdependence is the concept that all nation-states are interconnected and no single nation-state can truly act independently of others. Interdependence, some IR scholars argue, promotes cooperation because countries that are interconnected will hurt their own interests if they choose to engage in violent conflict. Interdependence contributes to globalization—and vice versa. These and other disciplinary concepts help us understand governments and their decision-making processes as well as political institutions, interests, values, and behavior.

Research Methods

Within political science, as noted above for the social sciences generally, we find two types of research: quantitative and qualitative. Political science is one of the disciplines that argues over which type of method is best. Ultimately, the discipline uses both, as does the subfield of international relations. For example, scholars can gather voters' opinions and attitudes toward foreign policy through qualitative focus groups—providing depth and detail about a few persons. On the other hand, quantitative "opinion polls, whether related to political elections or not, are pervasive in modern society . . . The ability to measure attitudes or opinions of a population through a relatively small representative sample is a powerful tool" (Ruel, Wagner, & Gillespie, 2016, p. 7). As another example, IR scholars studying conflict might consider qualitative case studies of particular wars at the same time other scholars undertake statistical analyses of datasets such as the Correlates of War project, which provides quantitative data on wars from 1816 to 2000s. As Shively (2013) concludes, "It is probably best that studies with varying degrees of quantification be carried on simultaneously in any given field of political research, for the different levels of quantification complement each other" (p. 22).

Political science and international relations research is published in a number of journals, including those of the American Political Science Association and International Studies Association: *American Political Science Review, Perspectives on Politics, Journal of Political Science Education, International Studies Quarterly, International Studies Perspectives,* and the *Journal of Global Security Studies.*

Theoretical Approaches

Within IR, some theorists seek to find a single theory that explains everything they want to study when they ask how the world works. Others believe that it is not possible to find a single, explanatory theory. This is because, whether political scientists study nation-states, organizations, or governments, they are ultimately studying people—and human behavior, individually and collectively, can be unpredictable. Both groups find theoretical approaches useful, they just disagree on whether theorists should work toward defining a single "grand theory" that explains all (or as much as possible) or accept that we may need different theories for different purposes. Either way, we seek theory as our conceptual frameworks in political science because we want to be able to describe and explain what has already happened and use that information to try to predict what might happen next, based on established patterns and trends. The ability to predict what might happen next allows governments, organizations, and leaders to make policy—either to promote or prevent a particular prediction about what may happen next.

Within international relations, a number of theoretical approaches exist and compete with one another. There are a variety of IR theories: realism, liberalism, constructivism, structuralism, feminism, and postmodernism, among others. The first three are more popular, and in IR realism and liberalism vied for position as *the theory* throughout the 20th century. Constructivism became popular in the 1990s. Within each IR theory there are divisions: Realism can be divided into classical realism, neo-realism, structural realism, and so forth. Again, for our purposes, we need only be aware of the theoretical approaches and how our sources use them. Detailed knowledge of each theory can come from additional courses or research on theoretical approaches.

Under the international relations theory of realism, political scientists assume that sovereignty and anarchy together create an international system in which nation-states compete to achieve their primary goal of national security and other national interests. Nation-states are the most important actors; realists may discount other global actors such as IGOs and NGOs. Realists see the system as one of self-help; without a higher authority to guide the behavior of nation-states, each is out for itself and can only trust itself. Going back to writings of Thucydides in the 5th century BCE, power is the most important tool, often military power. Realists see conflict as inevitable. They recognize that times of peace exist, but continually anticipate conflict, violent or otherwise. War has always been, for more than 2,000 years, and realists assume it always will be; the international system is one of continuity. Simply put, realists explain the world as it currently is (or as they currently see it). The ideas of classical realism are associated with Hans Morgenthau, those of neorealism with Kenneth Waltz, and those of offensive realism with John Mearsheimer.

An alternative theoretical approach to international relations is known as liberalism. The liberal theory of IR accepts that power and security are important to nation-states, but lengthens the list of national interests to include economic objectives, human rights, international development, international law, and the environment. Going back to ideas of Immanuel Kant published in the late 18th century, liberals acknowledge anarchy and conflict but believe both are managed through international cooperation. Countries work together and rely on one another more permanently—they are interdependent. They thus recognize more actors than nation-states; this is especially true of international institutions like the UN, through which liberals believe nation-states cooperate. Ultimately, liberals believe that cooperation and interdependence will lead to more peaceful international relations; the international system can change. Simply put, liberals accept the world as it is but see it as less conflictual than realists and also explain how the world could be. Robert Keohane and Joseph Nye are current liberal scholars credited with the development of neoliberalism, neoliberal institutionalism, and complex interdependence.

As a third major theoretical approach to IR, constructivism emphasizes identities and interpretation. The theory is associated with Alexander Wendt (1992) and his journal article "Anarchy Is What States Make of It." Constructivists question what realists and liberals take as given. They accept that nation-states and other actors are motivated by material interests, as realists and liberals do, but insist that global actors are also motivated by identity, interpretation, expectations, and interactions. While realists and liberals take national interests as given, for example, constructivists ask how

Which theory of IR is most biblical?

those interests came about and how they change; to constructivists, interests change over time because, like identities and interpretations, they are socially constructed. Constructivists argue that "many structures we take to be immutable in IR are actually embedded social relationships that are contingent to a large extent on how nation-states think about and interact with one another" (Sterling-Folker, 2013, p. 130).

For example, constructivists "argue that anarchy in international affairs is not a fixed, material condition. Rather *anarchy is what states make of it*" (Nau, 2017, p. 61; emphasis in original). If nation-states operate under the realist conditions of self-help and fail to trust others, then the system is one of anarchy. For constructivists, "relative identities, not relative power or institutional roles, determine whether countries behave as friends, rivals, or enemies toward one another" (Nau, 2017, p. 62). Although constructivism is a newer theoretical approach to IR, most scholars—whether critics or supporters—acknowledge its interpretive approach has had a significant impact on the field.

Theory in the subfield of IR demonstrates that while we can speak of a "political science perspective," we must also recognize variations within that perspective. If we utilize the lens metaphor, IR scholars may "see" many of the same things in the same ways, regardless of theory. At the same time, however, a realist lens would make power and nation-states more visible while a liberal lens would better see global institutions and rules and a constructivist lens would highlight identities, norms, cultures, and rhetoric.

The perspective of political science as a discipline—and especially IR as a subfield—contributes to Global Studies because it emphasizes power and decision-making based on interests and values by governments and among other global and transnational actors today. Anthropology also considers power, but often more so at the levels of kinship or cultural groups. History also considers decision-making by governments or other political actors, but in the past. The perspective of political science enables us to add information and insights regarding subjects of study and concepts such as power, governments, interests, values, and global political actors as we engage in Global Studies research about the present.

While brief, these descriptions of anthropology, economics, geography, history, and political science help demonstrate both the distinctive disciplinary perspectives and the overlap among them. All contribute to Global Studies because of the overlap, but also their distinct disciplinary perspectives. One way to envision the difference is which subjects of study are in the foreground and which are in the background for each discipline. Both anthropologists and human geographers study culture through fieldwork, and culture includes religious rituals and interpersonal relations such as marriage. For anthropologists, marriage and marriage traditions are the foreground, while the geographical environment within which they developed and the spatial distribution of common marriage traditions are likely background. For geographers, the reverse can be true. Marriage traditions also would be secondary, or background, for other contributing disciplines. Political scientists do not generally study marriage traditions first and foremost but do study policy—and many countries have public policies related to marriage, such as banning child marriages or defining tax policies as they relate to marriage. Economists also do not study marriage traditions or culture in and of themselves, but do study the economic impact of dowry, bride price, and arranged marriage—as well as tax policy. Each of the five contributing disciplines, then, can help us understand a single topic within Global Studies, whether their study of that topic is foreground or background.

Adequate Understanding of Contributing Disciplines

As noted in Chapter 1, common criticisms of interdisciplinary studies, including Global Studies, concern the breadth and depth of disciplinary knowledge required. How can a single student learn enough about each discipline? And how can each student, at the same time, learn enough about interdisciplinarity? What interdisciplinary researchers require is an "overall sense" of a discipline and its perspective (Repko et al., 2014). More specifically, for interdisciplinary researchers, "how much depth (i.e., command) depends, *just as it does for disciplinarians*, on the characteristics of the problem, the goal of the activity, and the availability of collaborators and the nature of their collaboration" (Newell, 2007, p. 253; emphasis added).

For Global Studies research, then, researchers are responsible for ensuring that they have an adequate understanding of the relevant disciplines to carry out their defined research project. (Determining which disciplines are relevant is in Chapter 3.) Global Studies researchers must be able to identify and "try on" a discipline's perspective—they must be able to see through its lens. If researchers cannot sufficiently understand books and journal articles published within a discipline to do so, they need to further develop their command of the subjects of study, concepts, theoretical approaches, and/or research methods in the discipline. So how does one evaluate and further develop their understanding of a discipline?

In *Becoming Interdisciplinary*, Tanya Augsburg (2006) develops "guidelines for researching disciplines" (p. 123). See Box 2.1 for a list of questions based on her guidelines. If you cannot thoroughly answer these questions for each discipline included in your interdisciplinary major or that you wish to utilize in Global Studies research, you need to further develop your understanding of the discipline. Doing so requires dedication to understanding as well as simply listing answers. Rely on disciplinary-specific sources when researching each discipline: "textbooks, professors, departmental websites at renowned universities, website of professional academics associations, and leading academic journals" (Augsburg, 2006, p. 122). Introductory textbooks for each discipline are extremely useful starting points, and then Global Studies researchers can move on to more advanced disciplinary textbooks on concepts, theoretical approaches, and research methods as needed. As you develop a sense of a discipline's perspective, check your understanding of the "lens" against recent publications for accuracy. Experts—professors—in each discipline are excellent resources, especially for ensuring you do indeed understand a discipline's perspective after researching that discipline. They can also help you understand the debates and disagreements within a field, which may lead to challenges or changes in disciplinary perspective over time.

For Global Studies, International Studies, and International Affairs majors, universities generally design required coursework to give you a basic understanding of several social science disciplines (even if not the same contributing disciplines included in this chapter). That understanding helps you develop command of disciplinary perspectives—and an understanding of one social science can help with developing command of others.

Research into many global events or issues, however, may also benefit from information and insights from disciplines outside the social sciences. As noted in Chapter 1, environmental problems are commonly global issues and research into them may require knowledge of the physical sciences such as biology or chemistry. In our upcoming case study on the global HIV epidemic, medical disciplines may be necessary to the study, depending on research question. In an academic setting, however, it isn't always easy to

BOX 2.1
LEARN MORE
Disciplinary Basics

To help you judge if you have an adequate understanding of relevant disciplines, research and answer the following questions thoroughly:

- What is an academic definition of the discipline?

- What are the subfields of the discipline? What are their purposes and goals?

- What is the discipline's subject matter?

- What are some of the key concepts associated with the discipline? How are they defined by this discipline? How would you describe them to someone unfamiliar with the concepts?

- What are the leading theories of the discipline? How would you describe each one to someone unfamiliar with it?

- What methods do researchers in the discipline use to answer their research questions? How would you explain them to someone unfamiliar with such research methods?

- Who are key thinkers, theorists, and/or practitioners in the discipline? How would you describe their contributions to the discipline?

- What are key books or seminal texts in the discipline? What is each about and why is it important to the discipline?

- What are the academic or professional journals in the discipline? Do they vary by subfield?

- What is/are the professional association(s) for the discipline? Review their websites to determine their purpose and goals.

Source: Guidelines for Researching Disciplines Worksheet *Becoming Interdisciplinary* (Augsburg, 2006, p. 123)

learn what we need to know across the social and physical sciences. While some students may major in Global Studies and minor in biology, due to an interest in countering bioterrorism, for example, the practicalities of prerequisite courses and other requirements can make it difficult to study both types of sciences.

This does not necessarily prevent social science students from using information and insights from the physical sciences, however. Books and articles written by scientists for general audiences may provide the basics needed when a physical science is relevant to a Global Studies research project. Asking questions of experts—professors, research scientists, and practitioners in the physical sciences—is also an option for social sciences faculty and students alike. Team research is another solution to crossing very different disciplines and can make for interesting undergraduate research experiences for students of both the social and physical sciences. There are, therefore, a number of ways for those within a social-sciences-based field such as Global Studies to successfully access information and insights from physical science disciplines and develop an understanding of their perspectives when necessary for a research question and research project.

Other Disciplines and "Interdisciplines"

Anthropology, economics, geography, history, and political science are five disciplines common to many universities' programs in Global Studies, International Affairs, or International Studies. No one should take this list of disciplines, however, as all-inclusive. For example, some Global Studies majors include the discipline of sociology, either in addition to or instead of anthropology. Other programs may incorporate additional disciplines such as communication/journalism, languages and linguistics, philosophy, or psychology.

Additionally, other "interdisciplines"—interdisciplinary fields of study like Global Studies—are also useful to understanding how the world works. These can include development studies, environmental studies, gender studies, religious studies, and area studies such as Latin American Studies or Asian Studies. There is little agreement among academic scholars as to whether interdisciplines can have their own perspectives; for now, it prudent to consider the information and insights found in already-interdisciplinary sources as exactly that—interdisciplinary. Chapter 3 discusses the difference and how to utilize them in Global Studies research.

Thus, the contributing disciplines described here only give us a starting point for understanding Global Studies and the Global Studies research process. Ultimately, it is the research topic or question that determines the disciplines relevant to any research project—and Global Studies students and researchers must be able to adequately understand the disciplines relevant to their research. As Repko, Szostak, and Buchberger (2014) point out, "In our quest for more comprehensive understandings of and, ultimately, solutions to the many complex problems confronting the worlds of nature and human society, *the disciplines are the place where we begin, but not where we end*" (p. 29; emphasis in original). Chapter 3 on the Global Studies research process explains how to build on the disciplines to get to an integrative, interdisciplinary end.

3 Global Studies Research Process

Novelist Zora Neale Hurston (1984)—who was also a trained anthropologist—wrote in her autobiography that "Research is formalized curiosity. It is poking and prying with a purpose" (p. 175). Disciplinary researchers poke and pry within their fields. Interdisciplinary Global Studies can then poke and pry among the disciplines to gather information and insights to carry out research on and better understand our complex world. As noted in Chapter 2, interdisciplinary research must build on disciplinary research.

Global Studies research "formalizes curiosity" through a step-based process. As Box 3.1 presents, there are four major steps, each with additional steps within them. The first is to prepare to research by selecting a research question and determining the relevant disciplines. Then a Global Studies researcher will gather disciplinary research from those relevant disciplines and consider the answers provided by each discipline to the overall question. Comparing the answers to each discipline comes next, and then the final step of combining—integrating—those answers. Chapter 3 presents the basic Global Studies research process; in Chapters 4 through 7 it is applied to and explained in detail for each case study: the global HIV epidemic and terrorism.

For any step-based process, it is important to note that research is rarely linear. It is uncommon to proceed smoothly from Step 1 to Step 2 to Step 3, and so forth. It is more common to need to backtrack and repeat steps. For example, no matter how thorough we might be in gathering a bunch of puzzle pieces, once we start to examine them in relation to one another and try to snap them together, we might discover we have gaps and need more pieces—more research. Or that we've accidentally gathered pieces that make up a different picture and are ultimately unnecessary—that research we've gathered is, in the end, not useful for or is unrelated to our topic.

Thomas (2007) presents several "general points" about research that further demonstrate its nonlinear nature. While we initially plan a research project, the "two-way relationship between ideas and evidence" requires "conceptualising and reconceptualising" our research. We select a research question based on certain ideas,

BOX 3.1
GLOBAL STUDIES RESEARCH PROCESS

- **Prepare**
  - Select a Global Studies research question
  - Determine the relevant disciplines
    - Know enough about each relevant discipline to utilize its information and insights
- **Gather**
  - Gather, through research, information and insights from the relevant disciplines
    - Sources: disciplinary, interdisciplinary, other
  - Answer the research question as each individual discipline would

- **Compare**
  - Criteria for comparison: the past, politics, economic resources, culture, and geography
  - Find similarities and differences between information and insights gathered from each discipline
- **Combine**
  - Integrate information and insights gathered from each discipline
  - Supplementary (similar) and complementary (different) information and insights

Sources: Adapted from Repko (2008, 2012), and Repko and Szostak (2017); also includes adaptations of ideas found in Klein (1990), Newell (2007), and Szostak (2002).

but the data we gather can challenge ideas and lead to new ones, thus requiring refinement of the research question. Thomas (2007) also suggests that researchers should be "uneasy" in the sense that we have to be prepared to find "odd pieces of data" that mean we are "finding out what [we] didn't know" and may need to reconsider the steps we've taken thus far (p. 18). So the steps in Box 3.1 are illustrative of the Global Studies research process but may need to be repeated before the process is finished (see Figure 3.1).

Prepare

Research Question

Research is guided by a **research question, which is quite simply the question you want to answer with your research**. "Research *can* examine questions about the *who, what, where, when, why,* and *how* of social life; it *can* explore 'so what' questions about the consequences of how the world is organized and the consequences of specific

FIGURE 3.1   Research is Nonlinear

Global Studies
Research Process

Prepare   Gather   Compare   Combine

Source: iStock/Fireofheart

human behaviors" (Loseke, 2013, p. 32; emphasis in original). Within Global Studies, there are more potential research ideas and topics than one could count, including facets of globalization, global actors and their interactions, and global issues—all these are complex topics that can benefit from interdisciplinary research and provide us with possible research topics. The topic of the research question becomes our jigsaw puzzle picture, and the research question guides our search for puzzle pieces.

Determining a research question usually starts with an idea or topic of interest, and then narrowing that topic down more and more specifically. Ultimately, a workable research question is one that makes a research project manageable—by being aware of and reasonable about limitations such as deadlines, maximum word or page length, the data available, the financial resources needed to gather that data, and so forth.

The global HIV epidemic is the first case study in this book (see Chapters 4 and 5). It is such a broad topic, however, that scholars could write book after book after book on the subject. I need to narrow that topic, and I can do so by asking myself what I want to know about the global HIV epidemic—by, quite simply, drafting a list of questions that interest me. For example:

- How and why is HIV a global problem? How has the world responded to the problem? Can HIV as a global problem be solved or must it be managed?

- How do developed countries like the United States and United Kingdom respond to the HIV epidemic? How do developing countries like Uganda or Botswana respond? How do other global actors like international governmental organizations (IGOs) and nongovernmental organizations (NGOs) respond?

- Do people living with HIV have any influence on the responses to HIV, either locally, nationally, or internationally?

- Does HIV create national security concerns for countries? Concerns about the impact on their economies? Does it hinder development in the Global South? Given the stigma that can be associated with HIV, is it treated as a human rights issue? What kind of international treaties and guidelines exist regarding HIV?

All of these could make interesting research topics, but I settled on one of the first to come to mind. The HIV epidemic is a complex global issue and thus a subject of study for Global Studies; it is present in most countries in the world and is thus of global concern. It can also be seen as a transboundary issue, when we talk about the spread of the virus from country to country. Given that, one interesting question we can answer is "How has the world responded to the global HIV epidemic?" I began my research at this point, starting with historical and political analyses of the HIV epidemic that would give me a "big picture" understanding of HIV as a global issue. The books I started with were Behrman's (2004) *The Invisible People: How the U.S. Has Slept Through the Global AIDS Pandemic, the Greatest Humanitarian Catastrophe of Our Time*; Engel's (2006) *The Epidemic: A Global History of AIDS*; and Lisk's (2010) *Global Institutions and the HIV/AIDS Epidemic: Responding to an International Crisis*. I also read the UNAIDS (2011) report *AIDS at 30: Nations at the Crossroads*.

My question remained pretty broad, however. While it was a good starting point for general research to get to know a topic, it is too broad to allow for an effective research paper in the end. Having done some initial research and reading, I narrow that further by asking myself what, specifically, I want to know. What do I mean by *world* and what do I mean by *response*? For world, I actually mean *which global actors?* and can consider actors such as countries and their government agencies, international governmental and nongovernmental organizations, national or local nongovernmental organizations, and even individuals. For my research question, I could list specific actors as I write it, or leave in *global actors*, because I know which I am studying—and that also leaves my question open to other actors that I may discover are important to the topic as I continue my research.

For *response*, I am asking what these actors have done (or not done) to address the global HIV epidemic, but still need to ask myself whether I mean what have they done cooperatively, individually, or both? For example, one responsibility of international organizations like the World Health Organization (WHO) and Joint United Nations Programme on HIV/AIDS (UNAIDS) is to set standards that require countries to undertake certain actions and report certain information back to WHO and UNAIDS—cooperative actions require individual actions on the part of countries. Can I study only the cooperative actions, or must I study both to learn what I want to learn about the global response to the HIV epidemic?

We already know that Global Studies explores complex problems, so I may also need to break down *the global HIV epidemic* in my research question. Do I mean the response to the global HIV epidemic as a medical problem? An economic one? A political one? A social or culture problem? Or all these, given that they are intertwined? A research question could list specific aspects such as economic and politics, although in the HIV epidemic literature I learn that the term *multisectoral* is used to encompass a range of common social and physical sciences aspects of the HIV epidemic as a global problem. The existing literature is always a necessary piece of crafting a research question. We can start with an idea, but often need to begin research—gather—to successfully refine it.

A more refined question, then, could be: "What activities have global actors undertaken to manage the multisectoral global HIV epidemic?" But is that question narrow enough to answer within the time and resources available to the researcher? It is narrow enough to begin more focused research, at least, that turns up the full range of global actors and many individual examples of each type, many activities, and many examples of actor cooperation or lack thereof within each activity. I now know the question remains too broad and can choose to narrow again based on types of actors or specific activities.

What seems an interesting question to start with—"How has the world responded to the global HIV epidemic?"—is actually quite complex and necessitates thought, refinement, research, and narrowing to craft a clear, specific, and manageable research question: "How are IGOs and NGOs involved in the global response to the multisectoral HIV epidemic?"

Relevant Disciplines

Generally, in interdisciplinary research, it is the subject under study and the research question that determine the *relevant disciplines*. Repko (2008) suggests "first identifying the disciplines potentially relevant to the problem before attempting to decide which of these are most relevant" (p. 160). Identifying potentially relevant disciplines

BOX 3.2
TAKE A STEP!
Write a Research Question

Following the guidelines above, select a research topic of interest to you and begin drafting a research question. It is okay to start with a broad or general question as you begin your initial research, but bear in mind you will likely have to narrow it to a clear and manageable question to guide further research and, ultimately, to answer.

involves somewhat the same thorough process as noted above to develop a research question: "think[ing] through the problem and attempt[ing] to identify its various components" (Repko, 2008, p. 161). Just as I considered what type of problem I meant by "the global HIV epidemic"—medical, economic, political, etc.—we can consider the potentially relevant disciplines: medicine, economics, politics, and so on. Once we have a list of potentially relevant disciplines, beginning to gather information and insights will help us determine which are, in fact, relevant; if they are relevant, they will have published scholarly research on the topic. Remember that relevance is guided by the research question, as well. While the medical disciplines are clearly relevant to the HIV epidemic, a specific research question that focuses on IGOs, NGOs, and the global response to the epidemic could make medicine less or not at all relevant.

In Global Studies, we have a head start. The relevant disciplines are partially determined for us, by those commonly contributing to the field and studied within the academic major, such as anthropology, economics, geography, history, and political science. Subdisciplines may also be relevant; for example, medical anthropology or health geography. Additional social sciences disciplines may be relevant to a specific research question, however. As noted in Chapter 2, for example, sociology is sometimes included in Global Studies majors and may be relevant to a research question that involves social behavior. It is also possible one of the five commonly contributing disciplines may be less relevant for a specific research question, particularly for emerging subjects of study such as cybersecurity or cyberwarfare. Also as noted in Chapter 2, we may determine disciplines outside the social sciences and/or that other types of interdisciplinary studies—such as environmental studies or area studies—are relevant. In those cases, return to the suggestions in Chapter 2 for how to develop an adequate understanding of the relevant discipline or interdisciplinary field.

Gather

To research complex problems in our world, we *gather* information and insights about the past, politics, economic resources, culture, and geography from the contributing disciplines through the basic research process. We utilize library, internet, government document, and other research resources to gather information (facts and data) and to gather insights, or scholarly analyses and explanations (Repko, 2008), from each Global Studies discipline to answer a research question. We poke and pry among the disciplines (Hurston, 1984, p. 175). Generally, we gather by searching library databases for pertinent disciplinary academic journals or using keywords appropriate to the topic along with the name of the discipline (such as terrorism geography or HIV politics). There may also be academic journals dedicated to global issues such as the HIV epidemic and terrorism, which could print both disciplinary and interdisciplinary articles. These and other tips for undertaking library searches can be found in Chapters 5 and 7, which provide concrete examples of how to gather using the case study topics as examples. For our puzzle metaphor, gathering information and insights is the same as finding the puzzle pieces, only instead of the necessary pieces being all packaged together in a single box on a store shelf, we must find our own puzzle pieces in the many boxes of the relevant disciplines.

As an interdisciplinary endeavor, Global Studies research differs from traditional disciplinary research in three ways: balance, organization, and point of view (Repko, 2012). *Balance* and *organization* help us ensure we gather information and insights from each discipline, without favoring one over others. We need roughly the same amount of information and number of insights from each discipline. We want to balance what we gather; balancing the number of sources is one way to do this, but it is rarely that simple. One source from geography may have as much information and as many insights as three sources from anthropology, or vice versa. Ultimately, we want to *avoid* gathering information and insights from one discipline to the exclusion or disadvantage of the others—we want to balance the material gathered from the relevant disciplines. Being organized helps us do this: We have to keep track of which sources are from which disciplines. This means consistently and carefully noting which authors, publications, information, and insights represent which disciplines. Researchers can usefully keep lists of disciplinary sources, interdisciplinary sources, and other sources as well as the disciplinary information and insights available within them (Repko, 2012). This can be done electronically (perhaps an Excel spreadsheet) or by hand in a hard-copy notebook.

Disciplinary Sources

Because for Global Studies we want to bring together different disciplinary perspectives into a comprehensive whole, we need to be sure that we have, in fact, gathered information and insights created from each discipline's perspective. There are several ways to determine which sources are from which disciplines. First and foremost is the author of the book, book chapter, article, or online document. Most academic sources will include a short biography of the author or we can look up the author online. We can usually tell which disciplinary perspective authors employ from their curriculum vitae (CV; an academic résumé) or biography, often available on faculty pages of a university website. Library search results webpages can also include identifying information.

The best indicator of disciplinary perspective is the author's PhD; that would be the discipline in which the author trained. Discipline of PhD helps determine an author's job title, which is another indicator. If an author is a Professor of History, we know she is trained in the historical perspective. If an author is an Assistant Professor of Political Science, we know he was trained in that perspective. Academic authors may also be associated with research institutes instead of universities, and biographies will identify their backgrounds as well. The purpose of the institute or think tank can also provide information about disciplinary perspective and they usually have online mission statements.

Another way to tell which discipline a source is from is the academic journal an article is found in; each discipline has its own major journals and publishes articles within them that are written from that discipline's perspective. Academic journals are those that publish the research and writings of professors through a process known as peer-review, in which each article is first reviewed anonymously by other specialists in the topic to determine if its methods and conclusions are legitimate. Generally, acceptance for publication by an academic journal indicates the perspective of the author matches the perspective of the journal, although not always. As well, both interdisciplinary authors and journals exist. (Chapter 2 includes major journals for each discipline.)

We would want to avoid or be very careful about using titles of books, articles, or documents to determine the disciplinary perspective: Titles can be vague or misleading. A title such as *AIDS in the Twenty-First Century: Disease and Globalization* does not immediately tell us which disciplinary perspective it presents; we wouldn't be undertaking balanced research if we guessed, so we would need additional information, such as author's biography, to be sure. And while a title such as "The Psychology of Terrorism: An Agenda for the 21st Century" would seem to indicate the discipline of psychology, it is actually written by political scientist Martha Crenshaw. We need more than the article title to determine from which disciplinary perspective the article is written. The journal title, *Political Psychology*, also fails to clearly indicate a discipline, so the author information included on page 1 of Crenshaw's article is best.

Interdisciplinary Sources

Some research resources already draw together information and insights from multiple disciplines. The book mentioned just above, *AIDS in the Twenty-First Century: Disease and Globalization* written by Tony Barnett and Alan Whiteside (2006), is in fact a source that draws together information and insights from a number of disciplines. We know this in two ways. First, as noted above, we can look at the author biographies. From the back of the book, we learn that Tony Barnett is Professorial Research Fellow in Development Studies, which is an interdisciplinary field of study that examines the processes and issues encountered as less-developed countries modernize and become more politically and economically developed. Alan Whiteside is an economist who specializes in the subfield of health economics. Interdisciplinary projects may draw together two or more authors with different disciplinary specialties.

Books that are intentionally interdisciplinary will often say so, in a preface or introduction. (This is also true for disciplinary sources; prefaces and introductions can also indicate which discipline a source is from.) Authors may clearly define their own project as interdisciplinary or may otherwise indicate the inclusion of several disciplines. While Barnett and Whiteside (2006) do not explicitly state "this book is interdisciplinary," they do write that "this book is about the social and economic impact of HIV and AIDS" (p. 3). Here, we can interpret "social" broadly, as in the social sciences, because in addition to economics the introduction makes direct reference to the disciplines of geography and history. Of course, it is a careful reading of any research resource that will prove it has combined information and insights from several disciplines and is thus interdisciplinary.

There are also multidisciplinary sources, and we must be sure not to confuse them with interdisciplinary sources. Anthologies bring together a number of chapters written by different authors—authors that may be from different disciplines. The volume *HIV/AIDS: Global Frontiers in Prevention/Intervention*, edited by Pope, White, and Malow (2009), brings together chapters written by anthropologists, geographers, historians, physicians, and psychologists. While such books may have interdisciplinary introductions or conclusions—which would thus be interdisciplinary sources—the chapters themselves are usually disciplinary sources and need to be considered as such for purposes of balance and point of view.

Additionally, more scholars are being trained in interdisciplinary fields. I mentioned Development Studies above. Scholars may have PhDs in such fields that provide them with interdisciplinary training and an interdisciplinary perspective. Or they may have multiple degrees in multiple fields and bring several perspectives together as a result. Additionally, some scholars choose to be interdisciplinary; despite training in a single discipline, they choose to gain expertise in multiple disciplines. Such scholars may make statements to that effect in prefaces or introductions to books and articles, or include it in their online biographies. Mark Hunter (2018), author of *Love in the Time of AIDS*, earned a PhD in Geography but clearly states on his website: "I try not to be constrained by disciplinary boundaries and draw inspiration from not only geography but anthropology, history, and sociology."

As we gather our information and insights, we need to remember that there are already many interdisciplinary books, journal articles, and research resources available. So while we must seek to balance what we gather from each discipline, we may find sources that have already done so for us. Such interdisciplinary information and insights are perfectly acceptable for Global Studies research, as long as we recognize from the start that they already draw together several disciplines in answer to a research question. We would not consider such a book or journal article as disciplinary. We would also, therefore, want to balance our interdisciplinary and disciplinary sources. An interdisciplinary book may combine two or three disciplines, but perhaps not all the Global Studies disciplines relevant to a research question. Additionally, we cannot know how well-balanced the interdisciplinary sources are. Therefore, we wouldn't want to rely too much on already-interdisciplinary sources just as we wouldn't want to rely too much on the sources from any one discipline. Additionally, we will need to consider how the interdisciplinary source relates to the disciplinary sources. An interdisciplinary source is like opening the box of a used jigsaw puzzle purchased at a garage sale or traded on the Facebook Jigsaw Puzzle Swap Exchange and then finding a cluster of pieces already locked together, because the previous owner did not sufficiently separate the completed picture before putting the puzzle back in its box. We can leave them stuck together, but we still have to figure out where in the picture that cluster of pieces goes and how the cluster fits with the pieces around it.

Other/Nondisciplinary Sources

Disciplines are academic categories, and we determine disciplinary (and interdisciplinary) sources based on author biographies, journals, and other indicators of academic disciplinary perspective. There are, of course, Global Studies research resources that are not produced or written from any academic disciplinary perspective. These could include government documents or reports; web resources posted by international organizations such as the World Health Organization; autobiographies and biographies; and journalistic or popular accounts of global actors, their interactions, and global issues. Utilizing *nondisciplinary* or other sources is acceptable as long as they are reliable and, in keeping with the need for balance, are used in conjunction with disciplinary sources. Examples of nondisciplinary sources can include the AIDS Fact Sheets published by the Joint United Nations Programme on HIV/AIDS (UNAIDS) and the World Health Organization or the UNAIDS report *AIDS at 30*. Nondisciplinary sources can also include work by respected journalists: Nicholas Kristof and Sheryl WuDunn (2009) traveled Africa and Asia and did extensive research to report on women's human rights in their book *Half the Sky: Turning Oppression Into Opportunity for Women Worldwide*.

All three types of sources can be valuable to interdisciplinary research. However, for now we set aside the interdisciplinary and other/nondisciplinary sources. Initially, the compare and combine steps will be presented only in relation to disciplinary sources. This is because our goal is to produce interdisciplinary research and we must utilize disciplinary sources to learn how to do so. We return to and discuss the remaining two types of sources later.

Disciplinary Answers to the Research Question

Once we have done our research and have gathered disciplinary sources, we need to thoroughly read and review the information and insights from each discipline. Before we can draw together the material from all our Global Studies disciplines, we need to evaluate each discipline's information and insights separately (Repko, 2012). First, we evaluate how the information and insights from anthropology allow us to answer the research question as if we were using solely research from anthropology to answer that question. Then we set aside anthropology and move on to economics: What answers do the information and insights from that discipline provide us? Then on to geography, and so forth. It is generally helpful to write out the answers for each discipline, either as formal essay or as detailed notes. This is why organization is so important: Unless we keep track of which source is from which discipline, we will have difficulty considering each discipline's answer to a research question. Doing this step achieves two things: It allows us to determine which information and insights are relevant to a research question and how each discipline's information and insights help provide an answer to that question.

With regard to relevance, we sometimes gather information that, while interesting, does not help us answer a research question, just as we might find a puzzle piece from another puzzle box mixed in with those for this puzzle. For example, an anthropologist's detailed story of an individual living with HIV in South Africa may be educational and even moving, but may not be relevant to a research question—or it may, in fact, be relevant if it helps us illustrate a global pattern among people living with HIV or bring a human face to data and statistics. If a puzzle piece is ultimately unrelated to our question, we must set it aside.

We must also, to offer William Newell's (2007) metaphor in "Decision Making in Interdisciplinary Studies," try on the different lenses of each discipline—or take on each discipline's perspective. Two things happen when we put on the lenses of a disciplinary expert. First, our view of the problem or research topic narrows, and we focus in on particular pieces of the puzzle. The focus results from utilizing a single discipline's perspective and applying its basic components such as subjects of study, key concepts, research methods, and theoretical approaches. This lens proves to be powerful (Newell 2007; Repko, 2012); the discipline's strengths bring into focus at least one puzzle piece within the larger picture. The second thing that happens, as the view narrows, is we see the gaps in the puzzle or weaknesses within that discipline. For as powerful as each discipline is, it is by definition too limited to explain or solve our global problem. To follow the Global Studies research process, we must be able to see the limitations as well as strengths of each discipline so that we don't get caught up in the narrower view of a single lens. For example, Newell (2007) points out that "a discipline such as sociology that focuses on groups doesn't see individuals clearly," whereas "psychology . . . is strong in understanding individuals [but] is thereby weak in understanding groups" (p. 254). Only by switching and eventually combining lenses—between psychology and sociology in Newell's example—can we see both.

This is when the third difference between traditional disciplinary and interdisciplinary research—*point of view*—becomes important. When evaluating how a single discipline answers a research question, it is easy to get caught up in that discipline's information and insights and forget that Global Studies benefits from several disciplines and perspectives. "Interdisciplinary research involves, among other things, looking for what disciplinarians have failed to see," and we risk that if we too blindly accept a single discipline's point of view (Repko, 2008, p. 178).

Compare

The Comparative Method

Once we are familiar with how each Global Studies discipline's information and insights would answer a research question on its own, we can combine those answers into an interdisciplinary and more comprehensive answer—we can bring together the various puzzle pieces into a fuller picture of how the world works. Before we combine them, we first *compare* the information and insights from each discipline with one another, to find interrelationships among the information and insights gathered from our Global Studies disciplines. Comparison is common within all

Global Studies disciplines—historians compare different time periods and economists compare different economic systems, for example—so it is also an effective tool for interdisciplinary efforts. To **compare (or to compare and contrast) is to find similarities and differences among the parts being analyzed**. In this case, we will be looking for similarities and differences in the information and insights each Global Studies discipline provides to answer case study research questions.

The act of comparison involves understanding each part, idea, or item being compared and then finding the similarities and differences between them. We usually want a rationale, or explanation, for why these items are being compared, which in our case has been established by the fact we are studying a complex Global Studies subject and are utilizing information and insights from Global Studies disciplines to understand, analyze, and, ultimately, explain aspects of how the world works. We also want to establish criteria or points for comparison.

Criteria for Comparison

We need *criteria* that allow us to find both similarities and differences in information and insights gathered from across the Global Studies disciplines of anthropology, economics, geography, history, and political science. Looking for similarities allows us to recognize that there is overlap among the social sciences, because at their most basic they all study some form of human behavior. Gathering information and insights resulting from each contributing discipline's perspective provides us with more information than doing so from just one discipline. Looking for differences allows us to recognize the unique contributions each discipline makes to Global Studies—it is the differences that allow us to gather not just more information, but more varied information.

Our common criteria for comparison are *the past, politics, economic resources, culture, and geography*. As noted above, social science research emphasizes the study of human beings, and these five topics have proven useful in describing and explaining not only people but also how the world they populate works. Each of our Global Studies disciplines can produce information on all these criteria, allowing for similarities but also the differences, or varied information, from unique disciplinary perspectives.

Gathering and comparing information and insights about *the past* allows us to examine continuity and change in how the world works as well as identify patterns and trends that explain the world as it is today. Looking for cause and effect is important to utilizing the past in Global Studies. In the discipline of history, examinations of continuity and change, patterns and trends, and cause and effect can be about politics, economics, culture, and/or geography of the past. At the same time, other disciplines also examine history. The discipline of political science considers the history of political development in a country to understand how it got to its political system today.

Politics is an important criterion for comparison because, at its most basic, it is about "who gets what, when, and how" (Lasswell, 1958). Power, political institutions such as governments or international organizations, government decision-making processes and the resulting policies, political ideologies, and the behavior of citizens within countries all have bearing on who gets what, when, and how throughout the world and, thus, on how the world works. The discipline of political science examines politics in the past as well as the present and across cultures and geographical borders. It also examines the role of the economic resources in politics, just as economists will consider government policies—politics—to understand their economic cost and impact on the market.

An economy, whether in a single country or the world as a whole, is a system of exchange, including goods and services and other monetary or financially based trans-actions. *Economics*—especially resources or the lack thereof—results from the struc-tures and functions of economic systems and institutions. Economics is a key feature of how countries behave in our world and thus a key feature of how the world works. The discipline of economics provides us with information and insights about not just economics, but also the impact of the past, policy decisions, culture, and geographical location on the distribution of resources. At the same time, the discipline of anthropol-ogy will consider how resources (or the lack thereof) and economics impact the daily lives of peoples and cultures.

Culture encompasses the many patterns of behavior that make up how people live their daily lives, including customs, religion, and family dynamics, among other things. The discipline of anthropology studies these patterns of behavior in the past as well as the present and as they relate to political systems, and economic systems. Geographers also look at culture, especially how geography impacts peoples—for example, the dif-ferences caused by living near an ocean as opposed to living in a desert.

Geography—including geographical space, place, and location—is a criterion for comparison because where we live affects human behavior and, thus, how the world works in different places and regions. The discipline of geography studies patterns of human behavior as they relate to factors such as physical location, climate, agriculture, migration, and population—both in the past and the present. Geography studies the interaction of geographical location with politics, economics and wealth, and culture. At the same time, the discipline of political science must consider geographical loca-tion with regard to military security, as a country with natural boundaries (such as mountains) can have very different security requirements than one with no natural boundaries and lots of neighbors.

When undertaking a comparative analysis and writing a comparative essay, the criteria or points for comparison are what we use to determine how the parts being analyzed are similar or different. The same is true when we are analyzing disciplinary information and insights through the Global Studies process. In addition, we use our criteria to determine what information and insights are relevant to our question and how we will combine them into our answer to a research question. Following through on our puzzle metaphor, we will be carefully examining each puzzle piece by itself and then in relation to the other puzzle pieces we have; we will be looking at the sides, angles, curves, tabs, and blanks (or cutouts) on each piece and, once we are familiar with each piece, we can see with which other pieces it might fit and interlock.

Using these criteria—the past, politics, economic resources, culture, and geography—we can compare the information and insights we have gathered. It is important to note that, like relevant disciplines, additional or different criteria may be useful depending on your research topic. As we will see in Chapter 6, adding another criterion can expand our understanding of a given research topic.

For now, we just want to find the similarities and differences; next we will use them to combine information and insights as we answer a research question. When some people put together jigsaw puzzles, they first sort through the pieces and group together on the table a handful that will likely fit together (all those that show portions of sky in a landscape picture, for example) but leave other pieces that will definitely not fit with the first group off to the side (those that show mountains, lake, trees, and houses for the landscape) and only then begin to lock likely pieces together. It is the same in Global Studies: We first analyze our information and insights, mentally grouping what might fit and what might not, and only then do we begin to combine them.

Finding Similarities and Differences

We already know that, because the divisions between disciplines are artificial if historically necessary, there is overlap among the social sciences disciplines. Where there is overlap, we can find both similarities and differences among information and insights. We know that the discipline of political science recognizes the impact of economic resources on government policies and actions, and therefore created the subfield of political economy. We could, for example, find the exact same dollar figures for global HIV funding in sources gathered from both of the partially overlapping disciplines of political science and economics. That is like finding duplicate puzzle pieces. But we could also find different figures for global HIV funding in political science sources than we do in economics sources. This is where knowledge of the disciplines is important; we need to examine the particular perspective and sources to determine how each discipline arrived at its figure. For example, a political science source emphasizing global funding for HIV could provide a figure for funding that includes only what developed countries allocate as foreign aid or official development assistance (ODA) for global HIV funding, while the economics source could provide a figure that includes domestic national government funding, ODA, and charitable donations. In this case, we have two puzzle pieces that are so similar that the tabs of both pieces *seem* to fit into the blank of the next piece of the puzzle, but we realize neither piece is actually a snug or correct fit. The two pieces are more similar than different, but not exact duplicates. (We solve this problem in the section on combining disciplinary research, below.)

Overlap between disciplines can also lead to very different information and insights. Consider the previous example of the concept of power, which is common to political science and anthropology. Power is defined as "the capacity to do things and in social situations to affect others to get the outcomes we want" (Nye, 2011, p. 6). Within the discipline of political science, particularly the subfield of international relations, we study the ability of one country to influence other countries, while within the discipline of anthropology we study the ability of individuals within families to influence other individuals. The concept would be the same, but the information produced and insights offered by the disciplines would be about very different subjects of study: countries or individuals.

Power is a key concept for most Global Studies disciplines, and there are many different ways in which power is important. Political science provides us with information about how an international organization such as the World Health Organization could try to influence a country's compliance in reporting transmission of HIV within that country. Anthropology provides us information about whether or not women within a given culture have the power to insist on the use of condoms as an HIV prevention measure. While each provides us with information related to power, the information and insights we gather may be very different. Going back to our puzzle metaphor, we would in this instance have puzzle pieces that are similar in color (the concept of power) but with different shades and from different areas of a landscape puzzle—all blue pieces, but different shades of blue: some pieces from the blue sky and some from the deeper blue of the lake.

There will also be disciplinary information and insights that are completely different; that is the advantage and goal of bringing multiple disciplines together in the first place. Given the discipline's emphasis on institutions, political scientists answering the question "How are IGOs and NGOs involved in the global response to the multisectoral HIV epidemic?" could likely focus solely on IGOs and their interactions with member actors such as countries, as those are common global actors for political science. They may not initially think of examining how, at the local level, NGOs help extended families in impoverished areas cope with orphans and other children made vulnerable by AIDS. But anthropologists could consider that part of the answer to the question, because the plight of such children is also a recognized parallel global issue. A political scientist and an anthropologist each bring not only different pieces to the puzzle but also different aspects of the picture. The political scientist might not, for example, choose a landscape with houses in it, whereas the anthropologist would. For our puzzle, we want a landscape with many aspects (lake, mountains, sky, and houses) because our goal is to create a more comprehensive picture. Within Global Studies, we want different disciplinary information and insights so as to create a fuller understanding of how the world works or more completely answer a specific research question. Comparing the information and insights we've gathered from Global Studies disciplines prepares us for combining the disciplinary insights and information into an interdisciplinary answer.

Combine

Once we have compared the information and insights about the past, politics, economics, culture, and geography that we've gathered from each discipline, we can begin putting them all together into a comprehensive answer to the complex question of how the world works—we can begin to piece together our puzzle's final picture. This step makes a research project truly interdisciplinary—it is the act of integration that makes a "smoothie."

To **combine is "to bring into such close relationship as to obscure individual characters"** (Combine, 2012). Describing exactly how to combine disciplinary information and insights is a challenge because, as a thought process, it is something we do without thinking about it. Think back to the example of choosing the best route to work when running late. Like me, you may consider weather, traffic patterns, time of day, location of construction zones, and possible routes to take and make your decision. Can you explain exactly how you considered all those factors and made your decision? Usually not, because we combine all that information and make our decisions intuitively. While we may consciously undertake certain steps, such as looking at the weather and traffic reports, in the end we don't stop what we are doing and purposely, consciously think through every possible combination of factors but instead subconsciously sift through the information until we identify the best route to take. The integrative process "is a combination of step taking, decision making, intuition, process, and creativity" (Repko, 2008, p. 300). Turning a sometimes-subconscious thought process into a carefully defined, step-by-step process for learning how the world works is a challenge, then, because it is difficult to explain *how* to be intuitive or creative.

One way to explain how to combine the relevant disciplinary information and insights we've gathered is ultimately about comparing and finding the relationships among them. As explained above, we can look for similarities and differences among each discipline's contributions (the compare step). Doing so allows us to determine whether the various discipline's information and insights are supplementary or complementary and thus how to combine them into a new whole. While it will vary by research topic, often information will be similar and supplementary while insights will be different and complementary.

Supplementary Integration

Supplementary is defined simply as "additional" (Neufeldt & Guralnik, 1991, p. 1345). If, during our comparative analysis, we discovered similarities between two or more disciplines' information and insights, it is likely that they supplement one another. Integrating information and insights that are similar can sometimes be trickier than integrating information and insights that are very different. Combining things that are similar may even seem pointless—why do we need duplicate pieces of a puzzle? Combining similar information and insights strains our puzzle metaphor. It is much easier to fill gaps than deal with overlapping information just as it is easier to fit tabs into blanks on puzzle pieces than to deal with duplicate pieces or two pieces that simply don't fit because they overlap or the fit is just slightly off. True puzzle enthusiasts will surely cringe at the thought of trimming one puzzle piece to fit it into another or otherwise modifying pieces, but in Global Studies research we can, in fact, do just that as we combine information and insights from many disciplines.

Think, again, of the example of global HIV funding. If we gather the exact same figure from more than one discipline, we have duplicate puzzle pieces. When building a puzzle, we do not need two of the exact same puzzle pieces, but in academic research we could. Finding the same information and insights from several disciplines—and drawn from different research methods, for example—allows us to validate the information and insights. To **validate is "to support or corroborate on a sound or authoritative basis"** (Validate, 2011). Validity is important; in general, most people are more likely to accept something as true when they find it in more than one source.

In the case of an existing fact such as allocated HIV funding, we may not need multiple sources. But what about if we are attempting to estimate how much funding the world needs to manage the global HIV epidemic in a future year? This figure could be controversial because different actors would have different priorities: How much would it cost if we emphasize educational prevention campaigns? Treatment with antiretroviral therapy? Both? How much should less-developed countries be expected to contribute? Wealthier, developed countries? There are different equations and economic models we can use to come up with the number, so when we put forward an estimate, we would want it to be a valid estimate. If we find that economists, political scientists, and geographers all separately come up with an estimate of the same range, say US$20–$30 billion, we can be confident that is a valid estimate. (According to UNAIDS [2017a], the annual estimate through 2020 was US$26.2 billion.) When building a puzzle, it doesn't make much sense to fill a gap with a puzzle piece, and then stack two more duplicate pieces on top of the first piece. In Global Studies research, however, it does make sense. Many readers would find a common figure garnered from different disciplines—each using their own perspectives based on theories and methods—more reliable, because the answer of one reinforces or validates the answers of others. To say economists, political scientists, and geographers agree that the world needs to spend between US$20–$30 billion to manage HIV worldwide next year may be accepted as more valid than to say simply that political scientists propose the world spend US$20–$30 billion to manage HIV worldwide next year. Supplementary disciplinary information and insights can validate answers to a Global Studies research question.

Disciplinary information and insights can also be supplementary when they are similar, but not exactly the same. I previously provided the example of when figures for HIV funding could vary based on what, exactly, is included in the figure: A political science source provides a figure for funding that includes only what developed countries allocate as foreign aid for global HIV funding, while an economics source provides a figure that includes national government, foreign aid, and charitable donations. I said we have two puzzle pieces that are so similar that the tabs of both pieces *seem* to fit into the blank of the next piece of the puzzle, but the first is perhaps very slightly too small and the second very slightly too large. We can solve our problem—integrate our information—by modifying either the pieces or the puzzle. My first choice in this example would be to modify the puzzle itself, because when our puzzle is a Global Studies research project, we can do so. We can enlarge the opening in the picture so *both* pieces fit, instead of just one. We can more completely answer the research question for the HIV epidemic case study, for example, if we remember there are a variety of global actors and we recognize that the global response includes funding from all, not just from developed countries. To do so, we could explicitly offer the distinction: If we measure only what developed countries throughout the world allocate as official development assistance, the 2008 figure was US$4.2 billion. If we measure what all actors, including what national governments spend domestically, official development assistance from other countries, and contributions from philanthropic organizations, the 2008 figure was US$13.7 billion (calculated using data from UNAIDS, 2009). The slightly different figures supplement one another.

Complementary Integration

Complementary is defined as "making up what is lacking in one another" with a complement being "either of two parts that complete each other" (Neufeldt & Guralnik, 1991, p. 285). If, during our comparative analysis, we discovered differences between two or more disciplines' information and insights, it is likely that they complement or complete one another. We can combine by filling the gaps left by one discipline's explanation of our topic with information and insights from another discipline. If we focus simply on two specific puzzle pieces, the tab of one fills the blank, or cutout, of another. If we focus on a complete landscape picture with mountains, lake, and sky, then the cluster of interlocked pieces that make up the lake fills in the gap between the clusters of interlocked pieces that make up the mountains, and the clusters of interlocked pieces that make up the sky fill the empty space above the mountains and lakes.

For example, both anthropology and economics study the problems of children who lose one or both parents to AIDS in developing countries. Anthropologists focus on the impact of such children on extended families, the daily lives of all involved, and the larger culture of communities. The anthropologists studying health and social impacts might find that while children made vulnerable by HIV are taken in and loved by extended family, the responsibility for the children affects the health and well-being of elderly relatives such as uncles or grandparents. Or given the unfortunate stigma associated with HIV, that by taking in the children the relatives become socially isolated within a community that fears HIV. Anthropologists do not ignore the financial impact, because that is part of daily life, but it may be one of many factors important to them.

For economists, however, that financial impact is most important to a study of children made vulnerable by AIDS, including the immediate impact of family finances, the role played by assistance from governments or international organizations, and the long-term impact on national economies. Economists studying the financial impact on family finances might discover that the extra financial burden of children made vulnerable by HIV prevents extended families from sending all children to school. To see just the economic impact or just the impact on daily life leads to interesting but incomplete answers to our question about responses to the global HIV epidemic, just as to piece together the mountains but not the lake of our landscape puzzle leaves a gap; to integrate information about the financial impact of orphans and other children made vulnerable by AIDS from both disciplines provides a fuller picture, just as to insert the cluster of interlocked puzzle pieces making up the lake comes closer to completing the landscape puzzle picture.

BOX 3.3
LEARN MORE
Writing Skills

Like any other type of essay, an integrative essay relies on good writing skills to effectively communicate the answer to a research question: a clear and appropriate thesis, organization and coherence, good development of and support for main points, effective sentences and paragraphs, and proper documentation of sources such as APA or MLA Style. Many colleges and universities have writing centers where students can receive assistance with writing challenges and may also have online writing resources, such as Purdue University's Online Writing Lab (https://owl.purdue .edu). There are many books on how to write effectively, both classic and new, including:

- Baker, S. (2005). *The Longman practical stylist: A classic guide to style.* New York, NY: Pearson.

- Goodson, P. (2017). *Becoming an academic writer: 50 exercises for paced, productive, and powerful writing* (2nd ed.). Thousand Oaks, CA: Sage.

- Osmond, A. (2015). *Academic writing and grammar for students.* Thousand Oaks, CA: Sage.

- Trimble, J. R. (2011). *Writing with style: Conversations on the art of writing* (3rd ed.). New York, NY: Pearson.

As we explain our answer to a research question—actually write a research paper—we are combining the supplementary and complementary information and insights we've gathered from each individual discipline. Again, Chapters 4 and 6 present integrated essays on the case studies of the global HIV epidemic and terrorism, then Chapters 5 and 7 detail exactly how I constructed those sample integrative essays. To briefly explain before you read these upcoming chapters, I wrote sentences and paragraphs that combine information and insights from relevant disciplines in much the same way that we snap together pieces of a puzzle or, as noted above, we end up stacking pieces one on top of another.

Going back to the hypothetical example of similar information on HIV funding (above), supplementary integration of information would be metaphorically stacking pieces one on top of another. For example:

> Estimates suggest that US$20–$30 billion would be necessary to manage the global HIV epidemic through 2020 (Economics source, 2018; Geography source, 2018; Political Science source, 2018).

In this sentence, we have three stacked pieces: the estimate from economics (US$20–$30) on top of the estimate from geography (US$20–$30) on top of the estimate from political science (US$20–$30). To provide the example *only*, I substitute the disciplines for authors in the APA Style parenthetical citation—we would of course cite the actual authors when writing an integrated essay (as I do in Chapters 4–7). And the sources are, in fact, the only way in which this supplementary integration is visible. As I noted earlier, the process of doing interdisciplinary research is best exemplified by the jigsaw puzzle metaphor but the end result—the integrated essay—fits the metaphor of a smoothie. I will mix the two here, hopefully instructively. Readers would not necessarily know from the sentence above that it combines three fruits because the fruits are blended together—by stacking three puzzle pieces. Careful readers could note that there are three sources, which shows reliability and validity.

Complementary integration blends information and insights by snapping different puzzle pieces together. In the hypothetical example of children made vulnerable by HIV, above, we saw that anthropologists and economists could come up with different insights. Anthropologists may learn of the personal and social impact on extended family adopting children made vulnerable by HIV while economics could study the impact on family finances. For example:

> When extended families take in children made vulnerable by HIV, it could impact the well-being and social status of relatives as well as limit their ability to afford education for the children (Anthropology, 2018; Economics, 2018).

In this complementary integration, our sentence was constructed not by stacking puzzle pieces, but snapping two disciplinary puzzle pieces together with the explanation or context for both insights: (1) the insight from anthropology and (2) the insight from economics.

- When extended families take in children made vulnerable by HIV, it could impact (context/explanation)

- The well-being and social status of relatives (anthropology piece of the puzzle) as well as

- Limit their ability to afford education for the children (economics piece of the puzzle)

Thus, in snapping together two different pieces of the puzzle, we have created a more comprehensive understanding than if we had insights from only one discipline. We have blended two different pieces of fruit into a smoothie, rather than just eating one on its own. One tip for ensuring balance and integration as you draft your essay is to put each different discipline's sources in different font colors—a visual reminder for the draft, only, of supplementary and complementary integration as you write.

Global Studies research thus allows us to develop more comprehensive answers to our questions about the world by providing us with an explanation of how to gather, compare, and combine information and insights from many disciplines.

Back to Interdisciplinary and Other/Nondisciplinary Sources

Global Studies research emphasizes and enables us to draw together sources written from disciplinary perspectives, but the same steps apply to interdisciplinary and other/ nondisciplinary sources. Once we have integrated our disciplinary sources into an answer to a research question, we can also integrate already-interdisciplinary sources and other/nondisciplinary sources in the same way, with attention to balance and point of view. We need to consider how the interdisciplinary or nondisciplinary sources that we gathered relate to the interdisciplinary answer to the research question we constructed. We integrate them into our interdisciplinary answer (research paper) by first comparing their information and insights, utilizing the same criteria for comparison, and then combining them as supplementary or complementary to the disciplinary information and insights. They are yet more puzzle pieces that expand or validate our jigsaw puzzle.

Chapters 4 through 7 encompass the case studies, as examples of how to carry out the Global Studies research process. Chapter 4 presents an integrated essay in answer to the global HIV epidemic case study research question that combines information and insights from relevant disciplines. Metaphorically, it is a completed puzzle picture, and in Chapter 5 I take apart and examine the puzzle pieces to explain how following the steps of the Global Studies research process allowed me to first prepare to research and then gather, compare, and combine the puzzle pieces to construct Chapter 4 (as a jigsaw puzzle picture). Chapter 6 is the integrated essay for the terrorism case study and Chapter 7 the explanation of how the Global Studies research process developed that essay. While Chapter 5 emphasizes the basic process, Chapter 7 introduces challenges and solutions researchers can encounter as they undertake the Global Studies research process.

BOX 3.4
TAKE A STEP!
Determine Relevant Disciplines

Once you have begun your research and refined your own research question, the next step is to determine which disciplines are relevant to your Global Studies research project. Following the guidelines above, consider the disciplines from which you may need to gather information and insights to answer your research question. Though the five contributing social sciences disciplines are a starting point, remember that other disciplines within or outside the social sciences may be potentially relevant. Those that are most relevant will become apparent as you find pertinent sources by gathering research. As you finalize the most relevant disciplines, ensure that you know enough about each discipline to utilize its information and insights (see Chapter 2).

4 A Complex Problem
GLOBAL HIV EPIDEMIC

B elow is a sample integrated essay that serves to introduce the HIV epidemic as a global problem; it is a completed puzzle picture. This essay resulted from gathering, comparing, and combining information and insights from the Global Studies disciplines of anthropology, economics, geography, history, and political science to describe at least part of the world's response to the HIV epidemic, in answer to the research question prepared in Chapter 3: "How are IGOs and NGOs involved in the global response to the multisectoral HIV epidemic?" Chapters 4 and 5 should be read together, because Chapter 5 explains in detail how undertaking the Global Studies research process allowed me to write this essay.

The Global Response to HIV

The Human Immunodeficiency Virus (HIV) and associated Acquired Immunodeficiency Syndrome (AIDS) came to the world's attention in the early 1980s, although this was well after the virus began spreading among humans and before scientists identified the virus, its origins, or the ways the virus spreads. Based on tests of stored blood and tissue samples, scientists know there was a confirmed case as far back as 1959. Medical histories, computer models, and other evidence suggest the virus may have infected humans as far back as the 1910s, primarily among Africans and Europeans who had been to Africa. Scientists discovered the Human Immunodeficiency Virus (HIV) itself in 1983. It was not until 1999, however, that we knew for sure that HIV jumped from chimpanzees and monkeys to humans in Africa,[1] with humans exposed to a gene mutation of simian immunodeficiency virus through the consumption of their meat and the handling of bloody remains of animals. Such gene mutations are common among viruses, although mutations do not always have such drastic consequences for our world (Engel, 2006; Harden, 2012).

Those with HIV are HIV-positive. When the immune system is compromised by the virus and a person becomes ill, the associated set of diseases and symptoms are

---

[1]Viruses commonly transfer from animals to humans; other examples include plague, SARS, avian or bird flu, and H1N1 influenza or swine flu (which actually mutated from both pig and bird viruses).

known as Acquired Immune Deficiency Syndrome or AIDS. The common term is now people living with HIV.[2] The virus is transmitted from person to person through bodily fluids. Most commonly, this happens through unprotected sex; from mother to child during pregnancy, birth, or breastfeeding; or through the sharing of needles, syringes, or other tools for injected drug use. Early in the global HIV epidemic, blood transfusions were a source of transmission but today most countries have safety measures in place to prevent this. Less common forms of transmission include when healthcare professionals accidentally stick themselves with needles used on patients with HIV or when someone with an open wound is exposed to blood from an HIV-positive individual. Once an individual is HIV-positive, the virus attacks the immune system, but slowly (Engel, 2006; Harden, 2012; Whiteside, 2008). During that time, people who do not know they are HIV-positive continue to live their lives, exposing sexual partners, spouses, and children to transmission. Testing so individuals know their HIV status is therefore very important.

While there is as yet no cure for HIV, there are medications known collectively as antiretroviral therapy available that reduce the impact of the virus on a person's immune system and delay development of HIV into AIDS. These medications are also effective in preventing mother-to-child transmission of HIV (Whiteside, 2008). As of late 2010s, there are also pre-exposure prophylaxis drugs (PrEP) available for those at high risk. These drugs reduce the likelihood of infection by 90% for sexual contact and 70% for injected drug use, but only when taken daily (U.S. Centers for Disease Control, 2018). Vaccine treatments would prevent HIV for extended periods (perhaps life), and efforts to find an effective vaccine continue. Over time, however, funding, ethical questions about human testing, and the scientifically difficult process of creating a vaccine against a rapidly mutating virus have limited vaccine efforts. Good news emerged in mid-2018, when a "mosaic" vaccine designed to fight multiple strains of HIV showed promise in human trials (Therrien, 2018).

In part because the history of HIV and AIDS in the United States and Europe began among men having sex with men or people who inject drugs—groups considered undesirable or politically unacceptable by many—there has been a persistent stigma attached to it. This is also true of other contagious and infectious diseases such as leprosy, pneumonic plague, and tuberculosis, so stigma and discrimination are also, in part, a common response to disease. Once scientists traced the origins of the virus to the continent of Africa, that stigma attached to the countries and cultures of

---

[2]People living with HIV seek to avoid stigma and thus deserve language and terms that are both accurate and respectful. Preferred terms change and evolve over time and across regions of the world. For example, people with AIDS (PWA) evolved to people living with HIV/AIDS (PLWHA) to recognize those who have HIV but not AIDS. Given antiretroviral therapy, fewer people living with HIV progress to AIDS, so people living with HIV (PLHIV) became more common into the early 2010s. Between 2011 and 2015, however, use of such abbreviations became seen as dehumanizing and the currently preferred terminology is people living with HIV. UNAIDS maintains updated terminology guidelines that can be found with an internet search for "UNAIDS terminology guidelines."

that continent. Governments in African countries reacted poorly to what they saw as blame for the global HIV epidemic—and to the sometimes ridiculous and culturally inappropriate speculation as to how the virus transferred from primates to humans. Many African governments viewed the stigma and blame as racist and damaging to the respect and dignity of their countries as well as to economies based in part on tourism. Some reacted by initially denying the virus existed in their countries, which slowed the response to and increased the impact of the epidemic in Africa.

Today, the scientific controversies are resolved; the global scientific community accepts the evidence that HIV transferred to humans from primates. Scientists, global health policy makers, and activists insist there is nothing to be gained by trying to assign blame for a naturally occurring gene mutation. We know that Africa has been hit the hardest because it was hit first—silently, unnoticed, for at least a decade (likely longer) before what would become known as HIV was noticed in the United States and Europe.

The United Nations Joint Programme on AIDS (UNAIDS) 2018 Global AIDS Update, *Miles to Go: Closing Gaps, Breaking Barriers, Righting Injustices*, offers very good news about the global HIV epidemic: From 1996 to 2017, the number of new HIV infections throughout the world fell by 47%. This includes a sharp decrease in new transmission rates among the eastern and southern sub-Saharan African countries, a region that has been extremely hard hit by HIV. Deaths have also dropped by 50% between 2004 and 2017, because access to antiretroviral therapy is becoming more widespread (UNAIDS, 2018c). This very good news, unfortunately, is tempered by less positive facts and trends. According to the UNAIDS 2018 Global AIDS Update, the estimated number of people throughout the world living with HIV in 2017 was 36.9 million, and, according to the World Health Organization (WHO), more than 35 million people have died of HIV-related causes so far. WHO's Africa Region accounts for about 66% of new transmissions (WHO, 2018). Funding provided by donors saw a large increase in 2016 but had remained flat for several years prior to that. During 2017, there were no new significant donations pledged and funding could even decrease due to domestic spending. Even with the increases, there is still a shortfall of 20% from the funds needed to achieve current goals (UNAIDS, 2018b).

As of 2014, UNAIDS set "fast-track targets" for 2020 and 2030, to end the epidemic. Under the "90-90-90 strategy," by 2020, UNAIDS seeks to ensure 90% of all people living with HIV get tested and know their HIV status, 90% of people living with HIV worldwide receive sustained antiretroviral therapy, and 90% of those receiving antiretroviral therapy will have suppression of HIV in their bodies. Also by 2020, the goal is to reduce new infections by 75%, to 500,000. By 2030, the respective targets are 95-95-95 and reduction of new infections to 200,000. For both targets, there is also a goal to reduce discrimination to zero (UNAIDS, 2018b). The 2018 Global AIDS Update notes that complacency regarding HIV is increasing among donor governments and average individuals; now that it is treatable, some urgency is gone. Knowledge of HIV and safe sex practices has dropped in many countries, especially among the young (UNAIDS, 2018c). There has definitely been

BOX 4.1
LEARN MORE
HIV and AIDS by the Numbers

Every year, countries and international organizations issue updates and annual reports on HIV and AIDS including statistics about transmission, deaths, people receiving antiretroviral therapy, and funding. To find the most up-to-date statistics and data, start with:

www.unaids.org (see especially Fact Sheets and Documents)

www.theglobalfund.org

www.who.int/topics/hiv_aids/en

www.aidsinfoonline.org (UNAIDS-sponsored database)

progress over the 30-plus years since HIV emerged, but there is more to do as our world responds to this global issue.

The HIV epidemic is both a parallel and transnational global issue. It requires a global response because it is present in most countries of the world and, due to globalization, stopping transmission of the virus—and its multisectoral impact—in one country isn't realistic unless transmission stops in all countries. The HIV epidemic as a global issue is complex and multisectoral because it affects daily life for millions throughout the world in ways varying from personal health, relationships with family and community, and personal finances to national health, national policies, and national economies to global health, international relations, and international aid. Until there is a cure, global actors cannot solve this complex global issue, only manage it.

All types of global actors (see Chapter 1) are involved in responding to the HIV epidemic and carry out a wide array of activities in response, making it productive to focus in on several of each. International governmental organizations (IGOs) like WHO and, later, UNAIDS coordinate the day-to-day work of developing and implementing the global response to HIV through emphasizing and monitoring national HIV/AIDS plans, among other activities; these lead organizations also engage directly with nongovernmental actors (NGOs) who both challenge and assist WHO and UNAIDS as the NGOs seek to influence the global response, such as the policy of universal treatment access. Funding for the global response to HIV has evolved into a public-private partnership, The Global Fund.

The Response Begins

Nongovernmental actors challenged governmental ones before there even was a global response—in efforts to end denial and prompt recognition of the HIV epidemic as a global issue necessitating a coordinated response. NGOs were not alone in this effort, as individuals and government agencies also demanded action. Initial international interactions were among scientists, healthcare professionals, and public health officials, who came together at conferences to discuss the emerging epidemic and compare progress on research. These interactions raised awareness among the government agencies, private businesses, IGOs, NGOs, and research entities for which they worked. Early on, the only interactions between governments were at the relatively low level of public health agencies, such as the U.S. Centers for Disease Control (CDC). Political leaders did not initially interact on this global issue. The World Health Organization itself was slow to respond. Because the first patients identified with the new virus were in wealthy countries such as the United States and Europe, an internal WHO memo from 1983 argues these countries had the financial resources and knowledge to respond effectively on their own (Behrman, 2004; Gordenker, Coate, Jönsson, & Söderholm, 1995). At that time, WHO chose to preserve its own resources and leave the response up to the high-income countries.

At the same time public health officials called for a response, however, so did people living with HIV and their concerned family and friends (Gordenker et al., 1995; Parker, 2011; Rau, 2007). As Parker (2011) asserts in "Grassroots Activism, Civil Society Mobilization, and the Politics of HIV/AIDS Epidemic," it is "impossible to overstate just how important grassroots pressure was—not only in the industrialized countries in North America and Europe, but also in more resource-poor settings in Africa, Latin America, and the Caribbean" (p. 24)—in prompting countries and IGOs to respond.

The first officially recorded cases of what would become known as AIDS were among men having sex with men and people who inject drugs in the United States and Europe. Both groups were at the time politically weak and rejected by mainstream society. Therefore, there was initially little political will to respond effectively, especially by the U.S. government. The U.S. civil rights movement of the 1960s and women's rights movement of the 1970s, however, helped create a culture of social activism: People were willing to speak out for their own needs and the needs of others, pushing the government and the public at large for change. This atmosphere was, at least in part, responsible for the unprecedented activism surrounding HIV and AIDS in the United States and other countries.

"Grassroots activists from communities directly affected by the epidemic were almost universally the first to respond" and, along with nongovernmental AIDS service organizations (ASOs),[3] "were also the first social actors to exert meaningful pressure on governments to take action" (Parker, 2011, p. 22). "For the first time in international

---

[3]Generally, use of the term NGOs denotes organizations that act in the HIV and AIDS issue-areas but for whom it is not their main reason for being. Partners in Health, for example, builds health capacity in developing countries and focuses on a number of health issues, diseases, and conditions—HIV is one of many. ASOs are solely dedicated to HIV and AIDS. There is an attempt to define ASOs as organizations offering care and services but not participating in politics (advocacy or activism). However, many organizations called ASOs do both, particularly later in the epidemic. (See section on universal treatment access, below.)

health work, patients themselves formed active and vocal groups" (Gordenker et al., 1995, p. 92). In the United States, LGBT communities first took to activism, like the organization ACT UP. In other countries, particularly in Latin America, it was LGBT communities in partnership with public health officials; activists concerned with social, economic, and political equality; Catholic-based communities; and the Liberation Theology Movement (Parker, 2011).

By the late 1980s, with information and demands from medical and health practitioner interactions, pressure from activists and NGOs, and data on HIV cases from national governments, WHO realized the potentially devastating, worldwide scope of the epidemic. The numbers of AIDS cases reported to WHO jumped from 408 in 1982 to 12,174 in 1984 to 71,751 in 1987; however, due to lack of testing and underreporting, estimates were that in 1984 5 million to 10 million were infected worldwide (Grmek, 1990; "History of AIDS," 2013). By 1988, the director general of WHO announced, "AIDS is 'the world's chief public health problem'" (Grmek, 1990, p. 182). WHO, other UN programs and agencies, and countries recognized the HIV epidemic as a global issue and began the global response.

Lead Organizations

Once any global issue is recognized, coordinating the global response often falls to UN organizations because IGOs have legitimacy, authority, and access to funding as governmental actors; they are forums through which member governments share information, express national interests, demand or agree to actions, and evaluate the effectiveness of those actions. In the case of the HIV epidemic, first the World Health Organization (WHO) and, later, the United Nations Joint Programme on HIV/AIDS (UNAIDS) took responsibility for the complex job of coordinating the global response to this multisectoral issue—coordinating the many actors and their many activities.

WHO and the Global Programme on AIDS

WHO started its Global Programme on AIDS (GPA, first called the Special Program on AIDS) in 1987; it became the "global vehicle" to coordinate the world's response to the new epidemic (Behrman, 2004, p. 40). GPA's goals were "exchange of information and provision of guidelines; public education; . . . assessment of diagnostic methodology; advice on safe blood and blood products; and coordination of research" (Lisk, 2010, pp. 16–17). WHO officials and others in the public health community recognized that the potential impact of HIV and AIDS went beyond the medical concerns to "wider non-health implications" including socioeconomic well-being and human rights (Lisk, 2010, pp. 16–17). Jonathan Mann, GPA's first director, focused on three broad areas: protecting the human rights of people living with HIV, coordinating the response within the UN, and coordinating the response at the national and international levels. GPA also sought to draw international attention to the HIV epidemic as a global issue; a first step was the London Declaration on AIDS Prevention issued in 1988 by an international meeting of health ministers, which emphasized the human rights of people living with HIV, the need for global cooperation to address the social as well as medical consequences of the virus, and the need for cooperation between developed and developing countries in funding the global response to the virus (Behrman, 2004; Lisk, 2010).

Joint United Nations Programme on HIV/AIDS

The GPA operated until the mid-1990s, when a combination of three factors led to a shift in the United Nations' response and the creation of the Joint United Nations Programme on HIV/AIDS (UNAIDS): lack of coordination and competition among agencies within the UN, dissatisfaction with GPA policies at the national level, and a broader climate for reform within the UN (Behrman, 2004; Gordenker et al., 1995; Harden, 2012; Iliffe, 2006; UNAIDS, 2011). First, GPA's goal of coordinating the response within the United Nations was problematic from the start. Because they recognized the HIV epidemic as multisectoral, WHO and GPA sought to work with other UN organizations involved in the response. For example, other relevant organizations and agencies included the United Nations Development Programme (UNDP), because of the economic impact of HIV and the probability that it would hinder efforts of developing countries to strengthen and industrialize their economies, and the United Nations Children's Fund (UNICEF), which provides emergency and development assistance to children and mothers, including those living with HIV.

Over time, tensions developed over funding for each group's particular activities and who was in charge when activities overlapped. By 1990, for example, UNDP and UNICEF were seeking donations to fund their own HIV programs, duplicating the efforts of and competing with WHO/GPA. Tensions increased further when changes in the leadership of WHO and GPA refocused efforts on primarily medical aspects of the HIV epidemic rather than the early multisectoral approach (Behrman, 2004; Gordenker et al., 1995; Harden, 2012; Iliffe, 2006; Lisk, 2010).

Second, countries also began to complain about GPA, both because of the inefficient duplication of efforts among relevant organizations and the one-size-fits-all guidelines provided by GPA for national AIDS plans. As countries (and WHO) recognized that HIV wasn't a short-term outbreak but a long-term global epidemic, they also recognized that prevention and education efforts would have to fit each country's circumstances and culture. For example, once WHO understood that the virus could be transmitted through contaminated needles, the guideline or medical best practice WHO prescribed was: Never reuse disposable needles in hospitals or clinics. The reuse of unsterilized or disposable needles didn't happen in hospitals or clinics in developed countries, so this seemed a simple, straightforward guideline.[4] In developing countries, however, where medical supplies can be difficult to obtain and afford, doctors often faced the choice of reusing needles or failing to treat patients at all (Engel, 2006).

---

[4]Reuse of unsterilized needles by people who inject drugs remains a mode of transmission in both developed and developing countries.

WHO thus adapted its guidelines to the circumstances faced in less-developed countries, emphasizing educating health care practitioners and patients about safe injection practices, including promoting single-use injections and avoiding unnecessary injections; reducing the costs of single-use needles; promoting government, hospital, and clinic planning and budgeting for single-use needles; and encouraging NGO, IGO, and country donors to provide funds for single-use injection equipment and training (Single Use, 2007).

Finally, tensions and criticisms surrounding GPA reduced its effectiveness, leading to the creation of the Joint United Nations Programme on HIV/AIDS, called UNAIDS. While the creation of a new UN program is not unique, UNAIDS was at the time. UNAIDS' unique structure and Programme Coordinating Board resulted from a willingness within the UN and the member countries to try something new. By the 1990s, the UN had become a large, unwieldy bureaucracy and member countries sought reform, either in general or specifically regarding the HIV epidemic. "The one commonality among donors was a willingness to break the mold" and UNAIDS came into being partly "as a trial for UN reform . . . a field test" (Behrman, 2004, p. 169). Peter Piot, the first director of UNAIDS, built on this willingness when he demanded that the Programme have regional offices and the power to run its own programs rather than working through other UN agencies. "Piot wanted to avoid the usual UN practice of making joint programs accountable to all the different UN agencies because Piot believed this would effectively kill the program's ability to act forcefully" (Harden, 2012, pp. 210–211).

UNAIDS began operations in January 1996 and has five basic functions: (1) coordinate the global response to the HIV epidemic, including the efforts of UN organizations and agencies, national governments, nongovernmental organizations (NGOs), the private sector, and individuals; (2) advocate on behalf of people living with HIV and promote awareness of the overlap between HIV, human rights, and gender equality; (3) gather and disseminate "political, technical, scientific and financial resources"; (4) provide information to ensure those resources are best utilized and assist prevention measures; and (5) reinforce countries' efforts to address HIV while helping them maintain or improve health and development ("About UNAIDS," n.d.).

UNAIDS is unique in structure because it is co-sponsored by 11 other UN organizations and agencies: UN High Commissioner for Refugees (UNHCR), UN Children's Fund (UNICEF), World Food Programme (WFP), UN Development Programme (UNDP), UN Population Fund (UNFPA), UN Office on Drugs and Crime (UNODC), UN Women, International Labour Organization (ILO), UN Educational, Scientific and Cultural Organization (UNESCO), World Health Organization (WHO), and the World Bank (Lisk, 2010; UNAIDS n.d.). These cosponsors jointly work to coordinate their activities in response to the HIV epidemic as they each carry out their specialized tasks and focus on their own larger goals. For example, the UN Office on Drugs and Crime provides information and assistance to countries working to prevent or reduce HIV transmission among people who inject drugs, prison populations, and those vulnerable to human trafficking. It does so through advocacy and support for effective national legislation as well as working in partnership with governments and non-governmental organizations to provide prevention, treatment, and care to these key populations.

The UNAIDS Programme Coordinating Board, which governs the Programme, further highlights its unique structure; in addition to the eleven UN organization and agency cosponsors, the Board includes representatives of 22 countries (all UN members) and representatives of NGOs, one for each of five geographic regions (Lisk, 2010; "NGOs/civil," n.d.). It is common for member countries to be represented, but it was definitely uncommon for NGOs to play a role. While also often dissatisfied with GPA—hence their challenges—NGOs did not play a driving role in the creation of UNAIDS; however, their unprecedented presence in the global issue-area helped prompt their inclusion in its creation. In developed countries early on, and developing countries within a decade, activist and advocacy NGOs pressured their governments for policies protecting people living with HIV from discrimination and for increased funding for HIV and AIDS research, prevention, and treatment. They pressured scientists to increase their efforts to find treatments, vaccines, and a cure. NGOs also pressured WHO to, in turn, pressure countries to respond as effectively as possible, to improve its own global response, to adapt to the different needs of different countries, and to maintain worldwide attention to the HIV epidemic as a global issue. Through their own activities and working with GPA, NGOs and ASOs have successfully influenced policy changes at the national and international levels, garnered funding, and offered vital services to those impacted by HIV and/or AIDS. These activities, along with the broader climate for reform in the UN system, allowed for inclusion of NGOs in UNAIDS.

UNAIDS' early days were hopeful but difficult. Ironically, as GPA was phased out, funding for HIV and AIDS decreased significantly. For example, U.S. contributions for GPA were approximately $40 million, but dropped by half with UNAIDS'

BOX 4.2
TAKE A STEP!
Identify Disciplinary Sources for HIV or Terrorism

Review the References associated with either Chapter 4, A Complex Problem: Global HIV Epidemic or Chapter 6, A Complex Problem: Terrorism and investigate the already-gathered sources until you have identified at least one disciplinary source from each of the five relevant Global Studies disciplines: anthropology, economics, geography, history, and political science. Remember, the References include other and interdisciplinary sources.

creation in 1996. While UNAIDS' unique structure was intended to diminish overlap and disputes between UN agencies, that took time—time during which some national HIV/AIDS plans suffered from lack of funding and guidance. UNAIDS' status as a new and unknown international organization also took time to overcome; it took about 2 years for the organization to gain the international recognition and authority needed to carry out its purpose (Behrman, 2004; Harden, 2012).

National HIV/AIDS Plans

Beginning in the early days of WHO's Global Programme on AIDS and continuing with UNAIDS' requirements today, each country should create, implement, and continually update a national HIV/AIDS strategic plan. WHO asked governments to prepare national HIV/AIDS plans to describe how they address and implement the procedures and priorities established first by GPA and later UNAIDS. GPA provided and UNAIDS continues to provide technical assistance for creation and implementation of national HIV/AIDS plans and to HIV/AIDS-specific agencies or personnel within each country's health departments or ministries (Behrman, 2004; Lisk, 2010).

The government plans include numerous aspects of national response. One is surveillance, which refers to developing and sustaining an effective way to identify cases of HIV. This allows countries to track in which regions or groups HIV is most prevalent and to target their national responses. A country faced with high rates of HIV among people who inject drugs will respond somewhat differently than a country faced with high rates among women. The first situation is affected by criminal laws and access to clean needles, while the second may be related to inequality, poverty, and access to education and prevention. National HIV/AIDS plans define prevention strategies, including awareness campaigns; treatment strategies, including decisions about provision of antiretroviral medications; and strategies for the care and support of people living with HIV, such as whether they receive government-funded health care and disability payments. Many national plans also address legal, social, economic, and political aspects of the epidemic (Behrman, 2004; Lisk, 2010). Developed countries such as the United Kingdom already had effective surveillance systems in place, although they may have had to adapt them to suit HIV. They also have basic health care services available and the capability to carry out effective awareness and prevention campaigns. Developed countries' national HIV/AIDS strategic plans, thus, involved adapting existing systems, services, and policies to HIV and AIDS, as well as addressing legal issues such as discrimination.

Many developing countries, however, not only needed to develop national HIV/AIDS plans but also to develop the surveillance systems, health services, and government policies to implement them—and needed to do so facing severe economic constraints, political instability, and even conflict. Low-income countries already lack the resources to improve the health of their citizens; HIV and AIDS only increase that problem. GPA thus also served as a source of funding for national governments in their development of plans and personnel specifically to address HIV and AIDS. WHO and its GPA supported more than 100 countries as they responded to the HIV epidemic within their own borders (Behrman, 2004; Lisk, 2010). Funding came from countries and other organizations—special donations specifically intended to support the response to the HIV epidemic.

The East African country of Uganda serves as an example. Immediately upon gaining power in 1986, President Yoweri Museveni of Uganda gave considerable attention to HIV and AIDS. Some historians of the HIV epidemic in Uganda question his motives—arguing that he was more interested in attracting international aid and reducing high rates of infection among the soldiers keeping him in power than in helping his country's people—but acknowledge he was the first African leader to undertake serious efforts to thwart spread of the virus (Kuhanen, 2008). The epidemic in Uganda was spread primarily through heterosexual sex and existed in the general population rather than in primarily marginal groups as in the United States and Europe. Uganda initially had one of the highest rates of transmission; at its peak, roughly one in six Ugandans had HIV. Uganda constructed one of the first national HIV/AIDS plans; following on GPA's guidelines at the time and accepting GPA funding, the Ministry of Health's National AIDS Control Programme emphasized establishing surveillance programs to track the spread and distribution of the virus, ensuring safe blood supplies, and education and prevention. HIV testing and AIDS treatment, care, and support became additional priorities over time. President Museveni's rapid response included numerous speeches on the HIV epidemic and the creation of a culture in which the virus, ways to prevent its spread, and sex could be openly discussed (Barnett & Whiteside, 2006; Behrman, 2004; Engel, 2006; Iliffe, 2006).

This high-level attention to the HIV epidemic in Uganda drew the interest of international organizations and other international donors. Decades of conflict had destroyed both the economy and the health care system of Uganda. There were few functioning clinics or hospitals to carry out the medical and technical procedures defined in the national plan. President Museveni therefore took advantage of the willingness of IGOs and donors to invest in rebuilding his country's economy and health systems, and that process is still ongoing.

Uganda is currently operating under its National Strategic Plan for 2015/2016–2019/2020. As of 2017, there are 1.3 million people living with HIV in the country, representing about 6.5% of the population. Seventy-two percent are receiving antiretroviral therapy. There were 50,000 new infections, down 45% since 2010. As of 2013, Uganda has lower numbers of new infections per year than numbers of new individuals gaining access to antiretroviral therapy per year (UNAIDS, 2018a). While encouraging, these numbers hide considerable social stigma and discrimination, particularly against men having sex with men and sex workers. In 2014, the World Bank and several bilateral donors threatened to withdraw their loans and foreign aid after the Uganda Anti-Homosexuality Act 2014 became law and instituted life sentences for same-sex relations, which were already illegal. Uganda's Constitutional Court later invalidated the law on procedural grounds, but LGBT discrimination is widespread and arguably increased due to the media attention surrounding the Act ("Uganda Court Annuls," 2014).

One expectation for GPA and the national HIV/AIDS plans was that they would raise awareness of the epidemic at all levels. To an extent, the plans—and NGOs/ASOs that assisted in their implementation—became "transmission belts," transmitting information both to and from the local level. Global and national actors became more aware of local-level efforts such as The AIDS Support Organization (TASO) in Uganda. Nongovernmental AIDS service organizations carry out educational campaigns to educate people about how to prevent HIV transmission, offer medical services to those who cannot afford or do not have access to them, and offer legal, psychological, financial, and other services to people living with HIV and their families. TASO in Uganda was one of the first AIDS service organizations in Africa. It was founded in 1987 by a small group of friends, either people living with HIV themselves or close to someone with HIV, who volunteered their time to assist those living with HIV (Iliffe, 2006). The friends sought to support each other in the face of discrimination, abandonment by family, and limited access to treatment and care. TASO now has a dozen service centers and offers counseling, medical services, and other support services to more than 100,000 each year. It also promotes AIDS campaigns to reduce AIDS discrimination within Uganda and cooperates with global efforts to address the impact of the HIV epidemic ("About TASO," 2015; Parker, 2011). As GPA and governments of other countries learned about it, TASO became a model ASO for other African countries.

In Thailand, the transmission belt of awareness went the other direction. As first GPA and then UNAIDS encouraged national HIV/AIDS plans to carry out campaigns informing people living with HIV of their human and political rights, ASOs enabled individuals to demand those rights. In "Healthier Geographies: Mediating the Gaps Between the Needs of People Living With HIV and AIDS and Health Care in Chiang Mai, Thailand," Vincent J. Del Casino Jr. reports on the development of ASOs in this province of Thailand between 1994–1997. All ASOs receive some level of government funding, challenging their identity as nongovernmental, and can access meeting space in government buildings such as hospitals or clinics. Del Casino (2001) found that some ASOs met in temples or private homes, either to access spiritual services or because individual members were too ill to leave their homes. While their reasons for meeting outside of government spaces may have been apolitical, the members of such ASOs were more likely to be activist:

> If using a site outside the public health care system, PLWHA [people living with HIV] can first organize their needs, prepare guidelines and policy, and then present these to local health and administrative officials. As such, PLWHA can assert their rights as consumers of health care . . . and as participants in the decision-making processes of local administrative organizations. (Del Casino, 2001, p. 416)

Engagement with NGOs

Having challenged the world to respond, grassroots activists and NGOs were eager to assist with that response. There was an unprecedented level of involvement by NGOs and ASOs in the global response to the HIV epidemic—higher levels than seen before on other important global issues and certainly higher than seen in other global epidemics. Given the activity of nongovernmental actors, GPA also sought to include NGOs in its coordinated response and by suggesting national governments include NGOs and ASOs in their national HIV/AIDS plans. This national inclusion was not always successful, as many countries feared empowering NGOs that could challenge national politics and policies while others co-opted NGOs through "directive rather than collaborative" national strategies (Gordenker et al., 1995; Rau, 2007, p. 171).

Determining the relationship between GPA and NGOs was no easier (Gordenker et al., 1995; Rau, 2007). GPA's own staff was divided over how to include them; some argued that NGOs and ASOs should only assist with implementation and service provision (their traditional role with WHO) while others argued that they should be involved in a wider range of activities. Buttressing the latter's position was the fact that NGOs were among the first actors to grasp the multisectoral nature of the HIV epidemic and, with Jonathan Mann's support, the latter group won (Gordenker et al., 1995).

Exactly how to include NGOs in GPA, however, remained uncertain. GPA settled on international meetings and creation of an umbrella organization to maintain contact with NGOs/ASOs. In 1989, WHO sponsored the First International Meeting of AIDS Service Organization in Vienna, drawing participants from more than 50 nongovernmental organizations. This meeting prompted the proposal and, later, planning and creation of a standing NGO advisory council: the International Council of AIDS Service Organizations (Gordenker et al., 1995; Zeiser, 1998).

The creation of the International Council of AIDS Service Organizations (ICASO) did not go smoothly, however. Even though we lump them all together as nongovernmental actors, there can be significant divisions among NGOs/ASOs. When it came time to vote on ICASO, at the 1990 Paris NGO Conference, arguments and protests emerged over the formality of the conference format, the priority given to different identity groups, and the "North-South divide." For example, LGBT groups, women's groups, and sex worker groups all complained their views were being ignored. Groups from Africa argued they'd been left out of the proposal drafting process. Some ASOs protested that other NGOs involved did not do enough work on HIV or AIDS to participate. ICASO finally came into being, after discussion and compromise, and was comprised of regional networks with a governing board to coordinate with GPA. The organization also increased opportunities for collaboration among NGOs/ASOs. Through ICASO, NGOs were included in policy planning, implementation, and review to varying degrees and were afforded some funding through WHO's GPA (Gordenker et al., 1995). (With the creation of UNAIDS and its Programme Coordinating Board, ICASO became irrelevant as an advisory council. ICASO still exists but is a Canadian organization rather than a network of regional organizations.)

The creation of ICASO and its relationship with GPA, however, did not always ensure NGO participation. When first announced in 1993, the 1994 Paris AIDS Summit excluded NGOs from participating and influencing the resulting Declaration— only high-level government officials and IGO representatives were invited. The advance notice, however, gave NGOs the opportunity to challenge WHO. Along with ICASO and the International Council of Women Living with HIV/AIDS (ICW), French NGO network Cellule des Personnes Atteintes par le VIH/SIDA lobbied WHO and the French government, as co-sponsor of the Summit. Through the Greater Involvement of People Living with HIV/AIDS (GIPA) Initiative, NGOs argued that the Summit would only be legitimate if they and people living with HIV were involved. They succeeded, and NGOs and people living with HIV were included in Summit planning, drafting of the Declaration, and as observers at the Summit (Delany, 1994; Zeiser, 1998). The participating countries committed to GIPA in all levels of the response to the HIV epidemic and to protecting the political and legal rights of people living with HIV (Behrman, 2004; Lisk, 2010). Specifically mentioning community-based organizations,[5] the Declaration "represent[ed] a significant public policy victory for PWA [today, people living with HIV] activists as well as NGO activists" (O'Malley, Nguyen, & Lee, 1996, p. 351).

UNAIDS' inclusion of NGOs on its Programme Coordinating Board (PCB) formalized their role in the global response to the HIV epidemic, though they participate as observers rather than voting members. The PCB is not without its critics, however, because there is discontent with the extent to which five regional NGO/ASO delegates can represent the interests of the diverse nongovernmental community. Some NGOs/ASOs end up unrepresented and left out. Formal inclusion of NGOs in UNAIDS also did not end nongovernmental challenges to the IGO and member governments, however. A clear example is the universal treatment access movement from the late 1990s into the 2000s.

NGO Challenge: Universal Treatment Access

In the mid-1990s, the availability of effective antiretroviral therapies altered the trajectory of the global HIV epidemic. These HIV medications changed testing HIV positive from a death sentence to a chronic but nonetheless manageable condition. Like the virus itself, the development of these drugs had implications far beyond physical health to global health. Formally announced at the 1996 International AIDS conference in Vancouver, participants celebrated effective antiretroviral therapy as a scientific success and people living with HIV were stunned at the opportunity to live

---

[5]Community-based organization (CBO) is yet another term for nongovernmental organizations, usually specifically those only active at the local level. The lack of clarity between NGO, ASO, and CBO, however, eventually made it difficult for nongovernmental actors to benefit from GIPA.

longer. People living with HIV, NGOs, and scientists from low-income countries, however, quickly realized that antiretroviral therapy would not be available to all. The medications cost US$10,000–$15,000 per year and would be far out of reach for those in the developing world—for roughly 90% of those with HIV (Behrman, 2004; Parker, 2006; Whiteside, 2008). This inequality of access would prompt a nongovernmental challenge as strong as the original efforts demanding recognition of the HIV epidemic as a global issue.

Antiretroviral therapies rely on a combination of medications that stop the human immunodeficiency virus from replicating, or making copies of itself within the body. This lowers the viral load, meaning there is less of the virus in a person's bloodstream. The lower the viral load, the less damage to a person's immune system and the less likely a person will advance to AIDS. A low viral load also makes it less likely that a person will spread the virus to another through contact of bodily fluids. Antiretroviral therapy does not cure HIV; it only reduces HIV's presence in the body. The virus can reemerge if antiretroviral therapy ends. Today's antiretroviral therapy has fewer side effects and is less likely to lead to drug resistance (Roxby, 2017; Whiteside, 2008).

Availability of antiretroviral therapy initially led to a drop in NGO activism in developed countries; activists had achieved much of what they were fighting for and could generally afford the medications. However, activism in developing countries mushroomed; many NGOs/ASOs previously focused on primarily service provision joined political advocacy and protest in favor of access to antiretroviral therapy. The fight was one of justice and equality: How could it be right to let millions die because they could not afford the medications that would extend their lives? NGOs in the United States and other developed countries joined in, and U.S. domestic NGOs began global activism for the first time, through the U.S. Health GAP (Global Access Project) Coalition (Behrman, 2004; Parker, 2011). Activist organizations from both developed and developing countries formed a transnational movement in favor of access for all, called universal treatment access, that faced and posed a big challenge in the response to the HIV epidemic.

In the late 1990s, several years after antiretroviral therapy became available, donor governments, WHO, UNAIDS, the World Bank, and other IGOs were against provision of antiretroviral therapy to developing countries. They considered relatively inexpensive prevention campaigns (emphasizing abstinence, being faithful, and condoms) more effective at reducing new infections and certainly more cost-effective. Given the expense of antiretroviral therapy and the fact that it enabled people living with HIV to live longer, the potential cost of universal access was huge and never-ending (Jones, 2004; Parker, 2011). Donor governments and IGOs added objections related to the medical aspects of treatment as well. They argued developing countries did not have enough doctors or testing facilities to administer the medications. They questioned poverty-stricken patients' abilities to adhere to strict protocols, such as the times of day when one should take the pills (Jones, 2004; Whiteside, 2008). Donor governments and IGOs also asked how developing countries would distribute limited supplies of antiretroviral therapy and avoid corruption. In Africa, especially, activist NGOs viewed these arguments as neo-colonialist—as if the advanced societies were setting policy for the backward societies, based on questionable assumptions about capacity and behavior. Life-saving treatment was "regarded as an uncertain bet and a luxurious alternative" (Jones, 2004, p. 397).

South Africa's Treatment Action Campaign (TAC), founded in 1998, sought to lobby its own government for provision of antiretroviral therapy, but found itself quickly drawn into the whirlwind of global effort (Parker, 2011; Robbins, 2006). The universal access movement utilized several different tactics at once: NGOs/ASOs advocated for a change in donor government and IGO positions, negotiated for lower antiretroviral therapy prices, encouraged production of generic drugs, fought discrimination, and used the media to raise awareness of their efforts among the general public (Robbins, 2006). While the movement succeeded in negotiating lower drug prices for developing countries, pharmaceutical companies fought back over production of generics based on drug patents and international intellectual property rights (Hunter, 2010; Parker, 2011; Robbins, 2006). A coalition of pharmaceutical companies sued the South African government for legislation encouraging the use of generic drugs, and TAC was at the forefront of a media campaign criticizing drug companies for putting profits before the lives of people living with HIV. The global attention and criticism embarrassed the drug companies into dropping the lawsuit. TAC then had to refocus its efforts on the South African government, which initially refused to offer antiretroviral therapy to all when it did become possible (Hunter, 2010; Parker, 2011). Eventually, WHO, UNAIDS, and NGOs/ASOs helped governments negotiate with pharmaceutical companies for licenses to produce generic antiretroviral therapy.

The universal access movement's various tactics paid off over time. First, drug companies agreed to drop the price of antiretroviral therapy for developing countries, first to roughly US$1,000 per person per year, which was an improvement but still beyond the means of most people living with HIV in developing countries. (Prices continued to drop over time; see below.) The movement won its years-long legal battle with the pharmaceutical companies, and production of generic drugs expanded. The activists galvanized public support. As donor governments and IGOs saw these successes, their positions began to change as well. In 2003, WHO announced its "3×5" initiative, setting a goal of providing antiretroviral therapy to 3 million people by 2005. While they knew there was more to do—WHO succeeded in tripling the number receiving antiretroviral therapy, but even that meant missing the goal and providing medications to just 1.3 million by 2005 (Whiteside, 2008)—NGOs/ASOs believed "the ideological battle had been won" (Parker, 2011, p. 33).

The practical and logistical battles continue, to implement access to antiretroviral therapy for all. However, there has been great progress: In 2017, roughly 22 million people living with HIV worldwide received antiretroviral therapy, representing 59% of all people living with HIV (UNAIDS, 2018b). The comparison between 2005 and 2017 is impressive. Other developments continue as well, helping more to access antiretroviral therapy: In 2017, ViiV Healthcare, holder of the patent for one effective antiretroviral therapy medication, negotiated with IGOs, NGOs, and national governments to allow generic production of the drug at a cost of $75 per year for 92 low- and middle-income countries (UNAIDS, 2017b).

Parker (2011) argues that while it still exists, the intensity of HIV and AIDS activism has declined following the successes of the universal access movement. NGOs/ASOs have shifted to assisting more than challenging, as they help implement and monitor treatment efforts. Nongovernmental actors advocate for improvements and change when monitoring shows ineffectiveness, but now are engaging in more technical assistance related to antiretroviral therapy access. However, the 30-plus-year history of the HIV epidemic suggests NGO activism can reemerge when necessary.

A Public-Private Partnership: The Global Fund

From the inception of GPA through today, global actors have known that funding is vital to respond to the HIV epidemic as a global issue. The priority for universal treatment access to antiretroviral therapy, even as prices drop, makes funding even more important. GPA initially had several hundred thousand dollars; today, The Global Fund to Fight AIDS, Tuberculosis, and Malaria (The Global Fund) makes billions available. The Global Fund demonstrates how governmental and nongovernmental actors can work together to reduce transmission of HIV and improve life for people living with HIV.

The Global Fund, championed by then-UN Secretary General Kofi Annan and American economist Jeffrey Sachs, was established in 2002. The Global Fund exists to provide financing for global health and is designed to be "independent, apolitical, results-and-performance based, and sensitive to national and local particularities" (Behrman, 2004, p. 261). Over the years of the global HIV epidemic, concerns had grown on the part of donor countries about effective and accountable use of the funds they were devoting to the global response to the HIV epidemic. On the part of recipient countries, concerns existed about the top-down nature of many guidelines for spending that allowed outside actors to determine priorities and programs for the funds—individual countries, regions, and towns were often unable to choose how best to spend HIV and AIDS funding for themselves. Concerns had also grown throughout the global health community about the gap between what was being invested in HIV and AIDS and what was needed to effectively respond, particularly in hard-hit Africa (Behrman, 2004; Lisk, 2010).

The Global Fund addresses these concerns for the HIV epidemic (and two other infectious diseases devastating developing countries) in innovative ways. Unlike WHO and the World Bank, the Global Fund exists outside the UN structure. This makes it independent and, hopefully, less subject to bureaucratic delays and organizational squabbles. The Global Fund has a mix of members in a public-private partnership, which means the Global Fund includes both nongovernmental (private) members and governmental (public) members; it combines numerous stakeholders including national governments, IGOs (including UNAIDS), NGOs and ASOs, privately owned businesses, charitable foundations (such as the Bill and Melinda Gates Foundation), communities affected by HIV, and people living with HIV ("Global Fund Overview," 2018).

To enable developing countries and affected communities to determine their own priorities and programs, proposals asking the Global Fund for funding are accepted only from the national or local levels. Proposals are then reviewed by an independent panel, to select proposals that reliably meet needs and to prevent politics from interfering in the decisions (Behrman, 2004; "Global Fund Overview," 2018); Lisk, 2010. For example, ideological and religious beliefs have caused American policymakers to limit bilateral funding for HIV prevention to programs that emphasize abstinence and exclude condom distribution, whereas many other countries do not accept these objections to condoms. The Global Fund's grant-making process is designed to eliminate such political bias from the multilateral funding process (Behrman, 2004). The panel and the proposal process are also designed to select workable proposals that limit opportunities for corruption and misuse of funds. In fact, the Global Fund can and has suspended grant financing to countries, such as Uganda in 2005, when it can prove funds are being misused due to fraud and corruption (Lisk, 2010).

In partnership with UNAIDS, the Global Fund also seeks to draw attention to the global response to the HIV epidemic, particularly to get developed countries, charitable foundations, and others to donate the money needed to effectively combat the HIV epidemic throughout the world and most especially in the hardest-hit regions such as Africa and, increasingly, South Asia. The wealthy countries of the world subsidize the responses of less-wealthy countries. The Global Fund depends entirely on donations, and most come from donor countries such as Canada, France, Germany, Italy, Japan, the United States, and the United Kingdom. Other donors include charitable organizations, businesses, and individuals (The Global Fund, 2017).

As of 2018, the Global Fund reports that 95% of funds come from countries and 5% from private donors. The Fund raises and grants roughly US$4 billion per year (for AIDS, TB, and malaria), and through December 2017 had disbursed a total of US$36.8 billion to health programs in 140 countries. Through June 2018, the private sector had contributed $2.3 billion. For the budget period 2017–2019, donors have pledged US$12.9 billion (The Global Fund, 2018a). The United States is by far the largest contributor to The Global Fund, primarily through the President's Emergency Plan for AIDS Relief (PEPFAR), which pledged US$4.3 billion for 2019–2019 ("United States Support," 2017). The Bill and Melinda Gates Foundation, the charitable organization of the founder of Microsoft, pledged $200 million to the Fund in 2018 (The Global Fund, 2018b).

Conclusion

Though not without its critics, particularly concerning delays in disbursing grants and funds wasted through corruption, The Global Fund provides upwards of one fifth of all international financing in the response to the HIV epidemic and its grants supported programs that provided medication and antiretroviral therapy to eleven million people living with HIV in 2017 alone (The Global Fund, 2017).

While IGOs and NGOs are only two types of global actors involved in the HIV epidemic, together they illustrate activities that make up the global response. IGOs like WHO and UNAIDS develop and implement guidelines, procedures, and policies that help manage the day-to-day work of the response. NGOs both challenge and assist IGOs, to influence the response. More recent developments like universal treatment access and the Global Fund portray cooperative efforts between the two actors. Together, IGOs, NGOs, and other global actors work to end the HIV epidemic—productively if not always seamlessly.

BOX 4.3
TAKE A STEP!
Gather and Identify Authors' Disciplinary Perspectives

Going back to your own research question and project, continue gathering information and insights, making sure to identify the authors' disciplinary perspectives as you go. This is to ensure balance and point of view, as explained in Chapter 3. You will likely find interdisciplinary and other/nondisciplinary sources, as well. All are useful!

5 Global Studies Research Process
GLOBAL HIV EPIDEMIC

Giving an account of the involvement of international governmental organizations (IGOs) and nongovernmental organizations (NGOs) in the global response to the HIV epidemic in the integrated essay in Chapter 4—a completed jigsaw puzzle picture—involves preparing, gathering, comparing, and combining knowledge about the history of infectious diseases, politics and policies, economies and resources, culture, and geographical locations. We can, therefore, use the HIV epidemic as an opportunity to learn the Global Studies research process. Metaphorically, in this chapter, we remove and examine individual puzzle pieces and how we put them together into the whole—to acquire and use the knowledge and skills necessary to study globalization, global actors, their interactions, and global issues.

Global Studies Research Process

Prepare

Research question

In Chapter 3, to explain how to design research questions, I went through the process of designing one for the HIV epidemic: "How are IGOs and NGOs involved in the global response to the multisectoral HIV epidemic?" The answer to that question becomes the main point of the sample integrated essay in Chapter 4:

> International governmental organizations (IGOs) like WHO and, later, UNAIDS coordinate the day-to-day work of developing and implementing the global response to HIV through emphasizing and monitoring national HIV/AIDS plans, among other activities; these lead organizations also engage directly with nongovernmental actors (NGOs) who both challenge and assist WHO and UNAIDS as the NGOs seek to influence the global response, such as the policy of universal treatment access. Funding for the global response to HIV has evolved into a public-private partnership, the Global Fund.

Relevant Disciplines

All five of the Global Studies disciplines are relevant to this research question and are reflected in the integrated essay in Chapter 4. As for other relevant disciplines, we are guided by the research question. Medical disciplines are, of course, relevant to HIV and AIDS. They are, however, not necessarily relevant to a research question that focuses on IGO and NGO response to the pandemic. Sources written by physicians and medical professionals can be useful to answering this research question, but in this case we can utilize them as other resources rather than accessing the medical disciplines' information and insights as a whole. This is practical as well as pedagogical: It would be difficult for most Global Studies undergraduates (and their faculty) to learn the minimum necessary to understand medicine as a discipline if it were a relevant discipline to our study. As noted previously, we can rely on explanations of the virus and its progression, efforts at vaccines, and other medicine-related subjects written for general audiences (by physicians or others). If we could not—if medicine were a discipline vital to our study and research question—team research or reliance on experts would be our best choices.

While all five disciplines are relevant to the HIV epidemic case study, for the purposes of demonstrating the Global Studies research process I focus on primarily two here: history and political science. The same steps demonstrated for these disciplines apply to all five, and I bring in other disciplines especially to demonstrate the *combine* step.

Gather

Gathering history information and insights

We can gather historical information and insights to answer the research question above. The discipline of history provides us with knowledge about politics, economics, culture, and geographical locations and, most important, how the past influences the global response to the HIV epidemic.

If we have an adequate understanding of the discipline of history and know the key academic journals, we can first search within them for HIV or AIDS (also HIV/AIDS) in general or for more specific topics like GPA or UNAIDS, as best suit the research question. University libraries have online databases allowing searches within subjects, and those subjects are usually disciplines. A computerized search of an online university library catalog for keywords such as history AIDS, history WHO, or history UNAIDS turns up hundreds of books, academic journal articles, and even documentary films. With this more general list of sources, especially, the information in Chapter 3, Global Studies Research Process, on gathering sources guides us, because we have to determine which sources are from the discipline of history, which are interdisciplinary, and which are other/nondisciplinary sources.

As noted in Chapter 2, Contributing Disciplines, historians rely on both primary and secondary sources. A library catalog search will turn up mostly secondary sources, which are sufficient for answering my research question: secondary sources provide us with historical insights—analysis or scholarly opinions—as well as information. A general internet search for the same keywords may turn up additional secondary sources as well as primary sources. International organizations such as the World Health Organization (WHO) and United Nations Joint Programme on HIV/AIDS (UNAIDS) post their documents and resources online; many of these would be primary sources, particularly those reporting statistics and activities as they happen, without analysis. Archived news articles and government documents regarding HIV and AIDS, available online, are also primary sources.

Many of the secondary sources that our library search produces may include information regarding the past, but are not necessarily written by historians or from the perspective of the discipline of history. There are two reasons for this. First, many books and articles on the HIV epidemic (indeed, any topic) include background and historical information to bring the reader up to speed. Second, there are still relatively few extensive historical surveys of the HIV epidemic by historians, globally or for hard-hit regions such as Africa. There has been a debate within the discipline because the HIV epidemic is "too new." Some historians argue that not enough time has passed, not enough primary sources exist, and points of view on the global epidemic are still shifting too rapidly to effectively describe and explain it. They are concerned that "history will go wrong on AIDS, and policies based on that history will in the worst case cost human lives" (Kuhanen, 2008, p. 304). This debate hasn't stopped historians from writing histories of the HIV epidemic but has limited the number of them, though more appear as time goes by.

Other available information about the past comes from other disciplines, interdisciplinary sources, or other/nondisciplinary sources. They may be written by scholars from other disciplines, activists, practitioners, journalists, doctors, or others responding to or reporting on the HIV epidemic. Such histories by non-historians may provide valuable and useful information about the past, but not scholarly insights from the perspective of the discipline of history. We can use non-historians' information about the past to answer the research question and write an integrated research paper, but would categorize them as disciplinary sources from other disciplines, not history, or as interdisciplinary or other sources as appropriate. Such information about the past from non-historians could be supplementary and complementary to what we find within the discipline of history. However, we do want to find information and insights from the discipline of history—to learn the process of integrating knowledge from disciplines and to ensure we include history's perspective. Only a few of the many sources we could gather about the history of the HIV epidemic are discussed here, as examples.

Disciplinary sources

Three examples of books from the discipline of history are Jonathan Engel's (2006) *The Epidemic: A History of AIDS*, Victoria A. Harden's (2012) *AIDS at 30: A History*, and John Iliffe's (2006) *The African AIDS Epidemic: A History*. Although the titles may be our first indication, we know we cannot determine disciplinary perspective based on title alone. The hard copy of Engel's book in my university's library does not have a biography in it. A quick internet search, however, turns up Engel's homepage at his university: He has a PhD in history and he is a professor of history—specifically history of medicine—and we can also see that his publications are histories, as well. Both the book jacket and "About the Author" page in Harden's book tell us that she is a trained historian and worked as an historian for the National Institute of Health, maintaining the history of that organization. Her online biography tells us she has a PhD in American History. On the back of Iliffe's book, his biographical blurb tells us he is a Professor of Modern History at University of Cambridge; his other publications are in the field of history. Therefore, we know that information and insights gathered from these three books provide us with history's disciplinary perspective because we know these three authors were trained in the discipline's subjects of study, key concepts, research methods, and theories.

Jan Kuhanen, identified in the journal as a history professor from Finland, published a scholarly article "The Historiography of HIV and AIDS in Uganda" in *History in Africa* in 2008. Kuhanen (2008) is critiquing the historiography (or existing histories) of the HIV epidemic in Uganda—by historians and non-historians alike. Because Kuhanen is a history professor, we know he provides information and insights from the discipline of history's perspective. We can thus categorize this journal article as a *history* source while we seek to balance our sources from each of the five disciplines.

In his article, Kuhanen notes that historians' reluctance—due to the lack of time that has elapsed since its start and the fact it is ongoing—or inability to produce histories of the epidemic in Uganda means that many histories have instead been produced by other social scientists, doctors, journalists, government officials, and activists. These histories "have approached the epidemic from different directions, with different agendas" (Kuhanen, 2008, p. 305) rather than from the perspective of history. Kuhanen considers the historical concepts of objectivity and bias (see Chapter 2) with regard to these other histories of the HIV epidemic in Uganda. For example, international organizations like WHO and UNAIDS as well as news sources around the world hold Uganda up as an example of a country that has successfully managed its HIV epidemic. Uganda succeeded in achieving sexual behavioral change through education campaigns, having a government that promotes open discussion of HIV and sex, meeting the guidelines and expectations of international organizations, and serving as a testing ground for antiretroviral treatments and other interventions. Following his review of a number of histories by non-historians, Kuhanen (2008) concludes:

> Although there is no reason to downplay Uganda's achievements, it seems that some interpretations are partially based on rather selective and occasionally uncritical readings of the evidence. Careless interpretations of numbers may have led to premature and unjustified conclusions, which may be been turned into axioms to be repeated from one publication to another without any critical assessment. (pp. 306–307)

Kuhanen is making a distinction between histories written from the perspective of history as a discipline and those that were written from other or nondisciplinary perspectives.

It is helpful to note that articles like Kuhanen's, which review existing publications, are useful not only for the information and insights they provide but also for the bibliographies. One of Kuhanen's stated goals is to survey books and articles on the HIV epidemic in Uganda; his list of references provides us with helpful resources that we may want to look up, if they fit the research question: "How are IGOs and NGOs involved in the global response to the multisectoral HIV epidemic?" Additionally, sources included in his list of references can help indicate key authors in this field of expertise.

Interdisciplinary sources

Elizabeth Fee and Daniel Fox's (1988) edited volume *AIDS: The Burden of History* is an example of an interdisciplinary source. Or, more accurately, it is a multidisciplinary collection of essays representing several disciplines' perspectives. Fee is a specialist in health policy. Fox is a professor of humanities, which we can determine includes history based on his past publications—which are histories—listed in the "Notes on Contributors" included in this book. The Notes tell us that contributors include political scientists, historians, art historians, and health scientists. If we use information from "Introduction: AIDS, Public Policy, and Historical Inquiry," coauthored by Fee and Fox, we would consider it an interdisciplinary source and eventually balance its information and insights with sources written solely by historians. Historian Guenter Risse's chapter "Epidemics and History: Ecological Perspectives and Social Responses" would be such a disciplinary source. Because the "Notes on Contributors" tells us that Risse is a historian, that chapter's information and insights come from the perspective of history even if not all chapters in Fee and Fox's book come from that same perspective.

Other/Nondisciplinary sources

For a topic like the HIV epidemic, there can also be extremely useful other or nondisciplinary sources that contribute to our understanding of the past and HIV. As noted in Chapter 3, these can include government documents or reports, publications and web resources from international organizations, autobiographies and biographies, and journalistic or popular accounts of the HIV epidemic. We are likely to find them while searching for HIV history or AIDS history, even if we cannot include them as disciplinary sources from History.

A Joint United Nations Program on HIV/AIDS (UNAIDS) report also titled *AIDS at 30* serves as an example. This report has no author indicated; it was produced by a team of UNAIDS staff. *AIDS at 30: Nations at the Crossroads* provides a brief history of the global response to the HIV epidemic, beginning with the U.S. Centers for Disease Control's first report through to 2011. The UNAIDS' report also includes analysis of the actions taken, globally, for the past 30 years. Throughout the report are a variety of global and national statistics, on HIV infection rates and AIDS deaths for example, that UNAIDS is responsible for gathering and reporting—making it one of the best sources for this information.

UNAIDS' *AIDS at 30: Nations at the Crossroads* provides valuable information and insights about the past, just not from an academic historical perspective. In this report, the insights come from the perspective of practitioners—people working for UNAIDS as that organization responds to the HIV epidemic. Such staff members draw their own insights about how the world has responded to HIV and AIDS, based on their everyday experiences at work rather than academic research based on training in subjects of study, key concepts, research methods, and theoretical approaches. While valuable, their perspective is different from that of an academically trained historian. For example, the UNAIDS report *AIDS at 30* includes four lessons that it (and, initially, WHO) learned between 1981 and 2000, which they call "the early years" of the pandemic: (1) the critical importance of leadership, (2) the transformative power of communities and people living with HIV, (3) the importance of scientific knowledge, and (4) the social dimensions of HIV (UNAIDS, 2011, pp. 15–19). The information and insights from UNAIDS included in their report *AIDS at 30* help us learn about the past and it is a valuable source for answering the research question. We would classify it as an other/nondisciplinary source and learn about the past from it along with academic information and insights from the discipline of history and interdisciplinary sources.

These few examples show that we can gather puzzle pieces—information and insights—from the discipline of history as well as interdisciplinary and other/nondisciplinary sources that also provide historical information. While all these puzzle pieces are about the past, many are also about other of our criteria for comparison: politics, economics, culture, and geographical locations. Harden (2012) and Iliffe (2006), for example, write about the political responses to the HIV epidemic within the United States and/or about how international organizations responded, which fall into the criterion of politics, but from the historical perspective.

Gathering Political Science Information and Insights

Just as we did with history, we can gather political science information and insights about our global HIV epidemic case study. We would follow the same library search steps, starting with political science or international relations journals and working through to more general searches if necessary. A general computerized university library search produces tens of thousands of books, academic journal articles, and other published sources. As we did for the discipline of history, we must determine which are from the disciplinary perspective of political science and which are interdisciplinary or other/nondisciplinary sources. Given the importance of government responses, government funding, and public health policies to the global response to the HIV epidemic, there is no dearth of political science sources. Again, only a few of the many political science sources we could gather are discussed here, as examples.

Disciplinary sources

Greg Behrman's book *The Invisible People: How the U.S. Has Slept Through the Global AIDS Pandemic, the Greatest Humanitarian Catastrophe of Our Time* (2004) provides a history of the epidemic from a political perspective as well as a political analysis of U.S. actions and policies regarding HIV and AIDS. Behrman's online biography tells us that he has a master's degree in international relations (a specialized political science degree). He has worked at the Aspen Institute, which is a think tank or research- and education-oriented organization focused on policy issues. His background and training place him within the discipline of political science.

Another book is *International Cooperation in Response to AIDS*, published in 1995 and written by Leon Gordenker, Roger A. Coate, Christer Jönsson, and Peter Söderholm. The book's back jacket tells us that all four are political scientists; the first three are professors and the fourth (at the time) a graduate student in the field. This biographical information assures that any puzzle pieces—information and insights—we gather from this book will be from the perspective of the discipline of political science.

One example of an academic journal article on HIV/AIDS is Marco Antonio Vieira's "Southern Africa's Response(s) to International HIV/AIDS Norms: The Politics of Assimilation" found in a 2011 issue of *Review of International Studies*. The bio included tells us that Vieira is a professor of international relations at a university in the United Kingdom. His article examines the response to the HIV epidemic in three southern African countries: Botswana, Mozambique, and South Africa. Vieira focuses particularly on the political culture of each country and how it has affected their responses to the policies and guidelines suggested or required by international actors such as UNAIDS. He also focuses on how the international policies and guidelines reflect the idea of HIV as a security issue. In the long run, however, this article ended up being an extra or unnecessary piece of the puzzle that I set aside—interesting but not useful in answering a research question specifically about the role of IGOs and NGOs in response to the HIV epidemic.

Interdisciplinary sources

AIDS and Governance, edited by Nana K. Poku, Alan Whiteside, and Bjorg Sand-kjaer (2007), is an interdisciplinary and multidisciplinary source on the global and national political responses to the HIV epidemic. This book appears in a general search for AIDS and politics but it is not written entirely from the perspective of political science even if all chapters in this book focus on government, political inter-actions, and policies. The book includes a List of Contributors with brief biographies. Authors of the chapters in this book range from political scientists to economists to sociologists. Some, like contributor Tony Barnett who specializes in Development Studies, have interdisciplinary backgrounds. Because the source is both interdisciplin-ary and multidisciplinary, we have to use it carefully. When we include a chapter by a political scientist in the answer to the research question, it would be a disciplinary source because it comes from the perspective of politics. When we use a chapter by an economist, it would be a disciplinary source but from the discipline of economics, because it comes from another discipline's perspective rather than the political science perspective. When we use a chapter by an interdisciplinary specialist, such as Barnett, we would consider it an interdisciplinary source.

Other/Nondisciplinary sources

Other/nondisciplinary sources regarding HIV and/or AIDS and politics are abundant. International relations includes international organizations as subjects of study and so documents and information from the UN, WHO, and UNAIDS are valuable other/nondisciplinary sources. The UNAIDS Global AIDS Update (2018c) titled *Miles to Go* is a good example; it provides an overview of the state of the epidemic that year as well as more specific information about the global response, including transmission patterns, treatment, gender issues, and resources. Newspaper and newsmagazine articles are also other sources that often report on the HIV epidemic and politics. A flurry of news articles usually surrounds World AIDS Day (December 1), releases of UNAIDS reports, or major political developments such as President Obama's October 2009 decision to lift the ban prohibiting HIV+ individuals from traveling to the United States, including as tourists.

As we did with history, we have now also gathered political science information and insights that serve as metaphorical puzzle pieces to complete our picture of how the world responds to the HIV epidemic. We would then move on to do so for the remaining Global Studies disciplines: anthropology, economics, and geography.

Part of gathering our information and insights is also considering how they add up to a *disciplinary* answer to the research question—so that we can later build an *interdisciplinary* answer that is more comprehensive and accounts for complexity. For the purposes of providing examples of this and later steps, we will narrow from the larger research question to a more specific point or subtopic within our integrated essay in answer to it: the creation of the United Nations Joint Programme on HIV/AIDS (UNAIDS). For this specific topic—and the sub-question "Why create UNAIDS?"—I present brief examples of disciplinary answers from history and political science using the sources gathered above.

Disciplinary Answers: Why Create UNAIDS?

History

Historian John Iliffe (2006), in *The African AIDS Epidemic: A History*, emphasizes two reasons for the creation of UNAIDS. First, he discusses the importance of a multisectoral response because to effectively address the HIV epidemic requires economic, social, and political development in conjunction with more specific health efforts. He notes that, on its creation, UNAIDS required that "each country must shift its HIV/AIDS programme from its Health Ministry to the Office of the President or Prime Minister" to emphasize that the epidemic is more than a health issue—to effectively address it requires economic, social, and political development in conjunction with more specific health efforts (p. 139). As noted in Chapter 4, the WHO Global Programme on AIDS (GPA), under its first director Jonathan Mann, initially advocated a broad, multisectoral response. Later, under other WHO and GPA directors, the response narrowed and focused almost exclusively on physical health, with less attention paid to economic, social, and political factors. UNAIDS' creation was, in part, a result of global actors' desire to again broaden the United Nations (UN) response to include all facets of the global epidemic.

Iliffe (2006) also introduces a second reason prompting the creation of UNAIDS: the fact that other international governmental organizations such as the World Bank were competing with WHO for funding and by instituting their own GPA-like AIDS programs. UNAIDS was, therefore, created to "coordinate, define, and publicise policies" recommended at the global-level of response as well as within countries (pp. 138–139). Harden (2012) includes the same reasons for creation that Iliffe does but adds to them information about the frustrations of countries donating money to UN agencies to fund HIV and AIDS efforts globally and, especially, in developing countries. Donor countries found that the competition and lack of coordination between UN agencies and other international organizations prevented effective action and wasted money.

Iliffe (2006) and Harden (2012) rely on the historical concept of exploring cause and effect in their discussion of the creation of UNAIDS—they are trying to explain how we got to where we are today by exploring why today's leading global-level actor in the international response to the HIV epidemic was created. Reviewing Iliffe's and Harden's footnotes reveals they utilize typical historical sources, including primary documents, secondary sources, and interviews, as the evidence on which they base their analysis of why UNAIDS was created (the effect). Their analyses help us understand that it was created because (1) the need for an effective multisectoral response went unmet when WHO was in charge and faced competition from other UN agencies such as the World Bank and (2) because of donor country frustrations (the causes).

Iliffe's (2006) and Harden's (2012) analyses build on information about the past to develop insights explaining why UNAIDS was created. In doing so, they provide knowledge about the past, politics, and economics—our criteria for comparison—of the actors involved in the creation of UNAIDS. These puzzle pieces encompass context and details about the operations of WHO and GPA, why those operations were found lacking, and with what the global community chose to replace GPA. The historians contribute information and insights about politics, because WHO and UNAIDS, as IGOs, are political institutions, and it was dissatisfaction with one political institution that led to the creation of a second. We also learn about the role of economics because it was, in part, developed countries' concerns over effective use of their donations to the HIV epidemic that prompted the creation of UNAIDS.

Political science

Both Gordenker et al. (1995) and Behrman (2004) highlight the creation of UNAIDS from a political perspective, focusing on international organizations as

BOX 5.1

TAKE A STEP!

Gather and Compose Disciplinary Answers for HIV or Terrorism

Choose at least two sources you identified, in Box 4.2, from the References associated with Chapter 4 or 6, each from a different discipline. Gather them yourself from your library and read them, then draft disciplinary answers to one of the research questions, either HIV or terrorism (see Chapter 3 or 7). When finished, you'll be ready for the next step: compare.

actors. Gordenker et al.'s 1995 book *International Cooperation in Response to AIDS* explains the review processes, task force committees, proposals, and reasons leading to its creation. The authors discuss the lack of coordination and even competition between organizations, the lack of efficiency in their programs responding to HIV and AIDS, and the ways in which the UN's structure and funding process decreased their incentives to work together.

As Gordenker et al. (1995) explain, the first review of WHO's GPA was initiated in 1989 as part of a standard review process, although by that time both donor and recipient countries as well as UN entities had begun complaining. The 1992 review report was complimentary of many GPA efforts, but critical of coordination among UN entities. That review was followed by an *ad hoc* review by UN personnel later in 1992 and by a GPA Global Management Committee Task Force in 1993. Both of these reviews proposed the creation of a new UN entity to coordinate among all UN family HIV and AIDS policies and programs. Outside of the UN, other stakeholders including NGOs sought to influence proposals. Donor countries discussed the reviews and proposals prior to the 1993 annual WHO meeting, known as the World Health Assembly, and at that meeting Canada formally proposed the creation of a new UN entity. Gordenker et al. (1995) then describe months of bargaining and negotiation between WHO, UN Development Programme, World Bank, countries, NGOs, and others—although they cannot finish the story because of when their book was written. They point out that Secretary General Boutros Boutros-Ghali supported what would become UNAIDS because it "fitted with his notions of UN reform" (Gordenker et al., 1995, p. 80).

In *The Invisible People*, Greg Behrman (2004) also details the creation of this UN entity from a political perspective, situated specifically within his analysis of U.S. action (and inaction) on the HIV epidemic. He includes many of the same reasons for UNAIDS creation as Gordenker et al. do: lack of coordination among UN entities, complaints from donor countries about lack of efficiency, and complaints from recipient countries about restrictions and overlapping reporting requirements. Utilizing interviews with key players, Behrman expands particularly on the way in which the creation of UNAIDS fit within larger discussions of UN reform. Given that his book focuses on the United States, he notes that "in the mid-1990s, anti-UN sentiment, which had been long fomenting, was reaching a boiling point in the United States" (Behrman, 2004, p. 169). This, combined with economic downturn, made the United States reluctant to pay its required UN dues, much less additional funding for UN programs—even those for HIV. Other countries may have had different reasons, but many were in favor of reform: "Everyone seemed to want to try something new. The appetite for constructing a new prototypical global vehicle had piqued, and, as another insider remembered it, 'AIDS just happened to be there'" (Behrman, 2004, p. 169).

Gordenker et al.'s (1995) and Behrman's (2004) books emphasize the political science/international relations concept of international organization (discussed more below) to explain the creation of UNAIDS. In doing so, they utilize primarily qualitative political science methods, relying on primary sources, such as WHO and GPA reports, interviews, and secondary sources analyzing the same topics. Their analysis of the creation of UNAIDS informs us about the past, politics, and economic concerns of the actors involved. In carrying out a political analysis of the structure and functions of WHO, GPA, and, eventually, UNAIDS, they tell us about the past of these organizations and programs and how that led to the creation of UNAIDS. Given that all policies must be funded, their attention to policies created or required by WHO and GPA—at the global and national levels—also enlightens us about the role of economic resources (and the lack thereof) in prompting the creation of UNAIDS, given concerns about efficient use of aid donated by developed countries and the economic needs of developing countries. Behrman (2004) further analyzes the culture in the United States, as it relates to political attitudes toward the UN.

Thus, I have constructed disciplinary answers to the research question—which we will use to craft an integrated answer. Again, we would follow the same steps for all our relevant disciplines—providing answers from each individual discipline to the research question. Knowing the information and insights on the creation of UNAIDS available to us from the individual disciplines of history and political science, we can now compare the puzzle pieces from history to those of political science, to help us learn how we can ultimately combine the information and insights from the two disciplines.

Compare

The next step in the Global Studies research process is compare, through which we must find the similarities and differences among the information and insights from all disciplines as well as interdisciplinary or other sources. Our full set of points or criteria for comparison includes the past, politics, economics, culture, and geographic locations. While our sample disciplinary sources, above, provide us with knowledge about the past, politics, economics, and, to a lesser extent, culture, in the interests of illustrating this step I will compare only the criterion of politics here and continue with the example of the creation of UNAIDS.

The Criterion of Politics: History and Political Science

The creation of UNAIDS is both a historical and a political development. As noted above, historically we learn about the political causes that contributed to its creation. Politically, we gain perspective on international organizations as a political science/international relations concept and how the actions of these organizations led to the creation of UNAIDS. Thus, both disciplines contribute to our understanding of the creation of UNAIDS. Box 5.3 reminds us of material from the Chapter 4 integrated essay on the global HIV epidemic, specifically the section on the creation of UNAIDS.

We previously gathered two historical sources that discuss the creation of UNAIDS as a subject of study: Harden's (2012) *AIDS at 30: A History* and Iliffe's (2006) *The African AIDS Epidemic*. Both rely on the historical concept of cause and effect (see Chapter 2) to explain the creation of UNAIDS—to explain how we got to where we are today. They identify reasons for its creation, including a return to a multisectoral response, lack of coordination, lack of efficiency, and dissatisfaction among countries. In looking at two political science sources we have gathered on this same subject of study—*International Cooperation in Response to AIDS* by Gordenker et al. (1995) and *The Invisible People* by Behrman (2004)—we find that they are also presenting information and insights about how we got to where we are today, but they utilize different concepts. Cause and effect are part of it, but Gordenker et al. and Behrman focus more so on the political science/international relations concept of international organizations.

As noted in Chapters 1 and 2, when political scientists study international organizations, they focus on the aims, scope, purpose, structure, and functions of international organizations as well as the attitudes of other actors toward them. This gives the political scientists a different lens than the historians used to examine the creation of UNAIDS. The political science sources explain the same reasons as the historians, but add a new and different reason. The historical sources utilized here did not report

BOX 5.2
TAKE A STEP!
Compare Information and Insights on HIV or Terrorism

Using the disciplinary answers you produced in Box 5.1, review the criteria provided in Chapter 3 and then find the similarities and/or differences for at least one criterion between the information and insights you found in the resources you gathered on HIV or Terrorism. You will use these similarities and differences in the next step, combine.

on the larger climate of UN reform or the ways in which UNAIDS was structurally unique. Harden (2012) notes the ways in which its first director, Peter Piot, wanted the program to be different, but her lens does not *see* or describe the larger climate of UN reform. In this case, it is from our political science sources we gain knowledge of how UNAIDS fits within the UN or the issue of UN reform.

International relations scholars are trained to examine the structure, functions, and interactions of international organizations like the UN and UNAIDS. Gordenker et al. (1995) was written at the same time as the challenges that led to the creation of UNAIDS and thus explains the interagency disputes and, eventually, bargaining that led to UNAIDS as we know it today. Writing specifically about interorganizational coordination in the early 1990s, they mention UN reform. Writing about the larger U.S. response to HIV later in the epidemic, Behrman's (2004) political science lens includes the United States' anti-UN attitudes, desire for UN reform, and how that affected the UN, WHO, and other UN family organizations as they negotiated the creation of UNAIDS. Because they rely on different concepts, political science sources add an element to our knowledge of the creation of UNAIDS that the historical sources utilized here did not—our disciplines contribute different as well as similar information and insights. We have found a few duplicate jigsaw puzzle pieces to pile atop one another, and also at least one distinctly different puzzle piece that will contribute to the overall picture by filling a gap or adding to the edge.

Back to Balance and Point of View

Having undertaken this comparison, we can see that we find both similarities and differences between the information and insights of history and political science. We use these similarities and differences, in our next step, to combine the two disciplines' information and insights into our integrated essay. We can pause in our process, however, to consider the differences between disciplinary and interdisciplinary research noted in Chapter 3: *organization, balance, and point of view. Organization* has allowed us to keep track of our disciplinary sources; as a result, we know that Iliffe is a historian and Behrman a political scientist. We keep track of insights regarding the creation of UNAIDS (and the larger research question), and know that the insight regarding competition among IGOs comes from both history and political science while the insight about UN reform only appears in political science sources. Using this tracking of disciplinary sources, we want to *balance* what we gather from each discipline, so as to have roughly the same amount of information and number of insights from each discipline. In the comparison of disciplinary sources on the creation of UNAIDS, we compare two sources from history and two from political science. More important than quantity of sources, however, is the overall amount of information and number of insights; the coverage of the creation of UNAIDS is roughly equal in the two history sources and Behrman's political science source. Gordenker et al. has less, because it predates the creation, but it provides vital real-time information and insights about the challenges that UNAIDS was supposed to solve. Thus, overall, the four sources provide a roughly balanced treatment of the topic—and that rough balance is enough to *avoid* relying on one discipline to the exclusion of others, which is the goal of balance.

Balance contributes to *point of view*. Balancing our disciplinary sources enables us to keep an interdisciplinary point of view—to remember that the benefits of the Global Studies research process enable us to see what a disciplinary researcher might not. In the example of the creation of UNAIDS, the sources from history saw a number of reasons for its creation, but missed one reason offered by a political science source. By utilizing not only history's perspective but also that of political science, we learn more about the creation of UNAIDS.

The Criterion of Politics: Interdisciplinary and Other/Nondisciplinary Sources

To this comparison of history and political science disciplinary sources we can add an other/nondisciplinary source: the 2011 UNAIDS report titled *AIDS at 30: Nations at the Crossroads*. The process for integrating interdisciplinary and other/ nondisciplinary sources is the same as doing so for disciplinary sources, always bearing in mind that the goal of interdisciplinary research is to integrate *disciplinary* information and insights, so just as we must balance between disciplines, we must also balance between disciplinary and interdisciplinary or other/nondisciplinary sources. We don't want to claim as integrated an essay comprised entirely of interdisciplinary and other sources. We cannot always be sure which relevant disciplines are represented in already-interdisciplinary sources and could miss disciplinary perspectives. We must also remember point of view; just as we must avoid getting caught up in the perspective of a single discipline, we would want to avoid getting caught up in an other/ nondisciplinary perspective to the exclusion of disciplinary perspectives.

I had already gathered, but did not include in the disciplinary answers, this other/ nondisciplinary source that provides information about the past of UNAIDS. To include it in our integrated answer, as well, we need to compare its contributions to those of the disciplinary sources on the criterion of politics. Information from UNAIDS itself about the creation of UNAIDS is descriptive: The reason is that the HIV epidemic required a multisectoral response. Iliffe (2006) and Harden (2012) add insights—scholarly analyses—that agree with UNAIDS' *AIDS at 30* about the need for multisectoral response. The contribution of the UNAIDS report, then, could be seen as unnecessary: we have disciplinary sources that identify this cause. UNAIDS, however, is one of the best and most comprehensive sources for facts and figures regarding HIV and AIDS. Thus, the UNAIDS report is a valid and validating source— particularly on its own creation. We should also recognize its limitations, however, especially in relation to the political science sources. Given that the UNAIDS Programme Coordinating Board is made up of WHO and other UN agencies, that organization's own history of its creation may not emphasize information critical of these agencies. It describes the facts, but does not always analyze them, whereas Gordenker et al. (1995) and Behrman (2004) do. While other/nondisciplinary sources such as

UNAIDS' *AIDS at 30* can be valuable, so are academic analyses from history and political science, which are written from the disciplinary perspectives and from outside UNAIDS and are, therefore, likely more objective about the organization itself.

The other/nondisciplinary UNAIDS report *AIDS at 30*, then, provides a validating piece of the puzzle by reinforcing similar reasons for the creation of UNAIDS found in our disciplinary sources from history and political science. The similarities and differences found through our comparison allow us to ultimately combine—integrate—the information and insights from two or more disciplines.

Combine

We can now combine our historical and political science puzzle pieces into a more comprehensive final picture. Having compared the information and insights, we can determine which are supplementary and which are complementary—and thus how to combine them.

Similar and Supplemental

As Chapter 3 explains, information and insights that are similar are additional or supplementary. The puzzle metaphor is strained a bit by supplementary material—when doing a jigsaw puzzle, we do not need duplicate pieces. However, in academic research, finding similar information and insights from two different disciplines serves to validate that material. Our historical sources and our political science sources (and other/nondisciplinary sources) all found similar reasons for the creation of UNAIDS: a return to the idea of a multisectoral response, lack of coordination and competition among agencies within the UN, and dissatisfaction with GPA policies at the national level. As we write up our answer to the research question, we can combine these reinforcing information and insights. Chapter 4 offers one possible essay in answer to our question "How are IGOs and NGOs involved in the global response to the multisectoral HIV epidemic?" If you review Box 5.3 on the creation of UNAIDS, you'll see that the sentence combines material and quotations from and cite both historical and political science sources for the supplementary material.

Different and Complementary

Information and insights that differ are complementary, or complete each other. The above comparison shows that a political science source, utilizing different concepts, found a reason for UNAIDS that history sources did not: the larger climate of UN reform at the time of its creation. Going back to our puzzle metaphor—and remembering that the global puzzle is one in which we never know exactly what the picture will be or how many pieces we'll need—political science has given us a piece of the puzzle we'd miss if we used only history sources. With just history, we don't lack an understanding of the creation of UNAIDS; it is sufficient and we could call the puzzle complete from that perspective. Political science, however, adds another puzzle piece, focused on the organizations themselves. Our jigsaw puzzle picture is more complete; as an example, perhaps envision an additional piece at one edge rather than a filled gap in the main picture.

Complementary material is combined more directly than supplementary material. Look again at the sentence summing up our material on the creation of UNAIDS in Box 5.3. The first block of text presents the supplementary information in the sentence, found in the disciplines of history and political science, as well as other material. In this sentence, we would lose one reason—the second block of text on UN reform—if we did not have the complementary information from political science. The supplementary information, on the other hand, is only indirectly visible through the multiple citations.

Moving beyond history and politics to economics and anthropology, we can see how complementary integration allows us to both make and support an assertion or argument. Box 5.4 presents another piece of the puzzle, a sentence describing the eventual success of NGOs and AIDS Service Organizations (ASOs) in their efforts

BOX 5.3
COMBINING PUZZLE PIECES

From Page 84 of Chapter 4 A Complex Problem: HIV Epidemic

The GPA operated until the mid-1990s, when a combination of four factors led to a shift in the United Nations' response and the creation of UNAIDS: a return to the idea of a multisectoral response, lack of coordination and competition among agencies within the UN, dissatisfaction with GPA policies at the national level, and a broader climate for reform within the UN (Behrman, 2004; Gordenker et al., 1995; Harden, 2012; Iliffe, 2006; UNAIDS, 2011).

The GPA operated until the mid-1990s, when a combination of three factors led to a shift in the United Nations' response and the creation of UNAIDS: lack of coordination and competition among agencies within the UN, dissatisfaction with GPA policies at the national level, and . . .	**Supplementary Integration** History Harden, 2012; Iliffe, 2006 Political Science Behrman, 2004; Gordenker, et al., 1995 Other UNAIDS, 2011
. . . a broader climate for reform within the UN.	**Complementary Integration** Political Science Behrman, 2004

to convince other global actors that offering antiretroviral therapy as well as prevention techniques could effectively manage the global epidemic. Whiteside (2008), an economist, provides us with specific figures to support anthropologist Parker's (2011) assertion that the efforts had succeeded (see Box 5.4).

Integration does not have to happen solely at the sentence level. In Box 5.5, we extract an entire paragraph containing pieces of the puzzle from Chapter 4. In this case, both supplementary and complementary integration allows us to combine information and insights from the disciplines of political science and economics into a paragraph describing the creation and goals of the GPA. Box 5.5 demonstrates the integration of information in this paragraph.

Combining supplementary and complementary information and insights, therefore, gives a more detailed picture through validation of similar material and inclusion of different material from our sources. History is not *wrong* for overlooking UN reform as a reason behind the creation of UNAIDS with its unique structure and functions. The history lens, emphasizing cause and effect but not, in this case, organization or structure, simply didn't see what the political science lens did. As we move forward into the other case study, we see that the political science lens fails to see information and insights that other Global Studies disciplines do. We find that history sees information and insights that other disciplines lack. This is the advantage

BOX 5.4
COMBINING PUZZLE PIECES

From Page 93 of Chapter 4 A Complex Problem: HIV Epidemic

While they knew there was more to do—WHO succeeded in tripling the number receiving ART, but even that meant missing the goal and providing medications to just 1.3 million by 2005 (Whiteside, 2008)—NGOs/ASOs believed "the ideological battle had been won" (Parker, 2011, p. 33).

Complementary Integration
Anthropology
Parker, 2011, p. 33

While they knew there was more to do . . . NGOs/ASOs believed "the ideological battle had been won"

WHO succeeded in tripling the number receiving ART, but even that meant missing the goal and providing medications to just 1.3 million by 2005

Economics
Whiteside, 2008

BOX 5.5
COMBINING PUZZLE PIECES

From Page 83-84 of Chapter 4 A Complex Problem: HIV Epidemic

WHO started its Global Programme on AIDS (GPA, first called the Special Program on AIDS) in 1987; it became the global vehicle to coordinate the world's response to the new pandemic (Behrman, 2004, p. 40). GPA's goals were "exchange of information and provision of guidelines; public education; . . . assessment of diagnostic methodology; advice on safe blood and blood products; and coordination of research." WHO officials and others in the public health community recognized that the potential impact of the HIV epidemic went beyond the medical concerns to "wider non-health implications" including socioeconomic wellbeing and human rights (Lisk, 2010, pp. 16–17). Jonathan Mann, GPA's first director, focused on three broad areas: protecting the human rights of PLWHA, coordinating the response within the United Nations (UN), and coordinating the response at the national and international levels. GPA also sought to draw international attention to the HIV epidemic as a global issue; a first step was the London Declaration on AIDS Prevention issued in 1988 by an international meeting of health ministers, which emphasized the human rights of PLWHA, the need for global cooperation to address the social as well as medical consequences of the virus, and the need for cooperation between developed and developing countries in funding the global response to the virus (Behrman, 2004; Lisk, 2010).

WHO started its Global Programme on AIDS (GPA, first called the Special Program on AIDS) in 1987; it became the "global vehicle" to coordinate the world's response to the new pandemic (Behrman, 2004, p. 40).	**Complementary Integration** Political Science Behrman, 2004
GPA's goals were "exchange of information and provision of guidelines; public education; . . . assessment of diagnostic methodology; advice on safe blood and blood products; and coordination of research." WHO officials and others in the public health community recognized that the potential impact of HIV/AIDS went beyond the medical concerns to "wider non-health implications" including socioeconomic wellbeing and human rights (Lisk, 2010, pp. 16–17).	**Complementary Integration** Economics Lisk, 2010

(Continued)

(Continued)

	Supplementary Integration	
Jonathan Mann, GPA's first director, focused on three broad areas: protecting the human rights of PLWHA, coordinating the response within the United Nations (UN), and coordinating the response at the national and international levels. GPA also sought to draw international attention to HIV/AIDS as a global issue; a first step was the London Declaration on AIDS Prevention issued in 1988 by an international meeting of health ministers, which emphasized the human rights of PLWHA, the need for global cooperation to address the social as well as medical consequences of the virus, and the need for cooperation between developed and developing countries in funding the global response to the virus.	Economics	Political Science
	Lisk, 2010	Behrman, 2004

to Global Studies—the more lenses, the better we see how the world works. (Lest I mix metaphors: the more puzzle pieces, the more detailed the puzzle picture.)

The integrated essay on the global HIV epidemic in Chapter 4 includes multiple lenses, and thus helps us better see that part of our world. To demonstrate the process, we have focused here only on two disciplines and one criterion for comparison. As we undertake the Global Studies research process for the terrorism case study, we utilize more and different disciplines and criteria.

BOX 5.6
TAKE A STEP!
Gather and Compose Disciplinary Answers

For your own research project, you began gathering information and insights in Box 4.3. When you believe you have gathered sufficient research, both to answer your question and for balance, utilize your sources to draft disciplinary answers to your research question for all relevant disciplines. When finished, you'll be ready for the next step, compare.

6   A Complex Problem
TERRORISM

Below is a sample integrated essay that serves to introduce the second case study of a complex global issue: terrorism. As another completed puzzle picture, this essay resulted from gathering, comparing, and combining information and insights from the common Global Studies disciplines plus another relevant discipline, psychology. It particularly focuses on causes of terrorism, in answer to the research question prepared: "How do the following potential structural and individual causes of terrorism describe motivations in the two different contexts of the IRA and Al Qaeda: (1) historical acceptance of political violence, (2) foreign or colonial occupation, (3) hegemony and power, (4) economic conditions, and (5) social alienation?" Chapters 6 and 7 should be read together, because Chapter 7 explains in detail how undertaking the Global Studies research process allowed me to write this essay.

Causes of Terrorism: Structural and Individual

Terrorism dates back centuries and yet continues to this day. The history of terrorism includes the Assassins in the 11th to 13th centuries and the 16th-century Anabaptists, a radical religious group in Germany. The term *terrorism* itself came into usage during the violent aftermath of the French Revolution (Miller, 2013). Scholars often date modern terrorism to the anarchists and nihilists in late 1800s Russia, who targeted political leaders for assassination. In Europe and the United States, other groups adapted anarchist ideals and adopted their tactics; President William McKinley was assassinated by an American inspired by anarchism in 1901 (Jensen, 2013). Prior to World War I and during the interwar period, left-wing and fascist groups engaged in terrorism. After World War II, terrorism was also a tool of national liberationists seeking an end to colonialism. Moving into the Cold War period, particularly from the late 1960s, there were a variety of groups undertaking terrorism: the Palestinian campaign of airplane hijackings, Marxist groups like the Red Army Faction in Germany and Red Brigades in Italy, and the Irish Republican Army in Northern Ireland. Following the Cold War, scholars consider the 1990s to be the start of catastrophic or mass-casualty terrorism, including the Oklahoma City bombing of 1995 and, most especially, the use of sarin gas in the Tokyo subways in 1995 (Nacos, 2016). Al Qaeda was active for more than a decade prior to 2001, although the September 11 attacks cemented perceptions of both mass-casualty terrorism and transnational or global terrorism.

After any terrorist attack, one of the most-asked questions is "why?" That one word can encompass why an attack happened, why the target was selected, and why do terrorists even do what they do. None are easy to answer, but perhaps the most difficult is the last: What motivates terrorists or what causes terrorism? While terrorism experts argue there are "no simple answers" (Nacos, 2016, p. 151), counterterrorism efforts must be based, at least in part, on the causes of terrorism to prevent it. Decades of study have produced lists of likely motivations—most of which are context-dependent. Social scientists seek to generalize, and yet for terrorism have been unable to provide a "universal model that identifies the conditions that breed group-based political violence and terrorists" (Nacos, 2016, p. 139). Proposed causes can be frustrating as well as interesting, given that one scholar will find a motivation to be explanatory while another will find the opposite. One of the most controversial proposed causes of terrorism is poverty; academic studies both support and dismiss it as a motivation (Abadie, 2006; Bahgat & Medina, 2013; Caruso & Schneider, 2011; Freytag, Krüger, Meierrieks, & Schneider, 2011; Jackson, Jarvis, Gunning, & Breen-Smyth, 2011; Kis-Katos, Liebert, & Schulze, 2011; Murphy, 2003; Mustafa, 2005; Nacos, 2016)—because it can be role-, situation-, and context-dependent (see below). Over time studies have become more sophisticated, breaking down the identity *terrorist* to consider such differences as lone-actor versus group terrorists, domestic versus foreign fighter, group leaders versus followers, and the specific tasks members of a group are willing to undertake. This has refined our understanding of motivations for terrorism, though the causes remain complex and context-dependent. Contexts can vary in many ways, including domestic or transnational terrorism. Two examples of different contexts for terrorism include the domestic terrorism of the Irish Republican Army in Northern Ireland and the transnational terrorism of Al Qaeda and its affiliates. Structural causes of terrorism such as historical acceptance of political violence, colonial or foreign occupation, hegemony and power, economic conditions, and social alienation as a potential individual cause all apply in the different contexts of the domestic terrorism of the IRA in Northern Ireland and transnational terrorism of Al Qaeda and its affiliates.

Definitions and Types of Terrorism

Exploring the causes of terrorism requires an understanding of terrorism—also not a simple task. There are many definitions of terrorism, yet none globally agreed on (or, often, nationally). There are many scholarly debates over the definition (see Jackson et al., 2011, and Nacos, 2016, for overviews). The statement "one man's terrorist is another man's freedom fighter" is a truism, but still points out that definition is a matter of perspective. Terrorism has changed over time; from the late-1800s to mid-1900s, terrorists often targeted political leaders or figures of authority for assassination, whereas today civilians are targeted. There is also considerable debate over whether a definition should be solely focused on non–state actors or also on state actors. Rather than provide a simple definition, many scholars now offer "characteristics of terrorism" or what some call "a core definition" (Bjørgo, 2005b; Jackson et al., 2011; Nacos, 2016) in which terrorists

- use or threaten to use premeditated violence that is politically motivated, and that violence
  - is "extra-normal" or "beyond the moral conventions regulating violence" (Caruso & Schneider, 2011; Rapoport, 2003, p. 39),
  - is mainly against noncombatants, and
  - sends a message to a broader audience than the specific targets or victims.

Post–September 11, some government agencies and scholars also characterize terrorism as an end in itself, such as suicide bombings, rather than a means to an end. However, that also remains debated, because it may fit the Islamic State and some Al Qaeda affiliates but does not necessarily describe active domestic terrorist groups throughout the world.

Rapoport (2003) seemingly blends history, definitions, causes, types, and goals of terrorism into his "four waves" of terrorism: the anarchist wave (late 1800s to early 1900s), the anticolonial wave (1920s–1960s), the "new left" wave (1960s–1970s), and the religious wave (1970s–present). The anarchists sought to overthrow modern society and moral conventions of their time, the anticolonial terrorists pursued independence, and the "new left" also sought to overthrow their modern society, particularly the existing system of capitalism. The ongoing religious wave began with the Iranian revolution of 1979 and, unlike earlier religious motives for terrorism, provides "justifications and organizing principles" for a new, religious global system (Rapoport, 2003, pp. 37–43). Rapoport's approach suggests that the religious wave including Al Qaeda and affiliate terrorists will break just as the others have, yet government rhetoric and popular opinion suggests it will be more enduring. Eubank and Weinberg (2010) present data that the earlier waves were shorter, even, than Rapoport thought and propose several factors that "may very well accelerate the waning of Fourth Wave terrorism over the next decade" (p. 601). Rapoport (2003) and Eubank and Weinberg (2010), however, caution that terrorism itself will not come to an end.

In addition to Rapoport's four waves, various political typologies of terrorism exist. These typologies are, at least in part, based on causes as well as goals of terrorist groups. Schmid (2005a) lists insurgent, vigilante, state/regime, and state-sponsored terrorism. He then further breaks down insurgent terrorism into social-revolutionary, right-wing and fascist, religious (sometimes religious/cultural terrorism), nationalist and separatist (sometimes presented as national separatist or national liberationist), and single-issue terrorism, also called special-interest terrorism such as "eco-terrorism" (Schmid, 2005a, p. 224). Other typologies exist and may, for example, separate left-wing terrorism from social-revolutionary (Medina & Hepner, 2013; Nacos, 2016). Ideological terrorism may be used as an umbrella term to identify the political orientation of groups, including right-wing, left-wing, national separatist, and religious terrorism. This is to differentiate political terrorism from terrorism linked to organized crime, such as "narco-terrorism." Other types may be based on methods used by terrorists, such as suicide terrorism and cyber-terrorism; the domestic or global/transnational level of activity; and whether the terrorist actors are nation-states/governments or non-state actors (Jackson et al., 2011, pp. 154–157). Some scholars employ the terms *territorial* versus *non-territorial*, although the uses can differ between identifying terrorists who seek to gain territory, such as national separatists, or those who control territory as "safe havens" (Bahgat & Medina, 2013). Other typologies include homegrown terrorists versus foreign fighters, lone actors versus group terrorists, and—when studying the individual level of analysis—types based on role within terrorist organizations: "bomb-maker," "bomb-planter," financier, or gunman (Gill & Corner, 2017, p. 235). The categorizations of new versus old, traditional versus transnational, and limited versus apocalyptic terrorism all seek to encompass perceived differences—and similarities—before and after the advent of mass-casualty terrorism, particularly September 11, 2001 (Bahgat & Medina, 2013; Crenshaw, 2000; Jackson et al., 2011).

Types or categories of terrorism are, like definitions and causes, controversial because they are political designations. To categorize by type is "simultaneously useful and profoundly problematic." Types classify together those that are similar from those that are different—yet there are no pure types. Categories overlap: There can be religious influences on a national separatist terrorist group, just as there can be transnational activity carried out by primarily domestic terrorists. When terrorist groups are categorized by type, there is often an emphasis on the similarities within groups and an associated lack of attention to differences. If differences are missed or ignored, this can impact not only scholarly understandings of terrorism but also public policies to counter terrorism. Types can lead to assumptions of causality: Ideological terrorism is caused by the ideology, so it is the ideology that is dangerous and must be prevented—when in fact most ideologies encompass far more peaceful adherents than terrorists. Such assumptions are not helpful in countering terrorism. Critical theorists will also introduce the question of knowledge and power as it relates to types of terrorism: "typologies can be seen as problem-solving tools, used to classify problems and suggest solutions aimed at protecting the status quo. . . . By categorizing a particular problem as a form of 'terrorism', states can then deal with it using extraordinary measures" (Jackson et al., 2011, pp. 158, 163).

Today, the category of religious terrorism is particularly controversial. In Northern Ireland, the conflict is commonly described as "Catholics versus Protestants," yet the situation is a frequently cited example of national separatist terrorism because, in fact, the conflict there is not about religion (Jackson et al., 2013; Nacos, 2016; Post, 2005; Reinares, 2005; Soderberg, 2005). Al Qaeda, on the other hand, is usually classified as religious terrorism (Freeman, 2008; Nacos, 2016; Post, 2005; Rollins, 2011; Soderberg, 2005)—despite clearly stated political goals (Jackson et al., 2011; Miller, 2013; Mohamedou, 2013) and increasing evidence that Al Qaeda and successor Islamic terrorists (particularly the foot soldiers) are not generally religious prior to their process of joining and may know little about their religion as members (Atran, 2016; Bouzar, 2016; Mink, 2015). As Jackson et al. (2011) caution, "categorizing a group as 'religious terrorists', for example, encourages the researcher to focus primarily on the group's religious aspects and hence to neglect its secular or political dynamics" (p. 159). Because of this, Mohamedou (2013) argues that many scholars and policy makers failed to note what he considers one of two truly new features of Al Qaeda: its "martiality." Many noted its transnational nature, but not "the militaristic empowerment of a non-state actor" or that "the material manifestation of this transnational terrorism was more so an approximation of a military conception of operational delivery underscored by an up-tempo battle plan proactively designed and explicitly communicated" (pp. 237, 242). American policy makers, he argues, failed to hear much of what Al Qaeda said because they focused on the religious rather than political and tactical messages sent.

Differing Contexts: The IRA and Al Qaeda

Despite the drawbacks, types of terrorism remain useful analytical tools when used carefully with attention to context. Classifying terrorist groups into types or categories helps examine patterns in their goals and tactics—understandings of which can help prevent or counter terrorism. However, specific histories, geographic locations, political and economic conditions, and cultural experiences and values together create the contexts within which terrorist groups operate. Context along with type helps highlight similarities and differences among terrorist groups, including the motivations that lead them to terrorism. For that reason, two different contexts—different sets of historical, geographic, political, economic, and cultural conditions—serve as examples in this discussion of causes of terrorism: the domestic terrorism of the Irish Republican Army (IRA) in Northern Ireland and the transnational terrorism of Al Qaeda and its affiliates.

The Irish Republican Army in Northern Ireland

Known from the British perspective as The Troubles, the recent conflict in Northern Ireland lasted from the late 1960s through the late 1990s and claimed approximately 3,600 lives. Northern Ireland is one region within the United Kingdom (UK), officially known as the United Kingdom of Great Britain and Northern Ireland. The roots of the modern conflict go back centuries to British conquest and colonization of the island of Ireland. The term *plantation period* describes the migration of English and Scottish into Ireland, particularly Northern Ireland, in the 1600s. These British immigrants were culturally, linguistically, and religiously different from the native Irish, who experienced oppression and discrimination over the centuries. Efforts toward home rule or even outright independence from the United Kingdom coalesced in the late 1800s and early 1900s, leading into the War of Independence, 1919–1921. As the British and Irish negotiated for Irish independence and an end to the war, the British descendants of the planters in Northern Ireland objected (often violently) to being left behind by the UK in an independent Ireland. The unionists—who sought to remain part of the UK—made up the majority of the population in the northeast, so the peace agreement between Britain and the Irish rebels included Partition, a division of the island between the 26 counties of the south, now Ireland, and six counties that became Northern Ireland and remained part of the UK. Partition was intended to be temporary, but lasts until today (McKittrick & McVea, 2002; Mulholland, 2002; Wichert, 1999).

The IRA fought the 1919–1921 War of Independence, then split over the peace agreement—particularly Partition—and devolved into a brief civil war in the Irish Free State and sectarian violence in the North. The pro-peace treaty forces won in the south, and an independent Ireland was established. Over time, violence in the North quieted, though occasional outbreaks occurred. In the late 1960s, however, that violence would increase and be sustained for roughly 30 years. At this time, the IRA split again; formally, the dominant IRA group in Northern Ireland during the Troubles became the Provisional Irish Republican Army (PIRA, as opposed to the Official IRA, which ended its campaign in 1972), so the literature also references the PIRA; however, over time the group in the North came simply to be called the IRA. The IRA considered itself in a declared war against the British; the British (and the United States as their allies) considered the IRA terrorists (McKittrick & McVea, 2002; Mulholland, 2002; Wichert, 1999).

A historical, nationalist desire on the part of the Irish in the North to separate Northern Ireland from the UK and reunify with Ireland is a major cause of the conflict, but is not the only one. Religion is *not* one of the causes; the conflict is not over theological beliefs or the right to practice one's religion. Although the two groups in conflict are called the Catholics and the Protestants, religion serves mainly as an identifier between the two communities that historically belonged to different religions. The Catholics are more accurately the nationalists and republicans, who seek reunification with Ireland, and the Protestants are more accurately the unionists and loyalists, who seek to remain in union with Britain. For the nationalists and republicans, given their goal of reunification, British colonialism is a perceived cause of conflict (McKittrick & McVea, 2002; Mitchell, 1979; Mulholland, 2002; Wichert, 1999).

The 1960s–1990s conflict grew out of an initially peaceful civil rights movement fighting political, social, and economic discrimination by the unionists against the nationalists—and thus discrimination is another reason for conflict, as are economic and social injustices. The majority unionists maintained political control of regional and local governments, through discrimination as well as gerrymandering, so access to political representation is also a cause. Together, these various causes also, from the perspective of IRA, justified their use of violence in their war against the British (McKittrick & McVea, 2002; Mitchell, 1979; Mulholland, 2002; Wichert, 1999). IRA methods included assassinations, bombings, kidnappings, shootings/sniping, smuggling, and robberies (Gupta, 2005). British military, police, civilians, and business properties were all targets of the IRA. Because of the violence, the UK government suspended the regional government, known as Stormont, and instituted direct rule from London (McKittrick & McVea, 2002; Mitchell, 1979; Mulholland, 2002; Wichert, 1999).

After several unsuccessful attempts at peace agreements, the 1990s peace process culminated in the 1998 Good Friday or Belfast Agreement, which created a power-sharing regional government, ensured human rights, and offered the possibility of a referendum on reunification. The government of Ireland also amended its constitution, to remove articles laying claim to Northern Ireland. Thus, there were compromises from both the nationalist and unionist sides. Within several years of the Agreement, which was brokered by the United States, the IRA disarmed and officially declared an end to its war against the UK. Occasional, isolated attacks are carried out by dissidents who oppose the Agreement but, for the most part, the conflict in Northern Ireland has ended (McKittrick & McVea, 2002; Mulholland, 2002; Soderberg, 2005).

The IRA violence against the British is primarily classified as domestic terrorism, although there were attacks against British military in mainland Europe. Northern Irish terrorism developed and was carried out within a democratic, industrialized country generally characterized as a strong state. The goals were political and territorial—to remove British political control from Northern Ireland, reunify with Ireland, and end discrimination against the nationalists as a result. IRA terrorism is considered to be traditional terrorism, where that type refers to primarily domestic and (relatively) limited attacks—as opposed to the transnational goals and activities of Al Qaeda, for example, which include mass-casualty attacks.

Transnational Al Qaeda and its affiliates

Al Qaeda generally dates to 1989 and was initially comprised of foreign fighters who joined Afghanistan's side of the Soviet-Afghan War, in which the Soviet Union invaded Afghanistan in 1979 to support a troubled communist regime that had overthrown the previous government a year earlier. It quickly became a proxy war in the Cold War with the United States providing funding and arms to the mujahedin, or rebels, fighting against the communist government of Afghanistan and the Soviets. This meant they were fighting against a secular and even anti-religious government, so the mujahedin also received support from Islamic countries.

The war attracted foreign fighters from Islamic countries, seeking to defend Islam as well as gain fighting experience. Though foreign fighters were from a variety of countries, they became known as the Arab Afghans (Mohamedou, 2013, p. 233). Debate continues as to how much these foreign fighters contributed to the Soviet withdrawal from Afghanistan in 1989, but some would go on to have catastrophic impact as global terrorists.

When the Soviets withdrew from Afghanistan, this left Al Qaeda as an armed organization made up of experienced fighters whose goal remained to fight on behalf of threatened Muslims. In Arabic, Al Qaeda means base or foundation (Medina & Hepner, 2013; Nacos, 2016; Rollins, 2011). Leaders Abdullah al Azzam and Osama bin Laden disagreed about its future; al Azzam reportedly sought to create an "Islamic 'rapid reaction force,' available to intervene wherever Muslims were . . . threatened" while bin Laden wanted to send the "activists to their home countries to try to topple secular pro-Western Arab leaders." Al Azzam died in late 1989, and bin Laden became the undisputed leader of the organization. Bin Laden eventually came to believe that corrupt governments in Islamic countries such as Saudi Arabia were protected by U.S. backing and that American backing would have to be removed before Islamic countries could become Islamic theocracies (Rollins, 2011, p. 6).

Al Qaeda's goals focused on Western, particularly American, encroachment into and dominance of Islamic countries, especially in the Middle East. Osama bin Laden was born in Saudi Arabia and was highly critical of his own government's cooperation with the United States. When the Saudis allowed the United States to station troops in the country during the Gulf War (1990–1991) and then to remain there afterward, bin Laden saw this as American occupation of Islamic holy lands containing the sacred cities of Mecca and Medina; that the United States supported Israel's control of Jerusalem and oppression of the Palestinians compounded his frustration. Other motivations for Al Qaeda include the perceived threat to Islamic identity posed by the global dominance of Western culture, values, and beliefs; American support for corrupt, repressive governments in the Middle East; and the economic disparities that accompany unmet expectations of modernization (Freeman, 2008; Medina & Hepner, 2013; Miller, 2013; Mohamedou, 2013; Nacos, 2016; Rubenstein, 2011). To these goals Al Qaeda added the potential of a future global Islamic order, though this particular motivation was poorly defined and would come only after the West had been driven out of the Middle East and the current, illegitimate governments had been replaced.

Later, post–September 11, 2001, U.S. interventions in Afghanistan, Iraq, Libya, and Syria would further add to the grievances of Al Qaeda and its affiliates.

Al Qaeda methods included car bombings, suicide bombings, other bombings, hijacking, shootings, rocket attacks, and hand grenade attacks (Gupta, 2005). These methods were not unusual; the transnational or global projection of them, however, was. Most terrorist attacks are against the *near enemy*, such as one's own government or people with the intent of changing that single government or its policies (Medina & Hepner, 2013). Al Qaeda sought to achieve its goals by targeting the *far enemy* and "attack[ing] the enemies of Islam on their own territories" (Mohamedou, 2013, p. 233). According to Mohamedou (2013), Al Qaeda

> was in effect deciding not to "waste" its terrorism on the governments of the Islamic world but rather to reserve it to target the mightier powers, the US primarily, which were regarded as both the masters of these regional governments and the ultimate, more consequential foes of Islam. (pp. 233–234)

Al Qaeda thus justified their attacks on the United States and other Western territories. They further justified their attacks on civilians—including mass-casualty attacks—because Western voters were as guilty as their governments through "alleged electoral support to aggressive policies" (Mohamedou, 2013, p. 238). Al Qaeda did not always claim responsibility for its terrorist attacks. In addition to the September 11 attacks on New York and Washington, it has taken or been assigned credit for the 1995 bombing of a U.S. military base in Saudi Arabia, the 1996 bombing of the Khobar Towers housing facility for U.S. air crews in Saudi Arabia, the 1998 attacks on U.S. embassies in Kenya and Tanzania, and the 2000 attack on the USS *Cole* while it was docked in Aden, Yemen (Mohamedou, 2013; Rollins, 2011).

Following the September 11 attacks, the United States and its allies responded with military force against Afghanistan, for offering a safe haven to Osama bin Laden and Al Qaeda. It would be 10 years before bin Laden himself was killed by U.S. forces. During that decade and since, Al Qaeda did indeed become the foundation of a global terrorist network. Other terrorist groups affiliated themselves with Al Qaeda, and there were eventually recognized branches or franchises: Al Qaeda in the Arabian Peninsula, Al Qaeda in Mesopotamia, Al Qaeda in Egypt, Al Qaeda in Afghanistan and Pakistan, Al Qaeda in the Islamic Maghreb, and Al Qaeda in Europe. Other militant Islamic groups such as Al Shabaab in Somalia, Boko Haram in Nigeria, and Abu Sayyaf in the Philippines allied themselves with Al Qaeda (Medina & Hepner, 2013; Mohamedou, 2013; Nacos, 2016; Rollins, 2011). The term *Islamist* terrorism or ideology is used to encompass Al Qaeda and its affiliates or successors who adhere to an extremist or military view of Islam. Core or corporate Al Qaeda has all but ceased to exist, the organizations within the network it built—the franchises—are now highly decentralized, and many have refocused on local rather than global change and back on the near enemy. As Mohamedou (2013)

BOX 6.2
TAKE A STEP!
Compare

For your own research project, now that you have drafted disciplinary answers to your research question (see Box 5.6), you can begin to compare. Utilize the criteria described in Chapter 3—or other criteria relevant to your topic—and, following the examples in this chapter, explore the similarities and differences between the disciplinary information and insights you gathered. You will use these for the next step, combine.

concludes, the philosophy of *Al Qaedism* has replaced the organization and now guides the network:

> Ultimately, the necessary elasticity al Qaeda adopted—partly voluntarily, partly as a way to adapt to the international post-9/11 counter-terrorism campaign—created an ever-growing distance with already independent units, which in time embraced opportunistically that autonomy, being now loosely inspired by al Qaeda, now acting on their own (even when, for the sake of publicity, they claimed al Qaeda links). (pp. 240, 242)

Al Qaeda as an organization under Osama bin Laden and today as a loose network of autonomous organizations is the epitome of transnational terrorism. Its goals of global change—the better-defined goal of ending U.S. dominance or the longest-term goal of an Islamic regional or global order—and its choice of mass-casualty targets demonstrate that it operates on a much larger scale than the domestically oriented and relatively limited activity of the IRA in Northern Ireland. Al Qaeda and the IRA serve as very different examples of contexts within which individual and groups can be motivated to terrorism.

Causes of Terrorism

Today's terrorism literature still relies and builds on Martha Crenshaw's (1981) influential "The Causes of Terrorism" and its categorization of causes into preconditions and precipitants. Preconditions are background, often structural, factors that "set the stage for terrorism over the long run." Permissive preconditions create "an environment in which terrorism is possible" and direct preconditions "positively encourage resistance to the state" by "provid[ing] terrorists with compelling reasons for seeking political change." Precipitants create opportunities through "specific events that immediately precede the occurrence of terrorism" (pp. 381–383). Preconditions "are of a relatively general and structural nature, producing a wide range of social outcomes of which terrorism is only one" while precipitants can "motivate or trigger the outbreak of terrorism," such as emergence of a charismatic leader, major political change, or loss of a war (Bjørgo, 2005a, 2005b).

A variety of potential causes can fit within these categories. Bjørgo (2005a) presents 14 causes on a loose continuum from precondition to precipitants, some of which overlap with Crenshaw (1981), yet he cautions the list is incomplete. His causes range from lack of democracy and rule of law to extremist ideologies to illegitimate governments to discrimination and social injustice. Additional causes can include aspects of individual psychology such as feelings of social alienation (Abrahms, 2008; Crenshaw, 2000; Gill & Corner, 2017; Horgan, 2016, 2017; Lloyd & Kleinot, 2017).

It is because, in part, there are so many potential causes that terrorism—and preventing it—is a complex global issue. The identification of so many potential causes is also a reason many scholars find the research of causes to be controversial. Cause is tied to the definition of terrorism and, as noted above, there is little agreement on that. Particularly, causes could differ between state and non-state terrorism, so definitions that exclude state terrorism are seen as biased (Mustafa, 2005). Different terms have also developed, such as *motivations* or *origins*, because *cause* can be deterministic—as if humans are bound to become terrorists rather than making decisions based upon multiple factors (Freeman, 2008; Jackson et al., 2011). Differing points of view also matter: as Sinai (2005) points out, the root causes identified by "insurgents, the threatened governments, and independent academic experts . . . are likely to differ and, in some cases, even clash" (p. 217). Counterterrorism efforts have little chance of succeeding if the causes identified by governments or experts do not match the causes seen by terrorists themselves. Critical theorists question "the way causal explanations can be used to depoliticize terrorists and legitimate specific counter-terrorism politics" (Jackson et al., 2011). As even the criticisms of research into the causes of terrorism make clear, however, understanding causes is vital to counterterrorism.

The five causes explored here are primarily preconditions to terrorism, per Crenshaw (1981). Historical acceptance of violence and economic conditions are structural causes. Bjørgo (2005b) introduces "motivational causes" as "the actual grievances that people experience at a personal level, motivating them to act." When ideologies, leaders, or circumstances "translate causes from a structural level to a motivational level," people may undertake terrorism. Thus, foreign occupation and hegemony may reflect and/or create global structures, but they can also be recent circumstances or changes that people feel at a motivational level (pp. 3–4). Psychological factors are individual preconditions, though they may by impacted by situations prompted by structural or motivational causes. As Atran (2016) points out, "When perceived global injustice resonates with frustrated personal aspirations, moral outrage gives universal meaning and provides the push to radicalization and violent action" (p. S199).

Historical acceptance of political violence

One proposed structural cause of terrorism is a historical precedent and acceptance of political violence (Crenshaw, 1981; Bjørgo, 2005a; Jackson et al., 2011; Lloyd & Kleinot, 2017; Miller, 2013; Reinares, 2005; Schmid, 2005b). As a permissive precondition for terrorism, historical acceptance of political violence does not predetermine terrorism but "make(s) those means appear morally and politically justifiable" (Reinares, 2005, p. 124). In effect, historical events and circumstances give permission and incentive for forms of political violence, including terrorism. This is particularly true for nationalist, separatist, and ethnic groups engaged in terrorism, where "landscapes of government injustice, repression, and neglect are believed to fuel popular support, sympathy, motivation, and increased likelihood of terrorist attacks" (Bahgat & Medina, 2013, p. 51).

The IRA in Northern Ireland is commonly used as an example of the historical acceptance of political violence (Crenshaw, 1981; Mitchell, 1979; Post, 2005; Reinares, 2005). The IRA originated with Ireland's War of Independence (1919–1921) against the British that led to the creation of the Irish Free State (later the Republic of Ireland) and the partition that left Northern Ireland in the UK. Violence by the Irish against the British went back centuries before that and John Hume, a proponent for nonviolent change in Northern Ireland and later Nobel Peace Prize winner, recognized that "for generations our people have been reared on a notion of patriotism as fighting and dying for Ireland" (Toolis, 1995, p. 331). Perhaps equally important to the historical fact and myth that makes up the story of Irish rebellion against the British is its success: That the Irish drove the British out of the south and gained independence was a powerful motivator for later violence in the north.

Al Qaeda was also born out of political violence during the Soviet-Afghan War (1979–1989) and also, from their perspective, out of successful violence given the Soviet withdrawal from Afghanistan. It was not, however, the generations of national-separatist violence seen in Ireland—at least not for the foreign fighters who would become Al Qaeda leaders and members. Sources vary as to the organization's founding date, but from the mid-1980s it was set up to recruit and provide logistical assistance to Muslim fighters joining the Afghan mujahedin and by the late 1980s Al Qaeda was an armed organization prepared to undertake violence in defense of Islam.

Though its actual organizational heritage may not go back centuries, Al Qaeda and its affiliates perceive a long battle between the West and Islam. The term *jihad* means struggle or striving, though that can be "*greater jihad*, as personal spiritual and moral struggle, and the *lesser jihad*, as a violent struggle for the good of Islam" (Nacos, 2016, p. 121; emphasis in original). It is jihad as the violent struggle—including terrorism—that most Westerners are familiar with today. The term *mujahedin* means a fighter engaged in jihad, particularly in battles against non-Muslims; today it is most associated with the Soviet-Afghan War, but in fact this meaning of the term has been in use since the mid-1800s, particularly in reference to Afghans fighting British colonization. Lloyd and Kleinot (2017) summarize literature on the role of shame and humiliation in motivating terrorism, and argue that in Islamic communities "the loss of cultural and Islamic pride due to centuries of colonialism and exploitation by both the West and their own leadership has been a powerful source of shame, particularly for young men" (p. 370). Islam, thus, has "historical traumas and triumphs that become the source of collective pride and shame" (Lloyd & Kleinot, 2017, p. 370) and, as in Ireland, these histories can contribute to the justification of terrorism.

Colonial or foreign occupation

A second potential structural cause of terrorism is colonial or foreign occupation of the insurgent groups' lands (Bjørgo, 2005a). This cause is associated with national separatist terrorism as a type of terrorism (Bjørgo, 2005a; Jackson et al., 2011; Nacos, 2016; Rapoport, 2003). With the end of World War II and the beginning of decolonization, national self-determination became a legitimate goal—those groups who felt they were being denied it entirely or were impatient with the pace sometimes resorted to illegitimate means. Northern Ireland is a classic example. From the Irish nationalist (Catholic) perspective, Northern Ireland is a remnant of British colonization of Ireland; they see Northern Ireland "as an unsatisfactory and even illegitimate state." The unionists (Protestants), on the other hand, see themselves as British and as "descendants of settlers who emigrated from England and Scotland ... to plant a loyal British garrison community to establish control" (McKittrick & McVea, 2002, p. 2). The nationalist and unionist communities lived essentially separate lives for centuries and this had an enduring impact on the politics, socio-economics, and psychology of Northern Ireland. "While Catholics nursed the grievances of a subjugated people, Protestants developed the siege mentality of colonists in a hostile land" (Mitchell, 1979, p. 182).

Bjørgo (2005a) points out that "despite their use of terrorist methods, some liberation movements enjoy considerable support and legitimacy among their own constituencies, and sometimes also from segments of international public opinion" (p. 259). Though the IRA was unable to gain much support even within Northern Ireland for brief campaigns against the British between the 1920s and 1960s, as The Troubles moved into the 1970s British army support for the unionists and counterterrorism policies such as internment, or imprisonment without trial, led to an increase in IRA membership and sympathy for their efforts among the wider nationalist community (McKittrick & McVea, 2002; Mitchell, 1979). There was also sympathy and support for the IRA abroad, particularly in the United States (McKittrick & McVea, 2002; Medina & Hepner, 2013). This included the Irish Northern Aid Committee in the United States, known as NORAID, which raised funds for IRA prisoners and their families and allegedly for the IRA and its operations.

Northern Ireland remains part of the United Kingdom, but the Good Friday Agreement gave the Irish in Northern Ireland the comfort of a voice for the Republic of Ireland in relevant discussions through joint British-Irish decision-making processes. The Agreement allows for self-determination: One provision of the treaty is the opportunity to hold a referendum on reunification of Ireland. (No referendum vote has been scheduled yet.) These compromises were enough for the IRA to end its campaign of violence even if the region remains part of the United Kingdom.

Al Qaeda also saw itself as fighting foreign occupation. As noted above, Osama bin Laden saw U.S. support for Israel and U.S. military bases in Saudi Arabia and elsewhere in the Middle East as well as interventions in Afghanistan and Iraq as a threat to Islam and particularly its holy cities in the region (Freeman, 2008; Medina & Hepner, 2013; Miller, 2013; Mohamedou, 2013; Nacos, 2016). While not a case of national self-determination in the same sense as Northern Ireland, Al Qaeda used foreign occupation to justify attacking the United States as the far enemy. Its 1990s attacks on U.S. military targets in Saudi Arabia and Yemen, noted above, were a manifestation of their opposition to what Al Qaeda perceived as foreign occupation.

Hegemony and power

To both the IRA and Al Qaeda, colonial or foreign occupation is related to another potential structural cause of terrorism proposed by Bjørgo (2005a): "*Hegemony and inequality of power*. When local or international powers possess an overwhelming power compared to oppositional groups . . . 'asymmetrical warfare' can represent a tempting option" (p. 259; emphasis in original). For the IRA in Northern Ireland, this was the overwhelming local power of the British government, against which they marshalled their limited resources to use terrorism to gain attention and fight the government.

For Al Qaeda and its affiliates, this is the hegemony, or global dominance, of the United States since the end of the Cold War. Politically, this dominance manifests as what Al Qaeda and its affiliates perceive as foreign occupation as well as other aspects of globalization. Differing points of view are important. The United States may see itself as a compassionate and well-meaning world leader, but others—including Al Qaeda—may see it as arrogant and self-interested as it seeks to promote democracy, capitalism, its products, and its culture worldwide and as it supports repressive regimes to do so (Flint, 2003a, 2003b; Nacos, 2016). The "hegemonic power of the United States can be a cause of considerable resentment on the part of those who are excluded or perceive to be threatened by globalization" (Mustafa, 2005, p. 84).

Al Qaeda objects to U.S. troops and bases in Saudi Arabia in part "because of the threat this occupation poses to the ability of Muslims to act devoutly" (Freeman, 2008, p. 47). From this point of view, U.S. dominance and globalization lead to cultural threats and economic grievances as well as political ones. Islam is a cultural identity as well as a faith (Flint, 2003a, 2003b; Freeman, 2008; Mustafa, 2005; Nacos, 2016). Cultural homogenization or imperialism threatens that identity and thus can create a precondition for terrorism. Freeman (2008) provides examples of Al Qaeda operatives, such as Mohammed Atta, who were radicalized in part due to perceived attacks on the dignity of Islam. Atta, a leader of the September 11 attacks, felt a planned "'Islamic Disneyland' for tourists" in Egypt was degrading to his religion and culture. Freeman (2008) concludes that Al Qaeda and its affiliates' "ultimate goal is to defend the Islamic identity and the ability of Muslims to practice Islam within the Islamic world from the encroaching forces of unbelief" (p. 48). Al Qaeda and its affiliates see globalization—and the resulting threats to Islam—as guided by the United States, so it "becomes the prime target of this new terrorism and its public seen as the one that should be made to suffer in order to become aware of the terrorists' grievances" (Flint, 2003a, p. 55). Many Islamic societies were horrified by the September 11 attacks; however, as with the IRA example, there were those sympathetic to Al Qaeda's goals, particularly its hostility toward U.S. interference in the Middle East and other Islamic countries (Murphy, 2003, p. 51). The decrease in this sympathy, particularly due to Al Qaeda affiliates' re-orientation toward local attacks in Muslim countries, may have hastened the decline of the original Al Qaeda organization if not the remaining network (Rollins, 2011).

Economic conditions

American hegemony and globalization also contribute to the perception that economic deprivation can lead to terrorism. As noted above, there is considerable and ongoing debate over the connection between and causality of poverty and terrorism. There is a link between poverty and other forms of political violence, including civil war, so that assumption was carried over to terrorism (Malečková, 2005). Some scholars find that poverty breeds terrorism, while others conclude that it does not (Abadie, 2006; Bahgat & Medina, 2013; Bjørgo 2005a; Caruso & Schneider, 2011; Freytag et al., 2011; Jackson et al., 2011; Kis-Katos et al., 2011; Murphy, 2003; Mustafa, 2005, p. 84; Nacos, 2016). Ultimately, the connection between economic conditions and terrorism is complex and dependent on factors such as context and individual roles held within the organization.

Recent studies of the link between poverty and terrorism have focused on international terrorism and found weak or no associations between variables such as GDP per capita and terrorism (Abadie, 2006; Kis-Katos et al., 2011; Malečková, 2005; Nacos, 2016). Level of education combined with poverty also fails to establish a link to terrorism. On the whole, international terrorists such as Al Qaeda members are middle to upper income and educated; arguably,

> international terrorist organizations may prefer highly education individuals with established careers and special skills to poor, unsophisticated and uneducated people . . . the more educated, experienced, and qualified individuals better fit into a foreign and strange environment, and thus have a better chance of success. (Malečková, 2005, p. 40)

The Al Qaeda operatives involved in September 11 are an example—none were impoverished and many were educated professionals (Mustafa, 2005). This may have changed over time and in the face of counterterrorism efforts to track and freeze financing for terrorism. Based on interviews with imprisoned terrorists and data on detainees collected by the Saudi Ministry of the Interior, Atran (2008) suggests that Al Qaeda franchises have less funding than core Al Qaeda itself and that members of the franchises are "younger, less educated and less financially well off" than earlier members of the network such as the Arab Afghans. There has been, however, some evidence of a link between unemployment and motivations for individuals to become recruits for Al Qaeda or related organizations; this may be more about individual psychology, the absence of hope for a brighter future, and marginalization (Malečková, 2005; Schmid, 2005; see below).

Scholars have found a link between income inequality and international terrorism (Bahgat & Medina, 2013; Flint, 2003b). It may not be economic deprivation in and of itself, but disparities and what Caruso and Schneider (2011) call "immiserizing modernization" that promotes terrorism (p. S38). Referencing Al Qaeda and its affiliates, specifically, Freeman (2008) similarly concludes it is the "raised and failed expectations" when "modernizing influences have either partly by-passed the Middle East or failed to achieve all of their hoped-for results" that create grievances motivating terrorism or creating support for it (p. 50).

Few studies examine the economic conditions of domestic terrorism and even fewer directly compare the contexts of international and domestic terrorism (Kis-Katos et al., 2011), so it is difficult to draw comparisons and conclusions between the two. One difference is that studies of domestic terrorism, unlike international, do not usually find connections between unemployment and terrorist violence (Mitchell, 1979; Nacos, 2016). However, the situation in Northern Ireland does evidence connections between socio-economic class and terrorism. Differences can exist not only between domestic and international terrorist organizations but also within types of domestic terrorism; Laqueur (2002) found that "the nationalist-separatist terrorist groups almost always consist of young people of lower social background than the socialist-revolutionary groups; the IRA is an obvious example" (p. 124). High numbers of IRA members, especially foot soldiers, were of the working class (Jackson et al., 2011). Policies such as internment further disadvantaged working-class Catholics, increasing their likelihood of joining the IRA (McKittrick & McVea, 2002; Post, 2005). Anecdotal accounts suggest that, because of internment, working-class community support for the IRA and its methods increased as well and, through quantitative analysis of 110 countries, Freytag et al. (2011) found that poor socio-economic conditions can lead to increased support for—as opposed to participation in—terrorism among communities.

Social alienation

Economic conditions along with the other structural causes considered here are preconditions that help set the stage for terrorism. Grievances created by structural-level causes of terrorism can interact with the individual level—with "aspects of the individual personality and emotional experience" (Lloyd & Kleinot, 2017, p. 369)—potentially contributing to the likelihood an individual will become a terrorist. The potential link between mental health and terrorism has both varied over time and reflected the competing claims common to other causes of terrorism such as poverty. Gill and Corner (2017) present four paradigms or somewhat-overlapping phases of how researchers viewed that link. First, in the 1970s, terrorists were declared psychopaths; second, into the 1980s, terrorism resulted from personality disorders. In both periods, based on little or solely anecdotal evidence, terrorists were deemed abnormal. Also in the 1980s, however, some researchers assumed that terrorists were rational actors, assessing and selecting options that would allow them to achieve their goals. Taking this competing view, Crenshaw (1981) insisted "the relationship between personality and politics is complex and imperfectly understood" and argued that "the outstanding common characteristic of terrorists is their normality" (pp. 389–390).

Gill and Corner's (2017) third phase began in the late 1990s and was a period in which researchers evaluated the information and insights produced in earlier phases; in the early literature, the common weaknesses were "no statistical data, no standardized psychological instruments, and no control groups." There was, thus, no evidence to back up the assumption terrorists were abnormal. Researchers in this phase, according to Gill and Corner, were careful to avoid saying there was no mental illness among terrorists, but rather that there was no *evidence* of it and therefore "the prevalence rates of various mental disorders are no different to those found in general society" (p. 233). Nevertheless, post–September 11, the popular U.S. narrative became that terrorists were normal—anyone and everyone could be a terrorist.

Gill and Corner's (2017) fourth and current phase posits again that mental illness and terrorism are linked but carefully "disaggregates" the experience of being a terrorist and searches for fine distinctions among the diversity of terrorists, terrorist groups, terrorist activities, and environments with which they interact. "No meaningful (i.e., having predictive validity) psychological profile has been found" because of this diversity (Horgan, 2017, p. 200). Scholars now produce information and insights that suggest, for example, that "lone-wolf" or lone-actor terrorists are more likely to have a history of mental illness than terrorists who belong to a group (Gill & Corner, 2017) and that individual terrorists' personal motivations and goals differ by background. Those without a criminal background who saw themselves as part of a "noble cause" were often attracted to terrorism because of feelings of humiliation and a desire to belong whereas terrorists with a criminal background could "launder their offending by a righteous affiliation" and seek status and dominance (Lloyd & Kleinot, 2017, pp. 372, 374). Disaggregated research like this into the varying experiences of being a terrorist is new and growing.

One focus of psychological research into motivations for terrorism is on an individual's experience of social alienation (Abrahms, 2008; Atran, 2016; Crenshaw, 2000; Lloyd & Kleinot, 2017; Mink, 2015; Nacos, 2016; Reicher & Haslam, 2016). Abrahms (2008) argues that "terrorists are rational people who use terrorism primarily to develop strong affective ties with fellow terrorists"—they are, in other words, seeking "social solidarity" (pp. 80, 94). He defines social alienation as "the feeling of loneliness, rejection, or exclusion from valued relationships, groups, and societies" (p. 96). Unemployment and economic exclusion can lead to feelings of alienation along with frustration (Abrahms, 2008; Caruso & Schneider, 2011). Perceived powerlessness and the "inability to create one's own identity" due to globalization can also create feelings of alienation (Flint, 2003b, p. 163). Identity is also important to Reicher and Haslam (2016), who argue that "'misrecognition'" or the "experience of having others misperceive or deny a valued identity" created distance between individuals and their society—as well as authorities and government. They do not assert this alone leads to terrorism but that it can "shift the balance" (p. 37).

Lloyd and Kleinot (2017) also discuss the desire for a sense of belonging and social solidarity, placing it and other emotional experiences of terrorists within the frameworks of clinical depression and personality disorders as well as psychoanalytical processes of projection and splitting. For example, those who feel socially alienated may "project into an extremist cause" their "deep-seated sense of personal humiliation and injustice." Additionally, those "who harboured a deep sense of grievance" may resort to defensive splitting, which "allows a *good self* to be constructed and maintained through the construction and maintenance of a *bad other*" (p. 369). Engaging with others through terrorism can provide an individual with "a way of making sense of the world that projected blame onto others" (Lloyd & Kleinot, 2017, p. 372). Psychological defenses such as projection and splitting as well as depression and personality disorders may be present in individual terrorists, but do not predetermine terrorism any more than the structural causes examined above. Individual psychology can be a personal precondition just as hegemony and power can be a structural one. Studies of psychology and terrorism must always associate "individual life histories to political and social environments" (Crenshaw, 2000, p. 409).

A sense of social isolation is a psychological factor visible through interviews with[1] and data on a wide variety of terrorist groups. Abrahms (2008) cites evidence that 80% of interviewed Al Qaeda and affiliate members were marginalized immigrants living in non-Muslim countries. Studies of terrorists, including both Al Qaeda and IRA members, suggest that they joined their respective terrorist organizations because a relative or friend was a member, they were unemployed, and to reduce social isolation (pp. 96–98). Members of the Al Qaeda network today are characterized as "mostly self-seeking young adults in transitional stages in their lives—immigrants, students, people between jobs or mates, or having left their native homes" (Atran, 2016, pp. S198–S199). Charles Mink (2015), a former U.S. military interrogator who debriefed hundreds of accused terrorists primarily from the Islamic State (ISIS), also found that a sense of belonging was a key motivation for joining. It was, he concluded, "the pursuit of social satisfaction, not the expression of political or economic frustration, much less the fulfillment of a religious imperative" that drew people to terrorism (p. 63). He acknowledges that the causes of terrorism are complex and no simple profile exists, but suggests that lack of identity and social alienation make individuals targets for terrorist recruitment. On the other hand, other scholars contradict these findings and suggest that the socially alienated may not be accepted into terrorist groups that are heavily reliant on trust, though relationships with existing members may offset that concern (Nacos, 2016).

---

[1]Most interviews occur with imprisoned terrorists or suspected terrorists. Scholars are careful to point out that it is difficult to determine if interviewees who experienced mental illness did so before joining a terrorist group, because of engagement in terrorism, or because of capture and imprisonment.

Conclusion

If social alienation and social solidarity are important to terrorist recruits, countries may need to reconsider their primarily military and security approach to counterterrorism and consider more societal responses to offset individuals' feelings of isolation. This is because, ultimately, whether they are structural or individual, identifying and understanding the causes of terrorism are vital to counterterrorism; countries and the international community cannot effectively prevent terrorism unless they enact policies that address the complex and context-dependent causes. There are many more potential causes to examine, including state stability, triggering events, and group dynamics. There are also other aspects of terrorism to study, such as the impact of attacks or how individuals can disengage from terrorism.

This brief discussion shows how both structural and individual causes can apply in differing contexts, such as the domestic terrorism of the IRA in Northern Ireland and the transnational terrorism of Al Qaeda and its affiliates. Terrorism in both contexts is at least partially explained by historical acceptance of political violence, colonial or foreign occupation, hegemony and power, economic conditions, and individual psychology. Nonetheless, there is, as yet, no answer why some people in a given context resort to terrorism when others do not.

BOX 6.3
TAKE A STEP!
Combine Information and Insights on HIV or Terrorism

Using the similarities and/or differences you found in Box 5.2, combine the information and insights you found in the resources you gathered on HIV or terrorism. Going back to Chapter 3, similarities result in supplementary integration and differences result in complementary integration. This is the last step in the process, and the sentence or paragraph you write as you combine information and insights is a sample of the final, integrated product you will produce for your own research project.

7 Global Studies Research Process

TERRORISM

Like the global HIV epidemic, terrorism is a complex global problem and another opportunity to learn the Global Studies research process. The integrated essay on causes of terrorism in Chapter 6 resulted from the process of first preparing, then gathering, comparing, and combining information and insights drawn from six disciplines. As in Chapter 5, in this chapter we remove and examine puzzle pieces and how we used them to build a completed puzzle picture. While Chapter 5 focused on the basic process, here in Chapter 7 I also highlight challenges and opportunities that can arise while undertaking the Global Studies research process.

Global Studies Research Process

Prepare

Research question

Like the HIV epidemic, terrorism is a broad topic of interest and I need to narrow that topic to formulate a workable research question. As Chapter 3 suggests, I start by listing a number of possible questions that might interest me:

- How is terrorism different from other types of political violence, like war?

- Why do people or groups resort to terrorism? What are the causes of terrorism?

- Is terrorism effective? How often do terrorists achieve their goals?

- Is terrorism different after 9/11 than before? Are there different types of terrorism in different time periods? Different causes?

- What impact can terrorism have on countries? Societies? Identity groups? The international system?

- How do various global actors respond to terrorism? What are the most/least effective responses? How are national counterterrorism policies formed? How do they differ from country to country?

Based on these questions, I lean toward researching the causes of terrorism and whether they differ pre– and post–September 11. I do preliminary gathering and reading. Walter Laqueur's (2002) *A History of Terrorism* is a reprint of a 1977 edition (with a new introduction) and, thus, gives me insight into studies of terrorism prior to 2001, as does Martha Crenshaw's (1981) "The Causes of Terrorism" from the journal *Comparative Politics*. *Terrorism and Counterterrorism* by Brigitte L. Nacos (2016) is an introductory textbook and thus provides an overview of the subject of study. *Terrorism: A Critical Introduction* is exactly that—an introduction to the subject from the perspective of critical theory (Jackson, Jarvis, Gunning, & Breen-Smyth, 2011).

What I learn from my initial research is that, while there is far more research on terrorism post–September 11, the possible causes of terrorism did not change across time periods—but there are many proposed and even competing causes of terrorism. If there is agreement on the answer to "what causes terrorism?" it is that there is no single answer. This makes me even more interested in the subject, so I decide on "what causes terrorism?" as my initial research question—a question that will have to be narrowed further after gathering to be manageable as a research project.

Further research and reading teaches me that discussions of causes can vary by types of terrorism (such ideological or national liberation) and that causes are specific to context and situations. Additionally, depending on the source accessed, there can be more than a dozen different causes listed. A question such as "what causes terrorism in different contexts" remains too broad. Thus, it makes sense for me to limit the number of causes I explore, the types of terrorism, and the contexts within which they operate. To make my project manageable, I decide, therefore, to provide a general discussion on causes but limit my research question to a sampling of five potential causes, four structural and one individual. I also limit my research to two contexts—the two very different types of terrorist groups, as explained in Chapter 6: the IRA in Northern Ireland and Al Qaeda and its affiliates. My research question is: "How do the following potential structural and individual causes of terrorism describe motivations in the two different contexts of the IRA and Al Qaeda: (1) historical acceptance of political violence, (2) foreign or colonial occupation, (3) hegemony and power, (4) economic conditions, and (5) social alienation?" The answers to that question become the main point and thesis of my integrated essay in Chapter 6:

> Structural causes of terrorism such as historical acceptance of political violence, colonial or foreign occupation, hegemony and inequality of power, economic conditions, and social alienation as a potential individual cause apply in the different contexts of domestic terrorism of the IRA in Northern Ireland and transnational terrorism of Al Qaeda and its affiliates.

Relevant disciplines

For this research question, the five contributing disciplines remain potentially relevant. Others may be, as well. Given a subject that involves what motivates individuals to violence, it seems logical that the discipline of psychology is potentially relevant. Also, given those individuals join groups and that terrorism has an impact on society, the discipline of sociology is potentially relevant. As I started reading to refine my research question, my initial library research also turned up sources from the discipline of criminology, making it potentially relevant. Particularly moving into the current period of Al Qaeda and Islamic State terrorism and their use of traditional and social media, the field of Communication may also be relevant.

As noted in Chapter 3, a potentially relevant discipline becomes definitely relevant if it offers a body of published research on the topic addressed by the research question. Despite the sequentially defined steps of the Global Studies research process, research is nonlinear; I must take a step forward to gather, then a step back to prepare to finalize relevant disciplines. For example, I discovered a growing literature on terrorism in the discipline of criminology and criminal justice, including sources on responses to terrorism, policing and laws (often at the county level), terrorist attacks, and analyses of criminal offenses (such as firearms offenses) by ordinary criminals compared to terrorists. Much of the criminal justice research, therefore, did not address my specific research question and I determined the discipline to *not* be relevant for this research project.

Psychology, on the other hand, does produce publications on the causes of terrorism, though fewer than one might expect. As I explain further below (under Gather), a number of journal articles and even books with titles including key words such as *psychology terrorism* were actually written by political scientists; Martha Crenshaw's 2000 article "The Psychology of Terrorism" is one example. I was puzzled by this, especially after utilizing the library database PsychINFO turned up many of the same articles by political scientists or other non-psychologists. I was concerned that I was perhaps failing to find the right journals, databases, and key words. Because it is the main professional association, I searched the American Psychological Association website and was reminded of the ethics, rarity, secrecy, and criminality of terrorism by DeAngelis' (2009) statement that "terrorists aren't likely to volunteer as experimental subjects, and examining their activities from afar can lead to erroneous conclusions." I emailed a colleague in the discipline of psychology, who acknowledged the limited research produced by the field and directed me to valuable research on exactly that topic.

In "A Call to Arms," psychologist John Horgan (2016) suggests "it is incredulous that psychology as a *discipline* has been virtually absent from a serious, systematic exploration of terrorist behavior" and goes on "for too long, the study of terrorism has been the concern of other disciplines, notably political science" (p. 27). Horgan (2017) expresses confidence in the growing literature of psychology research by noting that with rigorous methodologies and "armed with increasing insights from former terrorists willing the share their experiences with researchers, autobiographies, and court testimonies, psychologists have been afforded new insights into the process of becoming involved in, remaining involved in, and disengaging from terrorism" (p. 201). As well as confirming and explaining my discovery of somewhat limited psychological research on terrorism, Horgan's articles are also literature reviews of what publications do exist—allowing me to mine his bibliographies and gather additional psychology sources. In the end, I feel I have sufficient sources from psychology for balance and I include it as a relevant discipline.

Utilizing sources from the discipline of psychology, however, means I must ask myself whether I have an adequate understanding of the discipline to utilize its information and insights. Psychology is considered a behavioral science, which is related to the social sciences and the study of humans but generally considers a different level of analysis: the individual. Social sciences like anthropology and economics can consider individual behavior but usually aggregate it to draw conclusions about cultures, societies, economies, and countries—social systems as a whole, made up of the individuals. Psychology is not generally included in Global Studies majors, and I need to learn more about the discipline to integrate its information and insights. As noted in Chapter 2, I can take several steps. I first browsed *Essential Psychology* by Banyard, Dillon, Norman, and Winder (2015), an introduction to psychology textbook. The subdiscipline of social psychology is mentioned in several of the sources I gathered, so I also looked at *Social Psychology* by DeLamater, Collett, and Myers (2014). From that point on, I looked up specific terms, concepts, and diagnoses as needed. For example, in "Pathways Into Terrorism: The Good, the Bad, and the Ugly," Lloyd and Kleinot (2017) discuss the "psychoanalytic processes of defences, splitting, and projection" (p. 367). I reviewed the meaning and importance of these terms in textbooks and other journal articles, then ensured my understanding of them by talking with subject-matter experts, including a licensed mental health counselor. Given the interdisciplinary nature of terrorism studies, I was fortunate that both disciplinary and interdisciplinary authors on psychological factors write for informed rather than specialist audiences and many articles were easily understandable.

I asked myself the same question about an adequate understanding of the disciplines for sociology and communication. Given they are social sciences and there is overlap between subjects of study, research methods, and theory with my original discipline of political science, I felt I could utilize their research without the introductory study I gave to psychology. I was, however, prepared to look up and verify my understanding of concepts as needed.

Gather

Challenges in gathering information and insights

As I began gathering information and insights from the relevant disciplines, I quickly discovered two challenges to the goal of balance among disciplines. First, there is a developed interdisciplinary field of terrorism studies. Disciplinary scholars collaborate with others across disciplinary lines. Therefore, many clusters of interlocked puzzle pieces already exist. One example is "There and Back Again: The Study of Mental Disorder and Terrorist Involvement," which is coauthored by political scientist Paul Gill and Emily Corner, who (based on her faculty webpage at Australian

National University) has degrees in both psychology and crime science. Such team research is an asset to Global Studies—it produces more smoothies. It does, however, challenge our ability to balance *disciplinary* research within the Global Studies research process. Existing interdisciplinary research sources may include some but not all of our relevant disciplines. To follow the smoothie metaphor, we can share someone else's smoothie or remain committed to making our own both to ensure we have the fruits (disciplines) we want and to learn how to make better smoothies for ourselves. We acknowledge—and integrate—already-interdisciplinary studies but also continue to focus on gathering disciplinary information and insights ourselves.

The second challenge to a balanced, integrated essay is the fact that the discipline of political science dominates the study of terrorism. The disciplines of economics and history produce relevant literature, although within economics many of the studies on causes of terrorism focus primarily on poverty and other economic conditions. A few economics sources also consider political, cultural, and geographical variables that may influence the impact of the economy on terrorism. There are publications on terrorism in other disciplines, but sources are far less numerous in anthropology, geography, and psychology. Political scientists write not only on psychology, but also the geography and sociology of terrorism. Disciplines like anthropology, geography, and psychology certainly are not irrelevant to terrorism studies. For reasons of ethics, methodology, and critical analysis of the interplay between knowledge and power, however, disciplinary scholars may have opted out of terrorism research.

Like John Horgan (2016, 2017) in psychology, geographers Karim Bahgat and Richard M. Medina (2013) call for more geographical research of terrorism and suggest avenues of research. They also demonstrate, graphically, that non-geographers have produced much more geographic terrorism literature than geographers, though they do not specify how much is attributable to political scientists. That terrorism studies as a field is already interdisciplinary reinforces the importance of interdisciplinarity to such complex global issues. At the same time, if one discipline dominates, the inclusion of other disciplines in terrorism studies is important to offset the perspective of political science and ensure that there are a variety of disciplinary perspectives represented. This is true for individuals seeking to learn about causes of terrorism and also for the bigger picture. When counterterrorism policies are influenced by academic research, over-reliance on a single discipline can limit the policy options available as well as selected. Current criticisms of U.S. counterterrorism policies include that they are too focused on military and national security measures, which might be attributed to the perspective of political science (though political scientists also promote a wider ranges of policies). A variety of disciplinary influences potentially could broaden counterterrorism policies beyond the "politico-military" dimension to include human, economic, and environmental dimensions, as advocated by Bakker and Kessels (2012).

Because I found fewer sources on terrorism generally and the causes of terrorism specifically in the disciplines of anthropology, communication, geography, and sociology, I made several decisions. First, I acknowledged and accepted that my integrated essay on the causes of terrorism may not be as equitably balanced as I'd like. Second, I worked even harder to find useful sources from geography and anthropology, as common contributors to global studies. In the end, I believe I found a reasonable balance of information and insights for the sections of the essay where I explore the causes of terrorism—I might have had to work harder, but I found puzzle pieces.

Third, I decided sociology and communication were not relevant. Of the sociology sources I found, many were on terrorism as it related to social movements and group dynamics, with less on the causes of terrorism I chose to focus on. One exception was Stephen Vertigan's (2011) *The Sociology of Terrorism: Peoples, Places and Processes*, which reinforced what I was reading about causes in research from other disciplines and also noted the absence of and called for more sociological research into the motivations of terrorism. I verified with a disciplinary expert that, indeed, the discipline's literature on terrorism, particularly its causes, is still limited. To drop sociology as a relevant discipline was an uncomfortable decision—even experienced researchers worry that they are failing to find vital sources—but I made it with the input of a disciplinary expert and based both on the literature available to me and the manageability of the project. I am not saying that sociology is irrelevant to terrorism, but simply that its information and insights are currently less available and useful for my research project. The same is true for the discipline of communication, which I also left out. There is interesting and growing research on media and terrorism, but it is less relevant to my research question.

All that I learned and decided as I initially gathered—and went back to the "prepare" step by determining relevant disciplines—left me with the need to gather information and insights from six disciplines, as well as finding other/nondisciplinary and interdisciplinary sources. My first search was for books and ebooks in the university library catalog. Second, I searched disciplinary journals for *causes*, *root causes*, and *origins* of terrorism—refining my search terms as I went along and saw titles of useful

BOX 7.1
TAKE A STEP!
Combine

In Box 6.2, for your own research project, you explored the similarities and differences between the disciplinary information and insights you gathered. Now, use those comparisons to combine information and produce an integrated essay.

As explained in Chapter 3, similarities allow you to engage in supplementary integration while differences require complementary integration. Examples are available in Chapter 5 and here in Chapter 7, below.

books and articles. For example, a prominent economics journal is *American Economic Review*, and in it I found Alberto Abadie's (2006) "Poverty, Political Freedom, and the Roots of Terrorism." Using a general internet search and the bibliographies of sources I'd already found, I learned there are academic journals specifically on the topic of terrorism, such as *Perspectives on Terrorism* and *Studies in Conflict and Terrorism*. I also searched these, making sure to investigate the disciplinary perspectives of authors, as explained in Chapter 3.

Disciplinary sources

Anthropology sources are found in a multidisciplinary book, *Root Causes of Terrorism: Myths, Reality and Ways Forward*. Chapters in the book are by scholars from a variety of disciplines and it provides brief biographies of all contributors. It is edited by Tore Bjørgo, an anthropologist who also contributes the introduction and conclusion. In addition to the Abadie source noted above, Caruso and Schneider's 2011 article "The Socio-Economic Determinants of Terrorism and Political Violence in Western Europe (1994–2007)" from the *European Journal of Political Economy* provides economics information and insights. That they are from the discipline of economics is evident from the author information at the beginning of the article. Geography sources gathered include Bahgat and Medina's (2013) journal article "An Overview of Geographical Perspectives and Approaches in Terrorism Research" from *Perspectives on Terrorism*. Their bios are included at the end of the article. History sources include Mohammad-Mahmoud Ould Mohamedou's book chapter "Al Qaeda and the Reinvention of Terrorism" from the edited book *An International History of Terrorism*, which includes bios of each contributor. Another example is Miller's (2013) book *The Foundations of Modern Terrorism: States, Society, and the Dynamics of Political Violence*, which also provides a biography of the author with which to determine his disciplinary perspective.

I gathered several political science sources, including the already-mentioned seminal *Comparative Politics* journal article by Martha Crenshaw (1981), "The Causes of Terrorism." I found Michael Freeman's "Democracy, Al Qaeda, and the Causes of Terrorism: A Strategic Analysis of U.S. Policy" in *Studies in Conflict and Terrorism*. From his online vita available through the Naval Postgraduate School in Monterey, California, I learn that he has a PhD in political science as well as a teaching position in that field (see https://faculty.nps.edu). Books in political science include Nacos (2016) and Jackson et al. (2011), mentioned above.

Examples of sources from the discipline of psychology are listed above, such as the journal article "Pathways Into Terrorism: The Good, the Bad, and the Ugly," by Lloyd and Kleinot (2017); the author listing and abstract of which identify them: "[T]he first author is a forensic psychologist" in the School of Psychology at University of Birmingham, UK and "the second author . . . is a psycho-therapist and group analyst" in private practice (p. 367). It is not always easy to identify some authors; John Horgan, mentioned above, appears to be within the discipline of psychology but his information (in journal articles and online) also presents a specialty in political psychology and he is a coauthor on articles that clearly result from interdisciplinary team research. This could have made him interdisciplinary (as with the example of Mark Hunter in Chapter 5), so to be sure I emailed to ask him, even though I didn't know him. Kind enough to respond, Dr. Horgan answered that psychology is his discipline and he described his process when engaging in interdisciplinary research: "I guess I learn how other disciplines view terrorism, and do my best to figure out what that means for what I bring to the table" (personal communication, December 7, 2018).

Disciplinary answers

As explained in Chapter 3, once I have gathered information and insights from the relevant disciplines, I construct an answer to my research question from each discipline. This will provide me with the material for the next step, compare. My full task is to draft six disciplinary answers to the question "How do the following potential structural and individual causes of terrorism describe motivations in the two different contexts of the IRA and Al Qaeda: (1) historical acceptance of political violence, (2) foreign or colonial occupation, (3) hegemony and power, (4) economic conditions, and (5) social alienation?" These answers can be developed essays or detailed notes. As examples here, however, I provide excerpts of disciplinary answers about types of terrorism and social alienation.

Disciplinary answer excerpts: types of terrorism

Categories or types of political terrorism are necessary to understand causes of terrorism because they are related. For example, national separatist terrorism, as a type, reflects the causes as well as goals of a group: colonial occupation as a cause and gaining independence from it as a goal. As I answered my research question about five potential causes of terrorism, I therefore knew I would also have to discuss types of terrorism—the categories created by scholars in their attempts to identify patterns of similarities and differences among terrorist groups.

Anthropology. Few of the anthropology sources I gathered explicitly discuss types of terrorism. They appear to implicitly accept that there are types and discuss the radicalization—and deradicalization—of individuals within the confines of the category of religious terrorism, using also the terms *Islamist extremist* and *jihadi terrorism* (see, for example, Atran, 2008, 2016; Bouzar, 2016). The exception is Bjørgo (2005b), because he discusses how different types of terrorism will reflect different causes of terrorism; given his emphasis on causes, he does not spend time delineating or analyzing the different types of terrorism.

Economics. Economic sources apparently accept common categorizations of terrorism, implicitly referencing types without describing or analyzing them (see, for example, Caruso & Schneider, 2011; Freytag et al., 2011). Abadie (2006) and Kis-Katos et al. (2011) explicitly discuss the differences between international and domestic terrorism as these types relate to their research into economic and other variables that describe the causes of terrorism.

Geography. Geographers Medina and Hepner (2013) classify, describe, and provide examples of three different types of terrorism, particularly based on motivations: nationalist/separatist, cultural/religious, and ideological. They caution that the categories can overlap but they would place terrorist groups into categories based on their primary motivation. Bahgat and Medina (2013) also explicitly discuss categories of terrorism, including transnational versus traditional and territorial versus nonterritorial groups. Other geography sources, such as Mitchell (1979) and Flint (2003b), reference common types such as domestic or international without explicitly defining or discussing them.

History. Historian Walter Laqueur (2002) defines four categories of terrorism based on political ideology: social revolutionary, Marxist or leftist, nationalist, and right-wing. Miller (2013) presents common types of terrorism as he tells the history of terrorism; for example, he follows historical trends from the anarchists of Russia as social revolutionaries to the ideological terrorism of the Cold War through to Al Qaeda in the 21st century. Both Miller (2013) and Mohamedou (2013) are critical of "religious terrorism" as a category, emphasizing the political nature of the designation and ways in which the category hindered the West's ability to understand the political motivations of Al Qaeda and to create effective counterterrorism policies.

Political science. In their introductory textbooks, political science authors Nacos (2016) and Jackson et al. (2011) list, describe, and provide examples of types of terrorism. Along with religious terrorism, Nacos (2016) includes "nationalist/separatist, lift and/or revolutionary, right and/or reactionary, antiglobalization, and extreme environmentalists" (p. 46). She also makes the distinction between domestic and international terrorism. Jackson et al. (2011) provides the most comprehensive lists of types. They discuss ideological types, state versus non-state terrorism, methods-based terrorism, levels such as domestic and international, criminal terrorism, new versus old terrorism, and so forth. As critical theorists, Jackson et al. question categorizations such as new and religious terrorism, and the ways in which these terms can be used to support the political agendas of leaders or countries.

Psychology. None of the psychology sources I gathered explicitly discuss types of terrorism. Lloyd and Kleinot (2017) and Reicher and Haslam (2016) group Islamic extremist or jihadi terrorists together, implicitly adhering to that categorization.

Disciplinary answer excerpts: social alienation

The potential individual cause of terrorism explored in Chapter 6 was social alienation, particularly as it related to individual psychology and mental health. Studying the individual as a level of analysis must relate back to historical, cultural, geographic, economic, and political contexts, so all five of the common criteria for comparison in Chapter 3 could be useful. However, the addition of the discipline of psychology allows us to consider social alienation as not only a cause but also a criterion for comparing disciplinary information and insights.

Anthropology. Some anthropology sources I gathered made no mention of social alienation or isolation. Two sources by Scott Atran (2008, 2016) did so, emphasizing that jihadi or Islamist terrorism "is about youth culture, not theology or ideology" because young people "want to belong to something that is at once intimate, bigger, and more permanent than a person alone." When they feel isolated from family, friends, society, and/or job opportunities, terrorist groups can provide solidarity as well as respect (Atran, 2008).

Economics.   None of the economic sources I gathered made direct mention of social alienation as a potential cause of terrorism. Caruso and Schneider's (2011) "immiserizing modernization theory" indirectly addresses it, because these economists consider the opportunity cost of participating in terrorism. Individuals with more to lose—socially as well as economically—are less likely to engage in terrorism. Those who have more grievances, "frustration and poor expectations about future economic scenarios" have less to lose and may engage in terrorist activity (p. S48). Unemployment and economic frustration can be a part of social alienation, as discussed by Abrahms (2008).

Geography. Most geography sources gathered did not address social isolation. The exceptions were two articles by Flint (2003a, 2003b), in which he mentions the grievances that can result "from the disorientation of being either at the center of the maelstrom of change (such as globalization) or the frustration of missing out of its perceived benefits" (2003a, p. 55). He does not mean solely economic frustration, as he also describes exclusion as powerlessness and the "inability to create one's own identity—while, instead, being the victims of mechanisms that create 'refugee problems,' 'extremists,' 'rebels,' . . . and so on" (2003b, p. 163).

History. Two history sources referenced individual feelings, akin to if not directly social alienation, as motivation for terrorism. Laqueur (2002) takes a questionable tone when he suggests "idealism, social conscience or hatred of foreign oppression are powerful impulses, but so are free-floating aggression, boredom and mental confusion. Activism can give meaning to otherwise empty lives" (p. 128). Mohamedou (2013) does not dismiss social alienation itself but rather criticizes the simplistic and unproductive view of it taken when the media and even social scientists constructed a narrative of Al Qaeda as "impoverished ragtags, alienated drifters merely channeling their free-floating anger animated by homicidal animosity" (p. 238). This is within the context of his article critical of social science research that emphasized the religious irrationality and hatred rather than politics and strategy of Al Qaeda.

Political science. Early political science publications addressing individual motivations such as a sense of solidarity or belonging include Crenshaw's 1981

"The Causes of Terrorism" and 2000 "The Psychology of Terrorism." It is in "What Terrorists Really Want" that Max Abrahms (2008) develops the argument that "the preponderance of evidence is that people participate in terrorist organizations for the social solidarity, not for their political return" (p. 94). Nacos (2016) presents research both supporting and contradicting the idea that social alienation motivates individuals to join terrorist groups. Jackson et al. (2011) dismiss the historical view of terrorists as psychopaths or abnormal but do not engage social alienation specifically.

Psychology. The discipline of psychology does produce recent, nuanced research on social alienation as an individual psychological cause of terrorism. Post (2005) includes excerpts of an interview with an Al Qaeda member accused in the bombing of the U.S. embassy in Tanzania, which make clear he saw himself as "alone, friendless, isolated" until attending services at a mosque in Dar es Salaam and becoming radicalized (p. 61). Reicher and Haslam (2016) argue that "radicalization starts when something happens to undermine someone's sense of self and purpose: discrimination, the loss of a parent, bullying, moving, or anything that leaves the person confused, uncertain, or alone" (p. 37).

Lloyd and Kleinot (2017) place the idea of social alienation and a search for solidarity firmly in the context of individual psychology, discussing it and other emotional experiences of terrorists in relation to depression, personality disorders, and psychological defenses such as projection and splitting. Though they are careful to recognize that "our collective understanding of terrorist offending is still in its infancy," they also note that depression and other mental illnesses are not surprising "in those who have struggled to find their place in society" (pp. 375-376).

Interdisciplinary sources

As with the HIV epidemic example, once I have my disciplinary answers to the causes of terrorism research question, I can consider how the interdisciplinary and other/nondisciplinary sources I gathered provide answers to the question. I also consider the need for balance—not only between the disciplines but also with interdisciplinary and other sources. As noted above, one challenge with this topic is to ensure that interdisciplinary source information and insights do not overwhelm those from the disciplines—so we can make the smoothies we want rather than relying on others' mixtures.

Alex P. Schmid (2005a, 2005b) authored two interdisciplinary sources I gathered; his contributor bio in *Root Causes of Terrorism* describes him as interdisciplinary: "a historian by training but has later worked in the fields of sociology, political science, and human rights" (p. xiv). His chapter "Prevention of Terrorism" includes his seminal typology of terrorism, breaking political terrorism into categories such as insurgent, vigilante, state, and state-sponsored terrorism and thus contributes to my understanding of types of terrorism (Schmid, 2005a, p. 224). Another interdisciplinary source, "There and Back Again" noted above, is by political scientist Gill and interdisciplinary scholar Corner (2017). This journal article also adds to my understanding of types of terrorism in addressing the individual level; as noted in Chapter 6, this can include categories by terrorists' role: "bomb-maker," "bomb-planter," financier, or gunman (Gill & Corner, 2017, p. 235).

Other/Nondisciplinary sources

Other/Nondisciplinary sources are authored by journalists, government officials, and other non-academics. In Chapter 6 I referenced a Congressional Research Report on terrorism, written by staff member John Rollins. I also utilized *Making Sense of the Troubles*, about Northern Ireland, which is coauthored by journalists David McKittrick and David McVea. The information from these sources provides examples and details to demonstrate the analysis of causes of terrorism as applied to Al Qaeda and the IRA. We need to know what answers they provide, so we can later compare them. Charles Mink's article "It's About the Group, Not God" is based on his experience as a U.S. military interrogator in Iraq, primarily with ISIS detainees. In this article, he concludes people join terrorist groups for "a strong identity, a role to play, a proud affiliation, and an opportunity to share intimate experiences with others" (Mink, 2005, p. 79). (Mink's article indicates that he is a PhD candidate but does not indicate the field of study, and I could find no additional information online; given that his article was based partly on professional experience, I chose to identify it as *other/nondisciplinary*.)

Compare

As noted in Chapter 3, the *compare* step prompts us to search for similarities and differences among the information and insights gathered from relevant disciplinary sources, interdisciplinary sources, and other sources. We are closely examining our puzzle pieces to see if we have duplicate pieces to stack and/or unique pieces that will fit snugly together. All five general criteria for comparison presented in Chapter 3— the past, politics, economics, culture, and geographic locations—are useful for the research question on terrorism. However, I only provide one of these as an example here: politics. The case study on terrorism gives us the opportunity to consider the addition of another relevant criterion: social alienation. The addition of the discipline of psychology allows us to view social alienation as not just a cause but also a criterion for comparing the information and insights gathered, and this criterion also serves as an example of comparison.

Comparing information and insights on the political criterion of types of terrorism

While types of terrorism reflect aspects of culture, history, and politics, my research indicated it is usually a political decision regarding which type a terrorist group is designated. Thus, I treat types of terrorism as within the political criterion introduced in Chapter 3.

Economics and psychology sources did not contribute information and insights on types of terrorism. I found information and insights—puzzle pieces—about types of terrorism in the disciplines of geography, history, and political science, as well as an inter-disciplinary source (Bahgat & Medina, 2013; Jackson et al., 2011; Laqueur, 2002; Nacos, 2016; Schmid, 2005a). These sources provided similar information and insights about generally the same types of terrorism, or duplicate puzzle pieces, although geography put more emphasis on territorial types (Bahgat & Medina, 2013) and political science source Jackson et al. (2011) provided the most comprehensive list of types—offering new and different puzzle pieces. In acknowledging that religious terrorism is controversial as a category, I also wanted to compare what I had gathered about Al Qaeda as a religious ter-rorist group. I found political science and other U.S. government sources are more likely to call Al Qaeda a religious terrorist group (Freeman, 2008; Nacos, 2016; Rollins, 2011), while critical political scientists and historians differ by being more likely to question assigning Al Qaeda to that type (Jackson et al., 2011; Miller, 2013; Mohamedou, 2013).

These same three sources differ from the rest in noting that by treating Al Qaeda as a religious group, U.S. and international counterterrorism efforts may have been misdirected and may even have increased resentment against the United States. One entirely different insight emerged from the discipline of history: Mohamedou (2013) was the only source I gathered that argued the United States, by focusing primarily on the religious elements of Al Qaeda's agenda, entirely missed the "militaristic empow-erment of a non-state actor" (p. 242).

Different information and insights emerged from anthropology and one other/nondisciplinary source, both of which offered information about religious apathy among many incarcerated Islamist terrorists. This would seem to logically contradict the view of religious terrorism and particularly religious terrorists as irrational zealots (Atran, 2016; Bouzar, 2016; Mink, 2015).

These similarities and differences will allow us to utilize supplementary and com-plementary integration to combine information and insights when we reach that step. We will either snap together unique puzzle pieces or, where appropriate, stack up duplicates to provide validity.

Comparing information and insights on the criterion of social alienation

The disciplines of economics and history provided little information and few insights on social alienation, which only served to reinforce knowledge gained from other disci-plines. They provided duplicate puzzle pieces for validity. Geography offered duplicate puzzle pieces, but also a different insight on identity from those found in other disci-plines. The disciplines of anthropology, political science, and psychology offered a variety of unique puzzle pieces for the social alienation picture. It is a political science source, Abrahms (2008), that introduced a model of "terrorists as social solidarity seekers" (p. 96). Political scientists Crenshaw (1981, 2000) and Nacos (2016) provide similar information and insights. Psychology sources provide evidence and a framework of specific mental disorders that are different from the insights provided by other disciplines, but they also come to similar, if cautious, conclusions. This is particularly true of Lloyd and Kleinot (2017) and the puzzle pieces they contribute to the picture.

Combine

Combining information and insights on types of terrorism

Using the similarities and differences found under the compare step (above), I integrate information and insights following the guidelines in Chapter 3. Where I find similarities, I combine using supplementary integration, and where I find differences, I combine using complementary integration. Box 7.2 reminds us of a sentence from the terrorism case study that demonstrates both supplementary and complementary integration. As Box 7.2 illustrates, there are three parts to the sentence. Part one demonstrates supplementary integration, as authors Freeman, Nacos, Post, Rollins, and Soderberg (a mixture of political science, psychology, and other sources) all treat Al Qaeda as a religious terrorist organization. They provide us with duplicate puzzle pieces. The second part of the sentence demonstrates both complementary and supplementary integration. While critical political science and history authors Jackson et al., Miller, and Mohamedou all provide us with identical puzzle pieces, they are different from the pieces provided in part one because they assert Al Qaeda should be viewed as political rather than religious. Finally, the third part of the sentence reinforces the second part but does so with different information: that Al Qaeda perhaps should not be considered religious because group members simply do not see themselves as religious.

This puzzle piece is different from and can snap together with those from parts one and two of the sentences—but again we have three identical copies of this piece to stack one upon the other, two from the discipline of anthropology (Atran, Bouzar) and one from an other/nondisciplinary source (Mink).

The same paragraph of Chapter 6 that includes the sentence in Box 7.2 is also an example of paragraph-level complementary integration. As noted above under *compare*, Mohamedou (2013) added an insight about the martiality of Al Qaeda. This unique

---

BOX 7.2
COMBINING PUZZLE PIECES

From Pages 121–122 of Chapter 6, A Complex Problem: Terrorism

Al Qaeda, on the other hand, is usually classified as religious terrorism (Freeman, 2008; Nacos, 2016; Post, 2005; Rollins, 2011; Soderberg, 2005)—despite clearly stated political goals (Jackson et al., 2011; Miller, 2013; Mohamedou, 2013) and increasing evidence that Al Qaeda and affiliated Islamic terrorists (particularly the foot soldiers) were not generally religious prior to their process of joining and may know little about their religion as members (Atran, 2016; Bouzar, 2016; Mink 2015).

(Continued)

(Continued)

Supplementary and Complementary Integration

Part One: Supplementary Integration

Political Science, Psychology, Other/Nondisciplinary
Freeman, 2008; Nacos, 2016; Post, 2005; Rollins, 2011; Soderberg, 2005

Al Qaeda, on the other hand, is usually classified as religious terrorism

Part Two: Complements Part One and is also supplementary in that three sources provide the same information and insights

despite clearly stated political goals

Political Science, History
Jackson et al., 2011; Miller, 2013; Mohamedou, 2013

Part Three: Complements Parts One and Two and is also supplementary in that three sources provide the same information and insights

and increasing evidence that Al Qaeda and affiliated Islamic terrorists (particularly the foot soldiers") were not generally religious prior to their process of joining and may know little about their religion as members

Anthropology, Other/Nondisciplinary
Atran, 2016; Bouzar, 2016; Mink, 2015

piece of the puzzle complements and snaps into the already-integrated earlier part of the paragraph (see Box 7.3). Though types of terrorist groups are a political concept, Mohamedou adds an additional piece of the puzzle from a historical perspective—a piece that he argues political scientists failed to find.

BOX 7.3
COMBINING PUZZLE PIECES

From Pages 121–122 of Chapter 6, A Complex Problem: Terrorism

Today, the category of religious terrorism is particularly controversial. In Northern Ireland, the conflict is commonly described as Catholics versus Protestants, yet the situation is a frequently cited example of national separatist terrorism (Jackson et al.,

2013; Nacos, 2016; Post, 2005; Reinares, 2005; Soderberg, 2005) because, in fact, the conflict there is not religious (see below). Al Qaeda, on the other hand, is usually classified as religious terrorism (Freeman, 2008; Nacos, 2016; Post, 2005; Rollins, 2011; Soderberg, 2005)—despite clearly stated political goals (Jackson et al., 2011; Miller, 2013; Mohamedou, 2013) and increasing evidence that Al Qaeda and affiliated Islamic terrorists (particularly the foot soldiers) were not generally religious prior to their process of joining and may know little about their religion as members (Atran, 2016; Bouzar, 2016; Mink 2015). As Jackson et al. (2011) caution, "categorizing a group as 'religious terrorists', for example, encourages the researcher to focus primarily on the group's religious aspects and hence to neglect its secular or political dynamics" (p. 159). Because of this, Mohamedou (2013) argues that many scholars and policy makers failed to note what he considers one of two truly new features of Al Qaeda: its "martiality." Many noted its transnational nature, but not "the militaristic empowerment of a non-state actor" or that "the material manifestation of this transnational terrorism was more so an approximation of a military conception of operational delivery underscored by an up-tempo battle plan proactively designed and explicitly communicated" (pp. 237, 242). American policy makers, he argues, failed to hear much of what Al Qaeda said because they focused on the religious rather than political and tactical messages sent.

Already-Integrated: Anthropology, Political Science, Psychology, Other/Nondisciplinary

Today, the category of religious terrorism is particularly controversial. In Northern Ireland, the conflict is commonly described as "Catholics versus Protestants," yet the situation is a frequently cited example of national separatist terrorism (Jackson et al., 2013; Nacos, 2016; Post, 2005; Reinares, 2005; Soderberg, 2005) because, in fact, the conflict there is not religious (see below). Al Qaeda, on the other hand, is usually classified as religious terrorism (Freeman, 2008; Nacos, 2016; Post, 2005; Rollins, 2011; Soderberg, 2005)—despite clearly stated political goals (Jackson et al., 2011; Miller, 2013; Mohamedou, 2013) and increasing evidence that Al Qaeda and affiliated Islamic terrorists (particularly the foot soldiers) were not generally religious prior to their process of joining and may know little about their religion as members (Atran, 2016; Bouzar, 2016; Mink 2015). As Jackson et al. (2011) caution, "categorizing a group as 'religious terrorists', for example, encourages the researcher to focus primarily on the group's religious aspects and hence to neglect its secular or political dynamics" (p. 159).

Complementary Integration

Because of this, Mohamedou (2013) argues that many scholars and policy makers failed to note what he considers one of two truly new features of Al Qaeda: its "martiality." Many noted its transnational nature, but not "the militaristic empowerment of a non-state actor" or that "the material manifestation of this transnational terrorism was more so an approximation of a military conception of operational delivery underscored by an up-tempo battle plan proactively designed and explicitly communicated" (pp. 237, 242). American policy makers, he argues, failed to hear much of what Al Qaeda said because they focused on the religious rather than political and tactical messages sent.

History
Mohamedou, 2013

Combining information and insights about social alienation

Examples of integration in describing social alienation as a cause of terrorism follows the same process: Similarities lead to supplementary integration and differences to complementary integration. Box 7.4 presents a sentence from the section in Chapter 6 on social integration, which exemplifies supplementary integration—duplicate puzzle pieces. The understanding that unemployment or other forms of economic exclusion can lead to social alienation is found in both the disciplines of political science and economics; the supplementary integration is only indirectly visible through the multiple citations.

Complementary integration is visible in the partial paragraph in Box 7.5; it combines different information—particularly different evidence—from the disciplines of political science and anthropology along with an other/nondisciplinary source. Each source comes to same conclusion based on the same basic methods (interviews) but on different evidence from different populations of terrorists (Al Qaeda, IRA, ISIS). See Box 7.5.

As the examples of both types of terrorism and social alienation demonstrate, combining supplementary and complementary information and insights provides a fuller understanding of the answer to the research question: "How do the following potential structural and individual causes of terrorism describe motivations in the two different contexts of the IRA and Al Qaeda: (1) historical acceptance of political violence, (2) foreign or colonial occupation, (3) hegemony and power, (4) economic conditions, and (5) social alienation?" Integration does this through validation of similar material and inclusion of different material—duplicate puzzle pieces and unique puzzle pieces. The entire Global Studies research process provides the tools to answer the research question and build puzzle pictures, even when facing the challenges and opportunities inherent to research.

BOX 7.4
COMBINING PUZZLE PIECES

From Page 134 of Chapter 6, A Complex Problem: Terrorism

Unemployment and economic exclusion can lead to feelings of alienation along with frustration (Abrahms, 2008; Caruso & Schneider, 2011)

	Supplementary Integration
Unemployment and economic exclusion can lead to feelings of alienation along with frustration.	Political Science Abrahms, 2008 Economics Caruso & Schneider, 2011

BOX 7.5
COMBINING PUZZLE PIECES

From Page 135 of Chapter 6, A Complex Problem: Terrorism

A sense of social isolation is a psychological factor visible through interviews with and data on a wide variety of terrorist groups. Abrahms (2008) cites evidence that 80% of interviewed Al Qaeda and affiliate members were marginalized immigrants living in non-Muslim countries. Studies of terrorists, including both Al Qaeda and IRA members, suggest that they joined their respective terrorist organizations because a relative or friend was a member, they were unemployed, and to reduce social isolation (pp. 96–98). Members of the Al Qaeda network today are characterized as "mostly self-seeking young adults in transitional stages in their lives—immigrants, students, people between jobs or mates, or having left their native homes" (Atran, 2016, pp. S198–S199). Charles Mink (2015), a former U.S. military interrogator who debriefed hundreds of accused terrorists primarily from the Islamic State (ISIS), also found that a sense of belonging was a key motivation for joining. It was, he concluded, "the pursuit of social satisfaction, not the expression of political or economic frustration, much less the fulfillment of a religious imperative" that drew people to terrorism (p. 63).

Complementary Integration
Political Science
Abrahms, 2008

A sense of social isolation is a psychological factor visible through interviews with and data on a wide variety of terrorist groups. Abrahms (2008) cites evidence that 80% of interviewed Al Qaeda and affiliate members were marginalized immigrants living in non-Muslim countries. Studies of terrorists, including both Al Qaeda and IRA members, suggest that they joined their respective terrorist organizations because a relative or friend was a member, they were unemployed, and to reduce social isolation (pp. 96–98).

Members of the Al Qaeda network today are characterized as "mostly self-seeking young adults in transitional stages in their lives—immigrants, students, people between jobs or mates, or having left their native homes" (Atran, 2016, p. S198–S199).

Anthropology
Atran, 2016

Other/Nondisciplinary
Mink, 2015

Charles Mink (2015), a former U.S. military interrogator who debriefed hundreds of accused terrorists primarily from the Islamic State (ISIS), also found that a sense of belonging was a key motivation for joining. It was, he concluded, "the pursuit of social satisfaction, not the expression of political or economic frustration, much less the fulfillment of a religious imperative" that drew people to terrorism (p. 63).

BOX 7.6
TAKE A STEP!
Reflection

Having worked your way through the Global Studies research process twice—once with this textbook's sources and once with your own research project—it may be helpful to reflect on the process (Repko & Szostak, 2017). Did you find one particular step challenging? How often did you have to repeat steps, in the nonlinear process of research? Did you find yourself skipping or combining steps? Why? Did you have trouble with organization, balance, or point of view as you undertook research and wrote an integrated essay? Do you agree that your understanding of your research project is "fuller" because of combining disciplinary information and insights? The answers to such questions or other reflections can help improve your understanding of the Global Studies research process and your ability to undertake it again in the future.

8 Conclusion

The complexity of our world—including globalization, global issues, global actors and their interactions, and differing perspectives—means that research can be more fruitful when it is interdisciplinary, building on valuable disciplinary research. Using the jigsaw puzzle metaphor, completed puzzle pictures benefit from more and more-varied puzzle pieces through interdisciplinary research. We can define Global Studies, a subset of general interdisciplinary studies, as a process that utilizes the social sciences and other relevant disciplines to describe, analyze, and explain how the world works and prompt solutions for managing the complex global problems in our world.

The Global Studies research process is a tool for undertaking interdisciplinary research in the field of Global Studies. Based on the general interdisciplinary studies literature, *Global Studies Research* has presented a four-step process specific to Global Studies to offer students the research and comparative skills necessary to undertake integrative, interdisciplinary research. Integrative research combines the information and insights from disciplines in much the same way a smoothie blends fruit into a different form, texture, and taste (Augsburg, 2006; Nissani, 1995; Repko, 2012; Repko, Szostak, & Buchberger, 2014). Integrative research enables us to understand complex global issues such as global health, terrorism and security, human rights, environmental issues, migration and refugee flows, and international economic exchanges and crises. As examples, *Global Studies Research* presented two case studies: the global HIV epidemic and terrorism.

As explained in Chapter 3, the Global Studies research process starts like any other: preparing for research by developing a research question—and recognizing that any research process is nonlinear and may involve steps back as well as forward. Preparing for integrative research, however, differs in that it also involves identifying relevant disciplines. It is from publications in those disciplines, as well as interdisciplinary and other/nondisciplinary sources, that we gather information and insights and develop disciplinary answers to a research question. To do so, we must have a basic understanding of the relevant disciplines (see Chapter 2). We then compare the gathered disciplinary information and insights, using the common criteria of the past, politics, economic resources, culture, and geography—as well as other useful criteria as determined by a research project—to find similarities and differences that will allow us to combine the disciplinary knowledge into an interdisciplinary essay answering the research question. Supplementary integration enables us to combine similar information and insights by stacking duplicate puzzle pieces while complementary integration facilitates the integration of different information and insights through placing unique puzzle pieces into gaps in the picture.

The global HIV epidemic can be both a transnational global issue and a parallel global issue. It is not simply a health problem, but one that overlaps with historical and current culture, economics, geographic locations and patterns, and politics. Focusing on international governmental organizations (IGOs) and nongovernmental organizations (NGOs), Chapter 4 introduced how global actors respond to HIV as a global issue. Information and insights from the disciplines of anthropology, economics, geography, history, and political science combined to give us an understanding of activities undertaken by IGOs and NGOs as they respond to and help manage the global HIV epidemic. All disciplines contributed information and insights; to exemplify the basic process, however, in Chapter 5 I focused on the ways in which history and political science supplement and complement one another, with additional examples from economics and anthropology. In this way, I both crafted an integrated essay and explained how the Global Studies research process results in a completed puzzle picture.

Like the HIV epidemic, terrorism can be both a transnational global issue and a parallel global issue. It is a complex problem with controversies over the many definitions, types, potential causes, and consequences of terrorism. In Chapter 6, I limited my exploration to four structural and one individual potential causes of terrorism, applying them in the differing contexts of domestic IRA terrorism in Northern Ireland and transnational terrorism by Al Qaeda and its affiliates. In Chapter 7, I demonstrated not only the basic process but also the challenges and opportunities that can arise during Global Studies research. The challenges include already-integrated publications from the interdisciplinary field of terrorism studies and the dominance of political science as a discipline while the opportunities included adding the discipline of psychology as a relevant discipline and introducing social alienation an additional criterion for comparison. As with the global HIV epidemic case study, history and political science again complemented one another, this time with history adding an insight that the gathered political science sources did not include. The discipline of psychology allowed me to consider the link between structural and individual motivators toward terrorism, as well as social alienation as both a potential cause and a criterion for comparison; anthropology and political science, along with psychology, provided complementary evidence for supplementary conclusions that feelings of social alienation can be a potential cause of terrorism.

Student researchers' ability to understand and assess the complex problems in our world is improved by understanding and integrating information and scholarly analyses from different disciplinary perspectives. The Global Studies research process offers research, analytical, and comparative skills within a process to do so. These skills are also valuable for the research projects undergraduate students may encounter in going on to graduate school or the complex problems university graduates may encounter in their careers.

Surveys show that employers in the United States wish that 2- and 4-year college graduates were much better prepared for today's globalized working world than they currently are. Seventy-five percent of employers indicate that colleges are *not* yet doing enough to prepare students for careers in today's global economy. Employers want colleges and universities to work harder to ensure students achieve or understand the following:

- The ability to understand the global context of situations and decisions

- Global issues and development and their implications for the future

- The role of the United States in the world

- Cultural diversity in America and other countries (Hart Research Associates, 2010, p. 9)

Fifty percent of the employers responding to the survey expect "students to take courses that explore big challenges facing society, such as environmental sustainability, public health, or human rights" while 58% expect "students to learn about the point of view of societies other than those of Western Europe or North America" (Hart Research Association, 2010, p. 8).

In addition to having this global knowledge, employers want college graduates to have learned particular skills, including

- The ability to locate, organize, and evaluate information from multiple sources

- The ability to analyze and solve complex problems

- Critical thinking and analytical reasoning skills

- The ability to effectively communicate orally and in writing (Hart Research Associates, 2010, p. 9)

The Global Studies research process utilizes and reinforces these skills because integrative research develops the skills to assess, manage, or solve complex problems; utilize information from multiple sources; and present it in writing.

Employers clearly want college and university students (their future employees) to learn about our complex world and to develop skills that enable them to operate effectively in a global economy, and that is true for careers both at home and abroad. Such knowledge and skills are important to joining the U.S. Foreign Service and serving as a diplomat in American embassies all over the world. But knowledge of other cultures, countries, and global situations is equally important for jobs and careers in local communities: An elementary school teacher in Greensboro, North Carolina, will teach students from cultures as diverse as Vietnam and Mexico; a hotel manager in Reno, Nevada, will serve tourists from many different countries; and a police officer in Houston, Texas, may encounter refugees whose experiences of torture by police in their home countries dramatically affect their interactions with law enforcement here in the United States.

Interdisciplinary research of any type, including Global Studies, contributes to the acquisition of additional skills:

- Ability to identify and solve problems

- Ability to understand and be sensitive to other value systems

- Preference for diversity and ability to evaluate alternatives

- Flexibility or the ability to change one's opinion in the light of facts

- Ability to respond constructively to criticism (Augsburg, 2006, pp. 37, 95; Klein, 1990; Newell, 1983)

These skills are developed through the Global Studies research process because its strengths include an emphasis on the bigger picture, creativity, effectively addressing complex topics, and valuing a variety of points of view (Repko, 2008).

References

Abadie, A. (2006). Poverty, political freedom, and the roots of terrorism. *American Economic Review*, 96(2), 50–56.

About TASO. (2015). Retrieved from http://www.tasouganda.org

About UNAIDS. (n.d.). Retrieved from http://www.unaids.org/en/aboutunaids/

Abrahms, M. (2008). What terrorists really want: Terrorist motives and counter-terrorism strategy. *International Security*, 32(4), 78–105.

American Anthropological Association. (2018). *What is anthropology?* Arlington, VA: Author. Retrieved from http://www.americananthro.org/AdvanceYourCareer/Content.aspx?ItemNumber=2150&navItemNumber=740

American Association of Geographers. (2018). *What geographers do*. Washington, DC: Author. Retrieved from http://www.aag.org/cs/what_geographers_do

American Political Science Association. (2017). Political science: An ideal liberal arts major. Retrieved from http://www.apsanet.org/CAREERS/An-Ideal-Liberal-Arts-Major

Appleby, J., Hunt, L., & Jacob, M. (1994). *Telling the truth about history*. New York, NY: W.W. Norton.

Arnold, J. H. (2000). *History: A very short introduction*. New York, NY: Oxford University Press.

Atran, S. (2008). Who becomes a terrorist today? *Perspectives on Terrorism*, 2(5). Retrieved from https://jeannicod.ccsd.cnrs.fr/ijn_00505183/document

Atran, S. (2016). The devoted actor: Unconditional commitment and intractable conflict across cultures. *Current Anthropology*, 57, S192–S203.

Augsburg, T. (2006). *Becoming interdisciplinary: An introduction to interdisciplinary studies*. Dubuque, IA: Kendall/Hunt.

Bahgat, K., & Medina, R. M. (2013). An overview of geographical perspectives and approaches in terrorism research. *Perspectives on Terrorism*, 7(1), 38–72.

Bakker, E., & Kessels, E. (2012). The OSCE's efforts to counter violent extremism and radicalization that lead to terrorism: A comprehensive approach addressing root causes? *Security and Human Rights*, 23(2), 89–99.

Banyard, P., Dillon, G., Norman, C., & Winder, B. (2015). *Essential psychology* (2nd ed.). Thousand Oaks, CA: Sage.

Barnett, T., & Whiteside, A. (2006). *AIDS in the twenty-first century: Disease and globalization* (2nd ed.). Hampshire, UK: Palgrave MacMillan.

Behrman, G. (2004). *The invisible people: How the U.S. has slept through the global AIDS pandemic, the greatest humanitarian catastrophe of our time*. New York, NY: Free Press.

Benson, T. C. (1982). Five arguments against interdisciplinary studies. *Issues in Integrative Studies*, 1, 38–48.

Berg, B. L., & Lune, H. (2012). *Qualitative research methods for the social sciences* (8th ed.). Boston, MA: Pearson Education.

Bjørgo, T. (2005a). Conclusions. In T. Bjørgo (Ed.), *Root causes of terrorism: Myths, realities, and ways forward* (pp. 256–264). London, UK: Routledge.

Bjørgo, T. (2005b). Introduction. In T. Bjørgo (Ed.), *Root causes of terrorism: Myths, realities, and ways forward* (pp. 1–15). London, UK: Routledge.

Bonnett, A. (2008). *What is geography?* Thousand Oaks, CA: Sage.

Bonwell, C., & Eison, J. A. (1991). *Active learning: Creating excitement in the classroom*. ERIC Digest. ERIC Document Reproduction Service No: ED340272.

Bouzar, D. (2016). Escaping radicalism. *Scientific American Mind*, 27(3), 40–43.

Brown, J., Pegg, S., & Shively, J. W. (2006). Consensus and divergence in international studies: Survey evidence from 140 international studies curriculum programs. *International Studies Perspectives, 7*(3), 267–286.

Carr, E. H. (1961). *What is history?* New York, NY: Vintage Books/Random House.

Caruso, R., & Schneider, F. (2011). The socio-economic determinants of terrorism and political violence in Western Europe (1994–2007). *European Journal of Political Economy, 27,* 537–549. doi:10.1016/j.ejpoleco.2011.02.003

Chernotsky, H. I., & Hobbs, H. H. (2013). *Crossing borders: International studies for the 21st century.* Thousand Oaks, CA: Sage.

Combine. (2012). In *Merriam-Webster's online dictionary* (11th ed.). Retrieved from http://www.merriam-webster.com/dictionary/combine

Crenshaw, M. (1981). The causes of terrorism. *Comparative Politics, 12*(4), 379–399.

Crenshaw, M. (2000). The psychology of terrorism: An agenda for the 21st century. *Political Psychology, 21*(2), 405–420.

Cresswell, T. (2006). Place. In B. Warf (Ed.), *Encyclopedia of human geography* (pp. 356–358). Thousand Oaks, CA: Sage.

Danziger, J. (2009). *Understanding the political world: A comparative introduction to political science.* New York, NY: Pearson Education.

Dasgupta, P. (2007). *Economics: A very short introduction.* New York, NY: Oxford University Press.

DeAngelis, T. (2009). Understanding terrorism. *Monitor on Psychology, 40*(10). Retrieved from https://www.apa.org/monitor/2009/11/terrorism.aspx

DeLamater, J. D., Collett, J., & Myers, D. (2014). *Social psychology* (8th ed.). Boulder, CO: Westview Press. [eBook Collection (EBSCOhost)].

Delaney, M. G. (1994). Paris AIDS Summit: NGO representatives and world leaders gather in Paris. *AIDSLink 30.*

Del Casino, V. J., Jr. (2001). Healthier geographies: Mediating the gaps between the needs of people living with HIV and AIDS and health care in Chiang Mai, Thailand. *Professional Geographer, 53*(3), 407–421.

Del Casino, V. J., Jr. (2006). Theory. In B. Warf (Ed.), *Encyclopedia of human geography* (pp. 484–487). Thousand Oaks, CA: Sage.

Engel, J. (2006). *The epidemic: A global history of AIDS.* New York, NY: Smithsonian Books/HarperCollins.

Eriksen, T. H. (2004). *What is anthropology?* London, UK: Pluto Press.

Evans, R. J. (2002). Prologue: What is history? – Now. In Cannadine, D. (Ed.), *What is history now?* (pp. 1–18). New York, NY: Palgrave Macmillan.

Fee, E., & Fox, D. M. (Eds.). (1988). *AIDS: The burdens of history.* Berkeley: University of California Press.

Fellman, J. D., Getis, A., & Getis, J. (2007). *Human geography: Landscapes of human activities.* Boston, MA: McGraw Hill Higher Education.

Flint, C. (2003a). Geographies of inclusion/exclusion. In T. J. Wilbanks, D. Richardson, & S. L. Cutter (Eds.), *The geographical dimensions of terrorism* (pp. 53–58). New York, NY: Routledge.

Flint, C. (2003b). Terrorism and counterterrorism: Geographic research questions and agendas. *Professional Geographer, 55*(2), 161–169. doi:10.1111/0033-0124.5502004

Freeman, M. (2008). Democracy, Al Qaeda, and the causes of terrorism: A strategic analysis of U.S. policy. *Studies in Conflict and Terrorism, 31,* 40–59. doi:10.1080/10576100701759996

Freytag, A., Krüger, J. J., Meierrieks, D., & Schneider, F. (2011). The origins of terrorism: Cross-country estimates of socio-economic determinants of terrorism. *European Journal of Political Economy 27,* S5–S16.

Gill, P., & Corner, E. (2017). There and back again: The study of mental disorder and terrorism involvement. *American Psychologist, 72*(3), 231–241.

The Global Fund. (2017). *Results Report 2017.* Retrieved from https://www.theglobalfund.org/media/6773/corporate_2017resultsreport_report_en.pdf

The Global Fund. (2018a). *A smart investment.* Retrieved from https://www.theglobalfund.org/media/7527/corporate_theglobalfundasmartinvestment_brochure_en.pdf?u=636675998760000000

The Global Fund. (2018b). *Pledges and contributions to date* [Data file]. Retrieved from https://www.theglobalfund.org/en/government/#related-resources

Global Fund Overview. (2018). Retrieved from https://www.theglobalfund.org/en/overview/

Goldin, I. (2018). *Development: A very short introduction.* Oxford, UK: Oxford University Press.

Gordenker, L., Coate, R., Jönsson, C., & Söderholm, P. (1995). *International cooperation in response to AIDS.* London, UK: Pinter.

Grmek, M. (1990). *History of AIDS: Emergence and origin of a modern pandemic* (R. Maulitz & J. Duffin, Trans.). Princeton, NJ: Princeton University Press.

Gupta, D. K. (2005). Exploring roots of terrorism. In T. Bjørgo (Ed.), *Root causes of terrorism: Myths, realities, and ways forward* (pp. 16–32). London, UK: Routledge.

Harden, V. A. (2012). *AIDS at 30: A history.* Washington, DC: Potomac Books.

Hart Research Associates. (2010). *Raising the bar: Employers' views on the college learning in the wake of the economic downturn.* Retrieved from http://www.aacu.org/leap/documents/2009_EmployerSurvey.pdf

History of AIDS: 1987–1992. (2013). Retrieved from http://www.avert.org/aids-history-86.htm

Holm, H., & Sorenson, G. (Eds.). (1995). *Whose world order? Uneven globalization and the end of the cold war.* Boulder, CO: Westview.

Holt-Jensen, A. (2018). *Geography: History and concepts* (5th ed.). Thousand Oaks, CA: Sage.

Horgan, J. (2016). A call to arms: The need for more psychological research on terrorism. *Social Psychological Review, 18*(1), 25–28.

Horgan, J. (2017). Psychology of terrorism: Introduction to the special issue. *American Psychologist, 72*(3), 199–204.

Hunter, M. (2010). *Love in the time of AIDS: Inequality, gender, and rights in South Africa.* Bloomington: Indiana University Press.

Hunter, M. (2018). About me. Retrieved from https://www.markwhunter.net/about-me.html

Hurston, Z. N. (1984). *Dust tracks on a road: An autobiography* (2nd ed.). Urbana: University of Illinois Press.

Iliffe, J. (2006). *The African AIDS epidemic: A history.* Athens: Ohio University Press.

Jackson, R., Jarvis, L., Gunning, J., & Breen-Smyth, M. (2011). *Terrorism: A critical introduction.* New York, NY: Palgrave Macmillan.

Jensen, R. B. (2013). The first global wave of terrorism and international counter-terrorism, 1905–1914. In J. M. Hanhimäki & B. Blumenau (Eds.), *An international history of terrorism: Western and Non-Western experiences* (pp. 16–33). New York, NY: Taylor & Francis Group.

Jones, P. S. (2004). When 'development' devastates: donor discourses, access to HIV/AIDS treatment in Africa and rethinking the landscape of development. *Third World Quarterly, 25*(2), 385–404. doi:10.1080/0143659042000174879.

Kis-Katos, K., Liebert, H., & Schulze, G.G. (2011). On the origin of domestic and international terrorism. *European Journal of Political Economy, 27,* S17–S36. doi:10.1016/j.ejpoleco.2011.02.002

Klein, J. T. (1990). *Interdisciplinarity: History, theory, and practice.* Detroit, MI: Wayne State University Press.

Klein, J. T., & Newell, W. (1997). Advancing interdisciplinary studies. In J. Gaff, J. Ratcliff & Associates (Eds.), *Handbook of the undergraduate curriculum: A comprehensive guide to purposes, structures, practices, and change* (pp. 393–415). San Francisco, CA: Jossey-Bass.

Kristof, N. D., & WuDunn, S. (2009). *Half the sky: Turning oppression into opportunity for women worldwide.* New York, NY: Alfred A. Knopf.

Kuhanen, J. (2008). The historiography of HIV/AIDS in Uganda. *History in Africa, 35,* 304–325. Retrieved from http://www.jstor.org/stable/25483725

Laqueur, W. (2002). *A history of terrorism*. New Brunswick, NJ: Transaction.

Lasswell, H. D. (1958). *Politics: Who gets what, when, how*. New York, NY: Meridian Books.

Lattuca, L. (2001). *Creating interdisciplinarity: Interdisciplinary research and teaching among college and university faculty*. Nashville, TN: Vanderbilt University Press.

Lavenda, R. H., & Schultz, E. A. (2008). *Anthropology: What does it mean to be human?* New York, NY: Oxford University Press.

Lisk, F. (2010). *Global institutions and the HIV/AIDS epidemic: Responding to an international crisis*. New York, NY: Routledge.

Lloyd, M., & Kleinot, P. (2017). Pathways into terrorism: The good, the bad, and the ugly. *Psychoanalytic Psychotherapy*, *31*(4), 367–377. Retrieved from https://doi.org/10.1080/02668734.2017.1360380

Loseke, D. R. (2013). *Methodological thinking: Basic principles of social research design*. Thousand Oaks, CA: Sage.

Magli, I. (2001). *Cultural anthropology: An introduction* (J. Sethre, Trans.). Jefferson, NC: McFarland.

Malečková, J. (2005). Impoverished terrorists: Stereotype or reality? In T. Bjørgo (Ed.), *Root causes of terrorism: Myths, realities, and ways forward* (pp. 33–43). London, UK: Routledge.

Matthews, J. A., & Herbert, D. T. (2008). *Geography: A very short introduction*. Oxford, UK: Oxford University Press.

McKittrick, D., & McVea, D. (2002). *Making sense of the troubles: The story of the conflict in Northern Ireland*. Chicago, IL: New Amsterdam Books.

Medina, R. M., & Hepner, G. F. (2013). *The geography of international terrorism: An introduction to spaces and places of violent non-state groups*. Boca Raton, FL: CRC Press.

Miller, M. A. (2013). *The foundations of modern terrorism: States, society, and the dynamics of political violence*. New York, NY: Cambridge University Press.

Mink, C. (2015). It's about the group, not God: Social causes and cures for terrorism. *Journal for Deradicalization*, 5, 63–91. Retrieved from https://doaj.org/article/21428eadb309415f978733305d1ae91f

Mitchell, J. K. (1979). Social violence in Northern Ireland. *Geographical Review*, *69*(2), 179–201. Retrieved from https://www.jstor.org/stable/214963

Mohamedou, M.-M. O. (2013). Al Qaeda and the reinvention of terrorism: Social sciences and the challenge of post-globalization transnational political violence. In J. M. Hanhimäki & B. Blumenau (Eds.), *An international history of terrorism: Western and Non-Western Experiences* (pp. 230–244). New York, NY: Taylor & Francis Group.

Monaghan, J., & Just, P. (2000). *Social and cultural anthropology: A very short introduction*. Oxford, UK: Oxford University Press.

Mulholland, M. (2002). *Northern Ireland: A very short introduction*. Oxford, UK: Oxford University Press.

Murphy, A. B. (2003). The space of terror. In T. J. Wilbanks, D. Richardson, & S. L. Cutter (Eds.), *The geographical dimensions of terrorism* (pp. 47–52). New York, NY: Routledge.

Mustafa, D. (2005). The terrible geographicalness of terrorism: Reflections of a hazard geographer. *Antipode*, *37*(1), 72–92. doi:10.1111/j.0066-4812.2005.00474.x

Nacos, B. L. (2016). *Terrorism and counterterrorism* (5th ed.). New York, NY: Taylor and Francis Group.

Nau, H. R. (2017). *Perspectives on international relations: Power, institutions, and ideas* (5th ed.). Thousand Oaks, CA: Sage.

Neufeldt, V., & Guralnik, D. B. (Eds.). (1991). *Webster's new world dictionary of American English* (3rd college ed.). Cleveland, OH: Webster's New World.

Newell, W. H. (1983). The case of interdisciplinary studies: Response to Professor Benson's five arguments. *Issues in Integrative Studies 2*, 1–19.

Newell, W. H. (1998). Academic disciplines and undergraduate interdisciplinary education. In William Newell (Ed.), *Interdisciplinarity: Essays from the literature* (pp. 213–224). New York, NY: College Entrance Examination Board.

Newell, W. H. (2007). Decision-making in interdisciplinary studies. In Göktug Morçöl (Ed.), *Handbook of decision making* (pp. 245–264). New York, NY: Marcel Dekker.

Newell, W. H. (2010). Educating for a complex world: Integrative learning and interdisciplinary studies. *Liberal Education, 96*(4), 6–11.

NGO/civil society participation in PCB. (n.d.). Retrieved from http://www.unaids.org/en/aboutunaids/unaids programmecoordinatingboard/ngocivilsocietyparticipation inpcb/

Nissani, M. (1995). Fruits, salads, and smoothies: A working definition of interdisciplinarity [Electronic version]. *Journal of Educational Thought, 29,* 119–125. Retrieved from http://www.is.wayne.edu/mnissani/PAGEPUB/SMOOTHIE.htm

Nye, J. S. (2002). *The paradox of American power: Why the world's only superpower can't go it alone.* Oxford, UK: Oxford University Press.

Nye, J. S. (2007). *Understanding international conflict: An introduction to theory and history.* New York, NY: Pearson Longman.

Nye, J. S. (2011). *The future of power.* New York, NY: Public Affairs/Perseus Books Group.

O'Malley, J., Nguyen, V. K., & Lee, S. (1996). Nongovernmental organizations. In J. Mann & D. Tarantola (Eds.), *AIDS in the world II* (pp. 341–361). New York, NY: Oxford University Press.

Orvis, S., & Drogus, C. A. (2019). *Introducing comparative politics: The essentials.* Thousand Oaks, CA: Sage.

Parker, R. (2011). Grassroots activism, civil society mobilization, and the politics of the global HIV/AIDS epidemic. *Brown Journal of World Affairs, 17*(2), 21–37.

The Pew Global Attitudes Project. (2003). *America's image further erodes, Europeans want weaker ties.* Retrieved from http://people-press.org/reports/pdf/175.pdf

Poku, N., Whiteside, A., & Sandkjaer, B. (2007). *AIDS and governance.* Burlington, VT: Ashgate.

Pope, C., White, R. T., & Malow, R. (Eds.). (2009). *HIV/AIDS: Global frontiers in prevention/intervention.* New York, NY: Routledge.

Post, J. (2005). The socio-cultural underpinnings of terrorist psychology: "When hatred is bred in the bone."

In T. Bjørgo (Ed.), *Root causes of terrorism: Myths, realities, and ways forward* (pp. 54–69). London, UK: Routledge.

Rapoport, D. (2003). The four waves of rebel terror and September 11. In C. W. Kegley, Jr. (Ed.), *The new global terrorism: Characteristics, causes, controls* (pp. 36–52). Upper Saddle River, NJ: Pearson Education.

Rau, B. (2007). The politics of civil society in confronting HIV/AIDS. In N. Poku, A. Whiteside, & B. Sandkjaer (Eds.), *AIDS and governance* (pp. 165–175). Burlington, VT: Ashgate.

Reicher, S. D., & Halsam, S. A. (2016). Fueling extremes. *Scientific American Mind, 27*(3), 34–39. doi:10.1038.scientificamericanmind0516-34

Reinares, F. (2005). National separatism and terrorism in comparative perspective. In T. Bjørgo (Ed.), *Root causes of terrorism: Myths, realities, and ways forward* (pp. 119–130). London, UK: Routledge.

Remler, D. K., & Van Ryzin, G. G. (2015). *Research methods in practice: Strategies for description and causation.* Thousand Oaks, CA: Sage.

Repko, A. (2006). Disciplining interdisciplinarity: The case for textbooks. *Issues in Integrative Studies, 24,* 112–142.

Repko, A. (2008). *Interdisciplinary research: Process and theory.* Thousand Oaks, CA: Sage.

Repko, A. (2012). *Interdisciplinary research: Process and theory* (2nd ed.). Thousand Oaks, CA: Sage.

Repko, A., & Szostak, R. (2017). *Interdisciplinary research: Process and theory* (3rd ed.). Thousand Oaks, CA: Sage.

Repko, A., Szostak, R., & Buchberger, M. P. (2014). *Introduction to interdisciplinary studies.* Thousand Oaks, CA: Sage.

Risse, G. B. (1988). Epidemics and history: Ecological perspectives and social responses. In E. Fee & D. M. Fox (Eds.), *AIDS: The burdens of history.* Berkeley, CA: University of California Press.

Robbins, S. (2006). From "rights" to "ritual": AIDS activism in South Africa. *American Anthropologist, 108*(2), 312–323. Retrieved from, http://www.jstor.org/stable/3804793

Rollins, J. (2011). *Al Qaeda and affiliates: Historical perspective, global presence, and implications for U.S. policy* (CRS

Report No. R41070). Retrieved from https://fas.org/sgp/crs/terror/R41070.pdf

Roxby, P. (2017, May 11). HIV life expectancy 'near normal' thanks to new drugs. BBC News. Retrieved from https://www.bbc.com/news/health-39872530

Rubenstein, J. M. (2011). *The cultural landscape: An introduction to human geography*. Boston, MA: Prentice Hall.

Ruel, E., Wagner, W. E., III & Gillespie, B. J. (2016). *The practice of survey research: Theory and applications*. Thousand Oaks, CA: Sage.

Schmid, A. P. (2005a). Prevention of terrorism: Towards a multi-pronged approach. In T. Bjørgo (Ed.), *Root causes of terrorism: Myths, realities, and ways forward* (pp. 223–240). London, UK: Routledge.

Schmid, A. P. (2005b). Root causes of terrorism: Some conceptual notes, a set of indicators, and a model. *Democracy and Security, 1*(2), 127–136. doi:10.1080/17419160500321139

Scott, J. M., Carter, R. G., & Drury, A. C. (2019). *IR: International economic, and human security in a changing world*. Thousand Oaks, CA: Sage.

Shively, W. P. (2013). *The craft of political research* (9th ed.). Boston, MA: Pearson.

Sinai, J. (2005). A conceptual framework for resolving terrorism's root causes. In T. Bjørgo (Ed.), *Root causes of terrorism: Myths, realities, and ways forward* (pp. 216–222). London, UK: Routledge.

Snarr, M. T. (2008). Introducing globalization and global issues. In M. T. Snarr & D. N. Snarr (Eds.), *Introducing global issues* (4th ed., pp. 1–11). Boulder, CO: Lynne Rienner.

Soderberg, N. (2005). *The superpower myth: The use and misuse of American might*. Hoboken, NJ: John Wiley & Sons.

Soroos, M. (1990). A theoretical framework for global policy studies. *International Political Science Review, 11*, 309–322.

Starr, M. A. (2014). Qualitative and mixed-methods research in economics: Surprising growth, promising future. *Journal of Economic Surveys, 28*(2), 238–264.

Sterling-Folker, J. (2013). Constructivism. In J. Sterling-Folker (Ed.), *Making sense of international relations theory* (pp. 127–135). Boulder, CO: Lynne Rienner.

Szostak, R. (2002). How to do interdisciplinarity: Integrating the debate. *Issues in Integrative Studies, 20*, 103–122.

Therrien, A. (2018, July 7). HIV vaccine shows promise in human trial. *BBC News*. Retrieved from https://www.bbc.com/news/health-44738642

Thomas, A. (2007). Introduction. In A. Thomas & G. Mohan (Eds.), *Research skills for policy and development* (pp. 1–23). London, UK: The Open University in association with Sage.

Toolis, K. (1995). *Rebel hearts: Journey within the IRA's soul*. New York, NY: St. Martin's Press.

Uganda court annuls anti-homosexuality law [Video file]. (2014, August 1). Retrieved from https://www.bbc.com/news/world-africa-28605400

UNAIDS. (n.d.). UNAIDS cosponsors. Retrieved from http://www.unaids.org/en/aboutunaids/unaidscosponsors/

UNAIDS. (2009). *Fact sheet: AIDS funding 2008*. Retrieved from http://www.unaids.org/en/media/unaids/contentassets/dataimport/pub/factsheet/2009/20090209_fs_available funding_en.pdf

UNAIDS. (2011). *AIDS at 30: Nations at the crossroads*. Retrieved from http://www.unaids.org/unaids_resources/aidsat30/aids-at-30.pdf

UNAIDS. (2017a). *Country-reported HIV expenditure* [Data file]. Retrieved from http://aidsinfo.unaids.org/

UNAIDS. (2017b, September 21). *Press Release: New high-quality antiretroviral therapy to be launched in South Africa, Kenya and over 90 low-and middle-income countries at reduced price*. Retrieved from http://www.unaids.org/sites/default/files/20170921_PR_TLD_en.pdf

UNAIDS. (2018a). *Country factsheets: Uganda 2017*. Retrieved from http://aidsinfo.unaids.org/

UNAIDS. (2018b). *Global HIV and AIDS Statistics: 2018 Fact sheet*. Retrieved from http://www.unaids.org/en/resources/fact-sheet

UNAIDS. (2018c). *Miles to go: Closing gaps, breaking barriers, righting injustices*. Retrieved from http://www.unaids.org/sites/default/files/media_asset/miles-to-go_en.pdf

United States Support for the Global Fund to Fight AIDS, Tuberculosis, and Malaria. (2017). Retrieved from https://www.pepfar.gov/press/261920.htm

U.S. Centers for Disease Control and Prevention. (2018). *PrEP*. Retrieved from https://www.cdc.gov/hiv/basics/prep.html

Validate. (2011). In *Merriam-Webster's online dictionary* (11th ed.). Retrieved from http://www.merriam-webster.com/dictionary/validate

Vertigans, S. (2011). *The sociology of terrorism: peoples, places and processes*. London, UK: Routledge.

Vieira, M. A. (2011). Southern Africa's response(s) to international HIV/AIDS norms: The politics of assimilation. *Review of International Studies, 37*(1), 3–28.

Weaver, F. S. (2017). *Economic literacy: Basic economics with an attitude* (4th ed.). Lanham, MD: Rowman & Littlefield.

Weinberg, L., & Eubank, W. (2010). An end to the fourth wave of terrorism? *Studies in Conflict and Terrorism 33*, 594–602. doi:10.1080.1057610X.2010.483757

Wendt, A. (1992). Anarchy is what states make of it: The social construction of power politics. *International Organization, 46*(2), 391–425.

Whiteside, A. (2008). *HIV/AIDS: A very short introduction*. Oxford, UK: Oxford University Press.

WHO. (2018). *HIV/AIDS key facts*. Retrieved from http://www.who.int/news-room/fact-sheets/detail/hiv-aids

Wichert, S. (1999). *Northern Ireland since 1945*. New York, NY: Longman.

World Health Organization. (2007, May). Single use of injection devices. *Patient Safety Solutions, 1*(8). Retrieved from http://www.who.int/patientsafety/solutions/patientsafety/PS-Solution8-LowRes.pdf

Yin, R. K. (1994). *Case study research design and methods*. Thousand Oaks, CA: Sage.

Zeiser, P. A. (1998). *Influencing international processes: The role of NGOs in global social welfare policy making* (Doctoral dissertation). Retrieved from Proquest/UMI Dissertations and Theses. (UMI Number 9821517).

Index

Page numbers followed by b indicate box; page numbers followed by f indicate figure

Made in the USA
Monee, IL
09 August 2023